Why You Need a Foreign Language & How to Learn One

Second Edition: Revised and Expanded

Edward Trimnell

Beechmont Crest Publishing
Cincinnati, Ohio

www.beechmontcrest.com

Copyright 2005 Beechmont Crest Publishing
ISBN: 0-9748330-1-0

Table of Contents

Part I. Why You Need a Foreign Language

Part II. How to Learn a Foreign Language

PART I

WHY YOU NEED A FOREIGN LANGUAGE

INTRODUCTION: ENGLISH-SPEAKERS LOST IN TRANSLATION

The film *Lost in Translation* received considerable acclaim in 2003 for its portrayal of two Americans who meet in Japan. The movie primarily deals with the themes of loneliness, alienation, and the wistfulness of an unconsummated romance. However, *Lost in Translation* also makes some revealing (if inadvertent) points about the struggles that monolingual English-speakers face when they are forced to rely on the language skills of others.

    Lost in Translation casts Bill Murray in the lead role of actor Bob Harris. Bob Harris is a faded star who—not unlike many real-life actors whose glory days are behind them—is leveraging his earlier fame to earn money through television product endorsements. Harris is luckier than most Hollywood has-beens; he doesn't have to resort to peddling steak knives or abdominal machines on cable TV. In fact, Harris has landed a fat contract with the Japanese beverage giant Suntory. As the movie opens, the actor is making his way through the exotic streets of urban Japan, where he will appear in a series of television commercials.

    When Harris arrives on the studio set, he meets his director for the first time. The director speaks minimal English, and Harris will have to rely on an interpreter throughout the project. Although the actor appears to have some misgivings about the arrangement, he has obviously been through hundreds, if not thousands, of studio sessions before. He begins his first round of shooting with the confident air of an old pro.

    In order to give the commercial a relaxed, upscale atmosphere, the studio set has been designed to look like a private study in an elegant home. Harris is instructed to sit at a small table with a bottle of Suntory whisky and a glass of the beverage. When the cameras roll, he is supposed to lift the glass and deliver the lines, *"For relaxing times, make it Suntory time!"* Simple enough.

    But of course it will not be *that* simple. There are innumerable ways to deliver these lines, and a myriad of subtle messages that could be conveyed or garbled in the process. These are the nuances that directors are paid to manage, and Bob's director is in a managing mood. Before the shooting begins, the director approaches Harris and gives him a lengthy explanation of how he wants the actor to deliver the lines. The director rhapsodizes about mood and voice inflection, timing and feeling. He rambles on for several minutes. *In Japanese.*

Harris of course understands none of this, and he turns anxiously to his interpreter when the director has finally finished speaking. This commercial is important to his flagging career—not to mention his wallet. He *needs* to understand what the director said. He is therefore counting on his interpreter. He smiles at her uneasily, waiting.

To Harris's dismay, the interpreter gives him a single-sentence, ultra-simplified account of the director's instructions. In fact, she just repeats what he already knew. He is supposed to raise his glass and say, "*For relaxing times, make it Suntory time!*" Harris knows that the director said much, much more than the interpreter revealed, but he is entirely dependent on her abilities. He wants to ask someone to wait, to stop, to have the interpreter explain the instructions in more detail. But to whom can he appeal?

When the camera rolls, Harris delivers his lines, and the director stops him, then reprimands him in Japanese for not following directions. Once again, the interpreter provides a minimal explanation of what has been said. They shoot again, Harris fumbles again, and the cycle continues. This situation becomes one of the running jokes of the movie.

Every movie requires a romantic plot (or at least a romantic subplot); and actress Scarlet Johansson plays the role of Charlotte, Harris's romantic interest in the film. In one scene, he takes Charlotte to a Japanese hospital for treatment of a minor injury. In a continuation of the language barrier gag, Harris and Charlotte are completely unable to grasp what they see and hear. Hospital forms look like pages of random scribbles. The spoken words of receptionists, doctors, and orderlies are incomprehensible mysteries.

The misadventures of these fictional Americans illustrate a self-defeating fact about native English-speakers vis-à-vis the rest of the world:

> For the most part, native English-speakers do not learn the languages of others. Therefore, we are overly dependent on the language skills of others—and their willingness (or lack thereof) to use them to our benefit…

6

Notice that I used the term "native English-speakers" rather than "Americans." Americans have traditionally taken a lot of heat for our linguistic provincialism. Nonetheless, our British cousins are just as insular. The same goes for Anglophones in Canada, Australia, New Zealand, etc. Wherever people speak English as a primary, native language, most of the population can speak nothing else. The English-speaking world is almost universally hobbled by monolingualism.

No one imposed this condition on us. We have chosen to restrict our own options. In a competitive world where gaining insights about other markets and cultures is of increasing importance, we have voluntarily limited our mode of intelligence gathering and influence to a single language. As Shakespeare wrote in *Love's Labor Lost*, "They have been at a great feast of languages, and stolen [only] the scraps."

OBJECTIVES OF THIS BOOK

This book consists of two parts. Part I, *Why You Need a Foreign Language*, discusses the relevance of foreign languages for English-speakers. The chapters in this part of the book explore the concept of the lingua franca, the current status of various languages in the world, and probable trends for the future. In Part I you will find answers to questions like: Why did the language of tiny Britain become such a powerful linguistic force in the world? Why did Roman soldiers learn to speak Greek, when the language of Rome was Latin? How is the process of globalization likely to affect the worldwide usage of Chinese, Spanish, English, and Arabic?

Part II, *How to Learn a Foreign Language*, delves into the nuts and bolts of languages: What are language families? Which languages are relatively easy for native English-speakers to learn, and which present more of a challenge? How many tongues can you realistically learn? What are the basic characteristics of Spanish, French, Chinese, etc.? Part II also includes information about applying languages to your career and professional development.

Languages do not exist in a vacuum. They are influenced by geopolitics, social and demographic trends, and economics. This book therefore contains some necessary detours into topics like history, business, and current events. These subjects are not mere diversions. The rise of manufacturing in China, the backlash against globalization, and the history of Japan's ambivalent relationship with the West are just a few of the items that have shaped contemporary attitudes about languages.

The first edition of *Why You Need a Foreign Language & How to Learn One* was published in 2003. This edition has been significantly revised and expanded. While there are still several chapters that focus on the role of languages in the business world, the second edition takes a much wider look at the historical, cultural, and political factors that determine linguistic trends. The "how-to" chapters that deal specifically with language study are basically the same ones that appeared in the first edition, with a few minor updates and revisions.

As always, reader feedback is welcome. Please feel free to drop me a line at www.edwardtrimnell.com.

CHAPTER 1

DOES AN ENGLISH-SPEAKER REALLY NEED A FOREIGN LANGUAGE?

If you have picked up this book, then it is safe to assume that you already have your own reasons for wanting to learn another language. Perhaps your company is about to begin a joint venture with an Austrian company, and you are musing about brushing up on the German you studied in college. Alternatively, you might just be looking for one more "edge" to add to your resume. Or maybe you witnessed another English speaker rattling confidently away in a foreign language and you thought, "Wow, that looks like fun!—Could *I* learn to do that?" Whatever the source of your interest, you likely already have that first spark of motivation.

Nonetheless, enthusiasm for self-improvement initiatives often fades. (I wish I had a $10 bill for every New Year's resolution that I've broken over the years.) Although the novelty of a new undertaking can be intoxicating, at some point it becomes work—and you will need solid reasons to continue forward. Alternatively, a coworker or a relative may ask you, *"Why are you spending your valuable spare time learning French?"* After all, there is a lot to compete for your time. Moreover, you are about to begin an endeavor which will consume not only time—but effort, and a moderate amount of money. It is important for you to take your first step on the journey with a firm sense of commitment.

In the English-speaking world, the importance of language study is by no means accepted as self-evident. The percentage of native-born Americans who can actually speak a foreign language is abysmally small. The exact numbers are hard to come by, but ask yourself: among your friends, family members and professional colleagues who were born in the United States, how many could hold a conversation in any language besides English? Few readers will know more than one or two people who fulfill these criteria—and the majority will not know a single native-born American who can pass the test.

Volunteers at Oklahoma State University recently conducted a "Language Ambush" project in order to gain some measurement of language skills among students on the OSU campus. Language Ambush volunteers

9

approached OSU students and asked them a simple question (such as the time) in a foreign language like German, Japanese, or Spanish. Only six percent passed the test. Keep in mind: this experiment was conducted in an academic environment. In the general population, it is likely that fewer than one percent of respondents would have been able to pass the test.

Monolingualism has costs. In his 1987 book, *The Tongue-Tied American: Confronting the Foreign Language Crisis*, Senator Paul Simon reported that 200,000 Americans miss out on job opportunities because they do not know a foreign language. And that was in 1987—before the fall of communism, the rise of China as an economic power, or NAFTA. Given the growth of global business since the late 1980s, it is reasonable to assume that the number would be many times higher today. Moreover, missed job opportunities are only part of the economic cost involved. Monolingualism is a fundamental shortcoming that impedes American professionals who must manage, sell, and negotiate in the global marketplace.

Conventional wisdom would suggest that Britons would have high rates of bilingualism and multilingualism. After all, Great Britain is part of the linguistically diverse European Union. Such hopes are quickly disappointed by the data: The United Kingdom is the most monolingual country in the EU. When dealing with the rest of the world, the average Briton—like the average American—must rely on others to translate and interpret.

A study conducted by the British House of Lords in 2005 found that poor foreign language skills in Britain have begun to affect the nation's economic performance. A major British newspaper reported a "deeply disturbing" lack of language skills that threatens to leave Britain unable to 'protect our interests' abroad and to compete economically in Europe."

* * *

Why does this situation exist in the English-speaking world? There are a handful of reasons—some obvious, some more arcane:

10

THE BELIEF THAT "EVERYONE IN THE WORLD SPEAKS ENGLISH"

This misconception is vast and multifaceted, and the next chapter is dedicated to examining it in detail. As a preliminary remark, note two points: 1.) The whole world *does not speak English*. Rather, *much of the world knows some English*, and 2.) Even when you are dealing with people who have skills in English as a secondary language, there is much to be gained by the ability to resort to their language when necessary. (The full implications of this point will become clear in Chapter 7.)

ENGLISH-SPEAKING COUNTRIES ARE GEOGRAPHICALLY ISOLATED

Great Britain is an island. The United States is surrounded by oceans to the east and west; and our northern border is occupied by a sparsely populated country that also speaks English. Australia is an island continent in the Pacific Ocean. New Zealand and Canada are similarly isolated by geography, when compared to the interlocking, tightly clustered nations of continental Europe.

The Internet and modern air travel have made geographic isolation a less significant factor than it was at the beginning of the last century; but the psychological effects of geographic isolation have a long half-life. This is especially true in the United States, where much of the population still lives in relatively wide open, isolated spaces.

THE ENGLISH-SPEAKING WORLD REPRESENTS A DOMINANT CULTURE

The English-speaking peoples are arguably the freest, most prosperous people on Earth. I personally am thankful for this; I am not an apologist for the triumph of Western Civilization or American culture. Nonetheless, it would be myopic and ultimately delusional to ignore the rise of China, Japan, Brazil, and other non-Anglophone nations to world power status. This means that learning the languages of these nations is worth our time and effort.

11

A MISTAKEN PERCEPTION THAT LANGUAGES ARE ONLY FOR "LINGUISTS"

Japanese managers accept language skills as part of the "total package" that a modern professional should possess. I know Japanese managers who have learned English, Portuguese, Thai, and a host of other languages for business purposes. During the mid-1990s, I spent a great deal of time in Japanese-owned automotive plants throughout Mexico. Almost every Japanese manager I met was able to hold a conversation in Spanish.

Many American managers, however, believe that languages are too "artsy" for the hard-boiled world of factories and boardrooms. As one American manager whom I met expressed it, "If you exhibit foreign language skills, then you somehow get labeled a linguist rather than someone with business skills."

I have taken international business classes at the graduate level, and I have yet to find a textbook that considers the proper role of language skills for a modern professional. Under the current orthodoxy, there is an assumption that English-speaking professionals must rely on the language skills of others.

LEARNING LANGUAGES IS HARD WORK

A foreign language is certainly not something that you can master overnight. Unless you are unusually gifted (or have nothing else to do but study languages), you will need to spend a number of years on the endeavor. The exact amount of time required will depend on the language you choose (more on this later), the time that you can devote to the effort, and your enthusiasm for the project.

In most cases, the part-time, self-directed learner can achieve basic competency in one or two years. More advanced competency arrives with one to three years of additional effort.

Although the above numbers add up to as many as four years, an important qualifier is in order. Do not discourage yourself by imagining the journey as a long, fruitless struggle, at the end of which you will acquire the golden fleece of fluency. Language acquisition is a gradual process—and there are lots of satisfying milestones along the way.

You will begin to have fun with your skills after just a few months of study. At first you will be limited to greetings. Then you will be able to carry on simple conversations. Over time, your conversations will grow more complex. Finally, it will be a matter of moving from proficiency in your new language to the status of a highly articulate speaker.

Some may balk at the idea of spending two to four years to reach their goals in a language. But this is simply the price you must pay to learn any worthwhile skill. It takes at least a couple of years to learn how to program a computer, or to perform advanced accounting operations, or to do just about anything for which someone will pay you. Once you do learn your language, you will then have a skill that will never become obsolete. Moreover, you will be pleasantly surprised to discover that your language skills can be successfully combined with the expertise and experience that you have in other areas.

"YOU CAN ALWAYS HIRE AN INTERPRETER."

An interpreter is a good solution to your communication needs while you are still getting up to speed in your new language. When the language-related need is particularly urgent, and you don't yet speak the other language yourself, you have to call in specialized help. Interpreters (those who convert spoken content from one language to another) and translators (those who convert the written language) provide valuable assistance to thousands of businesses every year.

However, even the best interpreters have their limitations. Most business discussions require extensive knowledge about a particular industry. It may be difficult to locate an interpreter who has the knowledge and background needed. In order to use the interpreter's services effectively, you will probably have to spend some time briefing her about the details of your business, which takes more time, and leaves a considerable margin for error. If the discussions involve extremely complex matters, it may be impossible for you to give her enough background knowledge to handle the discussions smoothly.

Cost is also an issue. Experienced interpreters with expertise in a particular area charge a high hourly rate. Most interpreters work as independent contractors, so you will also have to pay for expenses such as mileage, parking fees, etc. If an international project is going to last for months or years, then an interpreter's services may be prohibitively expensive.

Moreover, an interpreter is an awkward medium for developing a rapport with someone. Although interpreters are sometimes hired to attend business dinners and other after-hours social events, communications through an intermediary usually have a stiff and artificial quality. Speaking directly in another language is much more personal—and much more effective.

CHAPTER 2

THE TRUTH AND THE HYPE ABOUT "GLOBAL ENGLISH"

There are many excuses for not learning a foreign language. However, the 800-lb gorilla among them is the "Global English" argument. This argument can be summed up as follows:

> *Why do I need to learn a foreign language when everyone in the world is learning English?*

This is not a stupid question, and we will answer it in depth in this book. As it turns out, the worldwide significance of English is undeniable, but the role of English as a "global language" is often misunderstood.

FRAGMENTARY ENGLISH IS EVERYWHERE

Get off an airplane in Brussels, Tokyo, or Taipei, and you will find signs written in English. In the same airport, the customs agent who asks you if you have anything to declare will probably ask the question in English. When you check out of your hotel, you will notice that a lot of English is written on the credit card receipt—especially if you have stayed in a major hotel in a large city.

If there is an antiwar protest somewhere in Europe this weekend, the protesters will mostly be holding signs with slogans written in the local language. Depending on the country, it might be *"Keine Krieg!"*, *"Pas de guerre!"*, or *"Geen oorlog!"* etc. But you will also be likely to see at least a few signs bearing the English equivalent: "No War!" The protesters realize that on an international scale, more CNN viewers will recognize these phrases in English than will understand the same words in German, French, or Dutch.

Many people who recognize fragmentary snippets of English could not begin to hold a real conversation in English. This makes sense when you consider that you also recognize many words and phrases in languages that

15

you don't actually "speak". Below is a sample of foreign words and phrases that many Americans have absorbed through the media and popular culture:

Word/Phrase	Language	Meaning
Vaya con Diós	Spanish	Go with God
Estás en tu casa.	Spanish	Make yourself at home
Insha Allah	Arabic	God willing
Sayonara	Japanese	Goodbye
Merci	French	Thank you
Bon jour	French	Good day
Excusez-moi	French	Excuse me; I'm sorry
Guten Tag	German	Good day; Hello

You probably recognize at least a few of these. And with a little practice, you could use them to hold basic conversations. If you held the door for a Spanish-speaker and she said "*Muchas gracias*," you would likely understand her meaning. Perhaps you would even be able to respond with the Spanish *De nada* ("You're welcome").

In fact, you probably know a *lot* of Spanish words: *sí, pronto, adiós, hóla,*etc. Spanish is the language in which most Americans would score the highest on a phrase recognition test. Many Americans understand fragments of Spanish because: a.) Spanish is a popular academic subject in the American school system, and b.) Latino culture has made significant inroads into the United States.

Because of these same factors, many non-English-speakers can recognize bits and pieces of English. English is a popular academic subject throughout the world, and American popular culture has a global appeal. Say "Hello" to someone just about anywhere in the world, and the odds are pretty good that they will understand that you are trying to be friendly. "Thank you," "Goodbye," and "My name is….," are also generally recognized throughout the world.

SPEAKING ENGLISH VS. *KNOWING SOME ENGLISH*

As a vehicle of concise messages, English is as ubiquitous as Latin was a thousand years ago, or as French was two hundred years ago. And in this role, English is indispensable. Since ancient times, there has always been a recognized need for a *lingua franca*—a common tongue that can be used for basic communication purposes by people who speak different languages. Throughout history, various languages have fulfilled this role. Depending on the time and place, Aramaic, Latin, French, Russian and Greek have enjoyed significant lingua franca status.

In recent decades, however, the undisputed lingua franca has been English. While English is not likely to lose its lingua franca status anytime soon, it is important to keep in mind exactly what a lingua franca is—and is not. Lingua francas are primarily useful for superficial, routine communications. It therefore makes sense that English is used worldwide for administrative miscellanea such as airport signs, customs transactions, etc. These subjects require a limited amount of vocabulary, and only a superficial knowledge of grammar.

If you have ever traveled abroad, then you may have had the following experience: You address someone in English within a limited conversational framework, and they seem to understand you perfectly. As long as you stay within a standard "script" of questions and answers, everything is fine. However, communications quickly break down when you attempt to broach more complex topics.

Consider the situation from the opposite perspective. Think back to your days of high school French class. You may have learned enough French to get an "A" in the course, and you may have been able to read basic texts. Nonetheless, your practical abilities in French were probably quite limited. Could you, for example, have passed your high school Calculus class if it had been taught entirely in French? And what if someone were to call you up this afternoon, years later, and start speaking French at you out of the blue?

"GLOBAL ENGLISH" IS "ENGLISH-LITE"

"Global English" is a stripped-down subset of the English language that is spoken by Americans, Britons, and other native speakers. The version of English heard in airports, corporate boardrooms, and hotels throughout the world is characterized by a restricted vocabulary and only the rudiments of grammar.

An article in the New York Times said that Global English is *"neither English nor American...It's some sort of operating language. It loses quite a lot of nuance."* In some situations, this loss of nuance presents

17

no problems. Streamlined versions of English have been around for years, and they have functioned well for limited interchanges. For example, airline pilots and ocean navigators have long used standard lines of English-based jargon for communicating with personnel in seaports and airports around the world. These situations lend themselves to a scripted approach.

When the practice is used for complex communications, however, the result is a breakdown in mutual understanding. And it doesn't take a conversation about astrophysics or existentialism to reveal the weaknesses of scripted English. Even a nonstandard exchange in an airport can quickly degenerate into mutual incomprehension. An Amazon.com reviewer of the first edition of this book recounted the following experience in France:

> *"Even as a mere tourist, I was told repeatedly before a trip to Paris that "everybody there speaks English" and that I would never need to use my beginning French. Wrong, wrong, wrong! Try losing your passport in the airport, as I did, and trying to negotiate what steps to take next, without knowing French. Thankfully, my far-more-fluent brother was with me, or I might still be there!"*

A guest who participated in a roundtable discussion on the Australian Broadcasting Corporation's "Lingua Franca" program had the following to say about Global English (or, as he calls it, "international English"):

> *"...the English that is spoken around the world as a second language by most people is an absolutely lousy English. It's appalling, there is this sort of international English whereby everybody thinks they can speak it...international English is really an absolute bastard of a language.... the fact that English is the world's second language is really debasing English."*

The commentator was admittedly taking a rather harsh stance. However, there is no doubt that the English being used abroad is a stripped-down version of what Americans or Britons would consider authentic English. At the very least, "Global English" is inarticulate English.

MEASURING LINGUISTIC ABILITIES

When a non-native English-speaker uses English, our first impulse is to think, "Oh, that person speaks English." This hasty conclusion overlooks an important fact: a person who speaks English as a second language may know only a tiny fraction of the language that we use on a daily basis. The measurement of linguistic abilities is complicated. An individual's abilities in a foreign language can seldom be appraised simply as "speaks X language" or "does not speak X language". Rather, language skills must be measured along an incrementally ascending continuum.

It is difficult to quantify how much English an individual needs to know before one can reasonably say that he or she "speaks English." A person who might easily pass for a competent speaker of English in a routine airport situation might not qualify as an English speaker if business or technical issues are involved.

Given the functional nature of language, "knowledge" must be distinguished from "capability." There are millions of people in the non-English-speaking world who have some knowledge of English. But it is equally valid to say that the average American high school graduate has some knowledge of Spanish, French, or German. However, few Americans can claim any real functional skills in these languages.

It is easy to jump to conclusions when practically everyone outside the English-speaking world seems to know "hello," "please," and "thank you." In a business situation, the issue is critical: A nonnative speaker of English who handles simple topics quite fluently might grasp less than ten percent of the sales presentation that you deliver in English.

A FUNCTIONAL APPROACH TO ENGLISH

Non-native speakers of English are quick to acknowledge the difference between a knowledge of English and functional skill in English. When Yukari Akiyama, a Japanese business/career consultant, hosted an online discussion about the necessity of English skills in the workplace, one thirty-six-year-old programmer responded: 英語が話せることと、英語を使って仕事をすることは違う。("There is a difference between the ability to speak English and the ability to use English to get the job done.") He then went on to explain that he and his colleagues really only need to decipher an occasional document in English. Their office deals primarily with Japanese customers, so there is no real incentive to pour lots of time and effort into learning English.

This minimalist approach to learning English is common abroad, where professionals often compare English to a utilitarian aptitude like accounting. This rule holds even in Western Europe, where English skills are generally higher than they are in Asia or Latin America. Subramanian Rangan is an associate professor of strategy in the Insead business school near Paris. In a 2002 *New York Times* article, professor Rangan described the use of English in European firms as "shallow." He elaborated: "I doubt it [English] is in the board room, and it's not on the factory floor…So it's a narrow sliver. It's not in labor relations, and it's not in customer relations."

THE DEGENERATION OF THE LINGUA FRANCA

In theory, English is an effective means of communication among non-native speakers of the language. In other words, if a French company and a German company are working on a joint project, they could use English—rather than German or French—as a working language.

Some European firms have implemented English as the language for cross-border communications between groups that do not speak it natively—often resulting in confusion. Global English typically loses its basic functionality when it is employed in situations in which there are no native speakers present. One Spanish engineer described the "descent into babble" that occurs when his colleagues in Spain and France attempt to discuss complex issues via email in English.

This is confirmed by my own experience in the multinational corporate environment. I have seen English-language email chains between Japanese and Thais that break down to the point where no group—neither the Japanese, the Thais, nor the Americans (who have been carbon copied)—understand the communication. I have also seen considerable confusion occur when Japanese and Thais attempt to verbally discuss complex ideas in English. They would be better off using either Japanese or Thai.

The tendency toward linguistic degeneration underlines a key limitation of any lingua franca. When native speakers of the language are not present, second-language speakers tend to modify the language at will. If I speak German with my German colleague, his native mastery of German will keep me from taking too many liberties with his language. On the other hand, if I try to speak German with my Japanese colleague, we will eventually be speaking something that only resembles German.

The degeneration of the lingua franca used by non-native speakers is a historical fact. The Latin spoken as a lingua franca in the Roman provinces of Gaul and Iberia eventually became so distinct from the real thing that French, Spanish, and Portuguese—three mutually unintelligible languages—emerged in its place.

This process was ultimately productive in the case of Latin, as several new languages were created over centuries of use and misuse of the Roman tongue. However, English is used internationally with the aim of establishing clear communications—not inventing new languages.

A quote from European Commission President Romano Prodi sheds light on the natural degeneration that occurs when English is used as a lingua franca on Continental Europe—where no one speaks English as a native language. Speaking to a reporter for *Helsingin Sanomat*, a Finnish newspaper, Prodi described the way in which the English spoken by European Union officials has been drastically pared down to express simple ideas. In many situations, fragments of other languages are even inserted into English sentences:

> *"'Everyday matters will be dealt with in a certain kind of Kitchen English in the same way that people spoke Latin in the Middle Ages', Prodi said.*
>
> *By 'Kitchen English' Prodi was referring to the fact that the English spoken at the EU is seldom perfect. Also, there is a tendency in the hallways of Brussels and Strasbourg to combine English and other languages. A German might say 'vielleicht' ("perhaps") in the middle of an English language sentence, or an Italian might say 'pronto' when asking that something be done quickly."*

A REALISTIC APPROACH TO LINGUA FRANCAS

None of this is meant to imply that foreigners who learn just enough English to get by are mere dilettantes. The mastery of a foreign language takes dedicated effort. Even basic proficiency requires some skill. And we

Anglophones are in no position to accuse others of linguistic provincialism. The average nonnative speaker of English still gets much farther than does the typical American or Briton with foreign language exposure.

However, it is a mistake to assume that all foreigners have received a genetic download of fluent English. This seems to be the assumption of Americans who return from abroad with claims that the residents in a non-English-speaking country "pretended that they didn't understand English," when in fact—they understood only a little. We should not be surprised when we are met with stares of incomprehension. All things being equal, it is as difficult for a French speaker to become fluent in English as it is for an English speaker to master *français*.

There are, of course, nonnative English speakers who have thoroughly mastered our language due to special circumstances, such as extended residence in Great Britain, or the opportunity to earn an advanced degree in Canada or the United States. However, such individuals are the exception, not the rule. In most overseas situations, you will need to talk to people who have had to study English in their own country, as just one more academic subject.

English is in fact a "world language"—for very basic communications. Limiting yourself to English therefore limits your capabilities to communicate with others. Even travelers who interact with the international tourist industry often find that English alone is insufficient to meet their communication needs. For businesspeople, the implications are even more important: English may be sufficient to help you find the baggage claim area in Narita airport, but it is not going to be enough to get your company a new contract with a potential client in Tokyo. If you want to share more complex, nuanced ideas with non-English-speakers, then you will likely need skills in another language.

CHAPTER 2 APPENDIX:
LANGUAGE AND POPULAR CULTURE

In 1956, the average American would probably not have understood the Spanish phrase, *Que será,será*. This minor obstacle didn't prevent the Doris Day song of the same title from appealing to an English-speaking American audience. The song's composers, Jay Livingston and Ray Evans, cleverly inserted the English translation of *Que será,será* into the refrain, so that non-Spanish speakers could immediately grasp the meaning.

In 1959, the Spanish-language song *La Bamba* was a hit in the American youth music market. *La Bamba* was Ritchie "Valens" Valenzuela's adaptation of a traditional Mexican folk song that is often sung by Mariachi bands. In the wake of the song's popularity, the Spanish interjection "*arriba*" enjoyed a brief period of popularity among American teens.

In 1987, the Mexican-American group *Los Lobos* produced a new version of *La Bamba* for a movie about the life of Ritchie Valens. The Los Lobos version of the piece became the first Spanish-language song to reach the #1 position on the American charts. Throughout the 1990s, a series of Latin crossover artists enjoyed similar success with Spanish-language titles in the American market: Los Del Rio, Jon Secada, Selena, etc. In some cases, these successes resulted in the popularization of certain Spanish words and phrases. Most Americans of a certain age group now have at least an inkling of what the words *la vida loca* mean. (However, no one would confuse this knowledge with real proficiency in the Spanish language. Ritchie Valens and Selena were among the artists who succeeded with Spanish-language songs although they did not speak the language well themselves.)

Similarly, the diffusion of American movies and music throughout the world has assisted the diffusion of fragmentary English. I recently saw a CNN report about a Bolivian rap group that peppers its Spanish and Quechua lyrics with bits of American English slang. Like some of their American counterparts, these rap artists felt free to adopt phrases of a foreign language that they do not necessarily speak.

In much of the world, English has even become a fashion statement of sorts. If you travel to Tokyo, Seoul, or Berlin, you will likely see tee shirts, baseball caps, and travel bags adorned with random English phrases. The examples I have noticed over the years include "Big Company," "Hello, my darling," and (my personal favorite) "Rock my Dogs."

We see examples of the same practice in the United States. Over the past ten years or so, Asian characters have become popular fashion statements. I was sitting in traffic the other day when I noticed a decal on the car in front of me that bore the following words:

高速

The above characters (*koosoku* in Japanese or *gao su* in Chinese) translate into English as "high speed." Given the the context, the driver likely knew the English translation of the characters on the decal. This does not necessarily mean that he could hold a conversation in Chinese or Japanese. The same goes for the many Americans who now have tattoos with the Chinese characters for love (愛), power (力), or freedom (自由).

Ding hao!

The Flying Tigers were a group of American fighter pilots who volunteered to fight against the Japanese in Burma and China in the early days of World War II, before the United States formally entered the war. The Flying Tigers often adorned the fuselages of their planes with the words "*Ding Hao!*" The Chinese word, (顶好), means "well done!" or "very good!"

Few of the Flying Tigers actually learned to speak Chinese. (They were otherwise occupied!). Nevertheless, this Chinese phrase became a popular exclamation among the pilots.

Foreignness Sells

In the non-English-speaking world, marketers often give a product an English (or quasi-English) name to give it an air of the exotic. I recently visited the website of the Japanese company NEC, and I saw product names like *Valuestar G* and *Smart Vision* targeted at the Japanese market. (NEC was also giving Japanese consumers a dose of French. One of its products is called *LaVie*.)

Once again, there are parallels within the English-speaking world. You may have noticed that many cosmetic products in the United States are given French names (or French-sounding names). Although only a fraction of the American consumer market has any reasonable command of French, cosmetics companies give their products names like *eau de parfum* and *eau de toilette*. (And if the cosmetics company happens to be European, it seldom anglicizes the name of the product for the American market.)

Restaurants also have a penchant for going Gaulish. In my home town of Cincinnati, there is an upscale restaurant called *The Maisonette*. In restaurant circles, one constantly hears raw French terminology like *nouvelle cuisine* and *haute cuisine*, even though these same ideas could be expressed in English.

French words are used in the above examples because giving a product a French name somehow makes it seem more refined, unique, or even exotic. French is by no means the only foreign language that is used for marketing purposes in the United States. Italian and Spanish names are also favorites. Consider the Ford *Fiesta*, the Honda *Del Sol*, and the Cadillac *El Dorado*.

"It doesn't go."

You may have heard the old story about the Chevy Nova, and the translation of this car's name in Spanish. The syllables *no va* mean "doesn't go" in Spanish. According to an often repeated urban legend, this embarrassing linguistic gaffe forced Chevrolet to pull the car off the market in Latin America. Latin American buyers reportedly confused Nova for *no va*, and rejected the vehicle.

However, there is no real evidence to support this story. In fact, the Chevy Nova actually sold well in several Latin American countries.

If you pointed to a car in a Spanish-speaking country and said "*no va*," people would understand what you meant. But a native Spanish-speaker would be more likely to use the phrase "*no funciona*" to describe a car that wasn't working properly.

Moreover, "Nova" is pronounced without a pause, as a single word. The correct Spanish pronunciation of *no va* distinguishes the division between the two words with a clear pause. In the same way, native English-speakers would be unlikely to confuse the pronunciation of the word "dragnet" with the words "drag net"—unless the speaker was making a deliberate attempt at phonetic ambiguity.

CHAPTER 3

THE 21ST CENTURY SPEAKS MANY LANGUAGES

THE [OLD] LINGUISTIC NEW WORLD ORDER

On January 29, 1991, President George H.W. Bush delivered his State of the Union address before the U.S. Congress. He spoke of a *"new world order"* as *"a big idea,"* in which *"diverse nations are drawn together in common cause to achieve the universal aspirations of mankind."* In many respects, the first President Bush was correct: during the 1990s, the global community did come closer to establishing universal norms of government, trade, and human rights.

The New World Order also had an impact on language. During the late 1980s, the bipolar world order of the Cold War years collapsed. Between 1989 and 1991, East and West Germany reunited, countries like Czechoslovakia and Poland jettisoned Communism, and the Soviet Union officially dissolved itself. In the absence of the bipolar conflict, the 1990s were dominated by the concept of *globalization*. Geopolitics, trade, (and the global use of language) was said to be heading down the path of homogenization. The only real powers in the world were the United States, and an amalgamation of smaller, weaker countries grouped together under the flag of the United Nations.

Almost by default, such an arrangement naturally favored the global usage of English. During the Cold War, half of the world was studying Russian as a second language. But now, English was the only second language that really counted.

NEW MARKETS FOR U.S. MULTINATIONALS

The business conditions that were emerging when George H.W. Bush delivered his "New World Order" speech in 1991 also favored the global dominance of English. During the 1990s, U.S. multinationals moved rapidly into new consumer and labor markets around the world. American companies had numerous advantages over any local competitors: access to cheap capital, management expertise, and brand recognition. In addition, many new players—like Russia and China—were still learning the basics of capitalism.

The Americans were offering not only products, but jobs as well. The 1990s was the beginning of the "outsourcing" or "offshoring" trend that would receive so much attention after the recession of 2001 and 2002. Multinationals discovered that they could significantly cut costs by moving production facilities to cheaper labor markets overseas. As a result, global hiring by U.S. multinationals soared during the 1990s. (For example, employment of Mexican nationals by U.S. companies more than doubled in the five years following the 1994 passage of NAFTA.) In much of the world, a job with an American company was seen as the surest path to personal prosperity. For the more desirable jobs, this usually meant learning English.

NEW TRENDS AND NEW CHALLENGES

There can be no doubt that the 1990s were an era dominated by the global usage of English. Nonetheless, three new trends are changing the global linguistic landscape—and making foreign languages more important to native English-speakers.

TREND 1: THERE IS A NEW GLOBAL BALANCE OF POWER

The United States remains the most prosperous nation on earth, and the other English-speaking nations are close behind. However, there has been a change in the *relative* position of the Anglophone world. At the end of World War II, nations like China and Japan were economic basket cases with little global impact. Today, China is the world's second or third largest economy (depending on how you measure economic size); and competitors from throughout the non-English-speaking world are gaining on American companies.

The automotive sector provides a striking example. A Japanese automaker—Toyota—now holds 12 percent of the U.S. automobile market. Many industry analysts are suggesting that Toyota will ultimately reach parity with the Big Three within the U.S. market. A 2005 industry study predicted that Toyota will supplant General Motors as the largest automobile manufacturer in the world by 2010. Toyota itself projects that it will corner 15 percent of the global automobile market by the same year. China was one of the world's poorest countries as recently as 1980. Today, China is home to 18 million millionaires, 400 million television sets, and 470 million cell phone subscribers. China now manufacturers two-thirds of the world's DVD players, copy machines, and microwave ovens. In its May 04, 2005 issue, *Newsweek* magazine openly asked "Does the Future Belong to China?"

Latin America was once dominated by totalitarian governments, high national debts, and almost universal poverty. Latin American living standards are still far below those of the United States, but purchasing power within the region is rapidly growing. The thirteen nations of South America alone have a total population of 330 million, and a combined GDP of $1.8 trillion. In Mexico, the second largest Latin American country after Brazil, ecommerce is booming; in a recent survey, more than 25 percent of Mexican consumers reported making an online purchase in the past ninety days.

Just as Sputnik generated fears of an American decline, the recent advances made in overseas economies are interpreted by some as a harbinger of doom. Others see the changes in a more optimistic light. Nobel Prize-winning Economist Milton Friedman has said that all countries will experience long-term benefits from the increase in prosperity in the developing world. Wealthy populations are typically less susceptible to extremist doctrines and dictatorship. This ultimately means fewer wars and terrorist attacks.

Cooperation between Non-English Speakers Diminishes the Usage of English

There is now large-scale cooperation between non-English-speaking economic entities. In the mid-1990s, I made numerous trips to *Nissan Mexicana*, Nissan Motor Company's Mexican division. Nissan owns a series of assembly plants, foundries, and research centers throughout Mexico. The Aguascalientes assembly plant produces engines and completed vehicles for the North American market. I spent most of my time in Mexico at this facility, and had ample opportunity to observe communications practices.

According to the theory of Global English, the Mexicans and the Japanese employed by Nissan should have used English as the daily "business language." However, this was almost never the case—even at the management level. Almost all conversations took place in Spanish.

The shift toward languages other than English has been accelerated by the rise of regional economic blocs. Mercosur is a union of Spanish- and Portuguese-speaking countries in South America. It therefore follows that these languages, rather than English, are used for business purposes at Mercosur functions. (When I visited the Mercosur website, the only language options available were Portuguese and Spanish.)

The hottest new language in Argentina and Chile is not English—but Chinese. In certain sectors, Beijing is poised to become the most significant trading partner of these two South American nations. Chinese language studies are booming; and some analysts have speculated that Chinese will be the most important foreign language in South America within five years.

China and Japan have not yet formed their own economic alliance, but there are signs that such an alliance may be formed within the next decade. At the end of 2002, Beijing and Tokyo began preliminary talks about the formation of a free-trade zone that would include not only their two countries, but also South Korea. Sino-Japanese trade is now growing faster than Japanese-American trade, or Chinese-American trade. China is already one of Japan's principle trading partners, and Japan has been China's largest trading partner since the early 1990s. Andy Xie, writing for Morgan Stanley's "Global Economic Forum" online newsletter in May, 2001, predicted that, *"Within ten years China and Japan could become each other's most important trading partners, replacing the United States."*

The relationship between China and Japan is entering a new, historically unprecedented phase. Dr. Jin Xide, a researcher at the Chinese Academy of Social Sciences, notes that in the past, Sino-Japanese relations have been defined by the relative weakness of one of the two countries. Now, however, *"..for the first time in history, Sino-Japanese relations are stepping into a new period of 'strong China and strong Japan.'"*

If the current pace of economic integration in East Asia continues, it is only a matter of time before businesspersons and government officials in China, South Korea, and Japan begin to show more interest in the languages of their neighboring customers and partners. While there are significant dissimilarities between Chinese, Japanese, and Korean, any one of these languages has vastly more in common with the other two than it does with English. Businesses in East Asia's three largest economies will always need some English speakers to communicate with the West; but it would be tremendously inefficient for these countries to use English to communicate with *each other*.

The bottom line is that the formation of regional trading blocks comprised of non-English-speaking countries will not favor a more extensive usage of English as a lingua franca. Businesspersons (and therefore, eventually, school systems) will have to devote more attention to the languages of their major trading partners. In such an environment, monolingual English-speaking businesspersons will be at a distinct disadvantage.

Businesses Speak the Languages of their Customers

Visit the website of almost any major company that provides goods or services to consumers, and you will likely find multiple language options. Ford Motor Company's English-language site has links to companion sites in more than a dozen languages—including such exotics as Indonesian and Vietnamese. Consumer goods manufacturer Proctor & Gamble provides online and offline materials in Russian, Turkish, and Hebrew, among many others.

Corporations like Ford and P&G exist to make money for their shareholders. Their investment in multilingual marketing materials is therefore motivated not by concerns of multiculturalism or political correctness—but a desire to tap the increasing purchasing power of the non-English-speaking world.

In previous decades, American corporations had minimal incentive to adopt foreign-language marketing campaigns abroad. Not only was the purchasing power of non-English-speaking consumers small, but there were few alternatives for the Chinese- or Spanish-speaking consumers who could afford to buy. Now U.S. companies face increasing competition from foreign firms who by default sell their goods and services in the local language.

It is also worth noting that the market incentive to go multilingual is not limited to household-name, multinational corporations. The area of Ohio where I live is home to many Japanese companies, and a large number of Japanese expatriates. This has prompted local real estate agencies, insurance companies, and travel bureaus to recruit employees who speak Japanese.

30

Improved access to foreign markets via the Internet has also enabled more small- and medium-sized businesses to enter the export market.

An English Internet?

Enthusiasts of the Global English theory once cited the Internet as evidence that the non-English speaking world was rapidly conforming to an English-speaking standard. In his Wall Street Journal article, "World Wide Web: Three English Words", Michael Specter wrote, *"If you want to take full advantage of the internet there is only one real way to do it: learn English."*

Given that the article appeared in 1996, Specter's statement cannot be written off as mere cultural chauvinism. As recently as 1997, about 80% of the content on the Internet was written in English. For a while, the Web seemed to be moving in a monolingual direction.

However, this trend is now reversing itself. It is estimated that as of 2002, less than 50% of the content on the Internet is written in English. Some experts anticipate that this figure will fall below 30% within the next few years. On a country-by-country basis, local languages are being overwhelmingly chosen as the medium for web content. In Japan, for example, more than 90% of all web content is written in Japanese. In Spanish- and French-speaking countries, this number is probably around 98% or 99%.

The Internet's major corporate players have recognized linguistic diversity as a dominant market trend. All the major portal and ecommerce sites—MSN, Amazon, Yahoo, etc—offer mirror sites in multiple languages. Yahoo even provides services in such arguably minor languages as Danish and Catalan.

Language and Technology Transfer

The linguistic patterns of the scientific and technological realms have largely followed those of the wider world, with a few minor variations. German never became a universal global language, but it did attain lingua franca status inside the scientific community. Before America's ascendancy as the world's foremost industrial power, Germany was widely regarded as the leader in scientific and technological research. A hundred years ago, a young person who aspired to a career in science would have likely studied the German language. Germany's technical universities were regarded as the finest in the world; and Germany's lead in patents and technical research

31

meant that many of the breakthrough research papers of the day were published in German. A disproportionate number of the scientific luminaries of the 19th century and early 20th century were German-speakers: Max Planck, Max Born, Albert Einstein, etc.

Germany is still the technological powerhouse of Europe, and the German language has retained a certain cachet among science and technology students. Even today, science and engineering faculties in the United States continue to recommend the German language for students who must complete a general studies language requirement.

Despite the continued popularity of German, English has become the language of technological research and development since the postwar era. In the decades following World War II, the United States developed into the world's primary source of groundbreaking research and new patents.

However, there is now evidence that the pendulum of technological supremacy may be swinging again. The United States now awards 25% fewer bachelor's degrees in engineering than it did in 1985. China graduates more engineers than the United States; and Asia as a whole graduates eight times as many engineers as the United States. In recent years, researchers in China, Japan, South Korea, and elsewhere have been making revolutionary strides in biotechnology, computer science, and related fields. Only a portion of this research material is being translated for foreign consumption. In the near future, American researchers may find that the ability to read a foreign language is essential to keeping up with the latest developments in their fields.

TREND 2: DEMOGRAPHIC CHANGES

Language and population are inextricably linked. Language is intimately tied to actual human beings; and languages either grow or shrink with populations.

In a March 2004 interview with the Voice of America (VOA) program "Coast to Coast," British linguistics scholar David Graddol noted that while the total number of English-speakers continues to grow, our population growth rate lags behind speakers of other languages. According to Graddol, this will lead to English falling to a secondary place as a world language by the middle of this century. After Chinese, English will likely occupy a mid-tier position along with Arabic and several other tongues.

32

Most English-speaking countries are part of the developed world, which is characterized by low birth rates, and low overall rates of population growth. In the United States, growth rates are still near the 1 percent threshold due to immigration. (The native population of the United States is now reproducing at a rate below the replacement level.) But the population growth rate in Great Britain is less than 0.5 percent. The population growth rates of Canada and Australia (both of which attract many immigrants) approach those of the United States; but both have comparatively tiny population bases. There are only 32 million Canadians, and 20 million Australians. When added together, Canada and Australia still comprise less than half the population of Mexico.

In the developing world—which largely speaks languages other than English—population growth rates are much higher than they are in the developed world. Some parts of the developing world have population growth rates near 3 percent. Moreover, many of these countries are growing from base populations that are already large. It has become a cliché to note that there are 1.3 billion people in China; but the considerable populations of Egypt, Brazil, and the rest of Latin America receive far less press. And Indonesia, the giant of Southeast Asia, is practically ignored by the Western media—the coverage of the 2002 terrorist bombings in Bali being the exception which proves the rule.

Demographic factors alone cannot give a language worldwide clout. On balance, German is still a more significant global language than Bengali. Germany's population of 83 million is now shrinking; it had no population growth in 2004. Bengali is spoken by twice as many people; and the average population growth rate of Bengali speakers is above 2 percent. Nonetheless, Germany's gross domestic product (GDP) is $2.362 trillion, compared to $275.7 billion of Bengali-speaking Bangladesh.

The impact of large population numbers is arguably most significant in those parts of the world which have high rates of economic growth *and* a large and/or rapidly increasing population. We will begin with the two most significant examples in this regard: China and Latin America.

China

As most readers have undoubtedly heard, China's population is the largest in the world—1.3 billion. This is more than four times the current size of the population of the United States. One in every five people living on earth is Chinese.

China's population has been large by Western standards for centuries. In the early 1300s, China already had a population of more than 120 million, when the total population of Europe was 170 million. China's population was subsequently halved by a bubonic plague outbreak in the 1330s. (The same outbreak would hit Europe in 1347 and reduce the European population by one third.) Despite this setback, China's population had reached 420 million by 1850, about five times its post-plague lows. (At the same time, there were 16 million souls in England, and 23 million in the United States.) The accounts of Westerners who visited China in the 1800s often make reference to the vastness of the country's population.

By 2010, it is estimated that China's population will exceed 1.4 billion. If the nation continues its current path of economic reform and development, then the sheer numbers of prosperous Chinese-speaking consumers in the world will dramatically increase the prestige of the language over the coming decades.

The Growth of Spanish and Portuguese

John F. Copper is a professor of International Studies at Rhodes College in Memphis, Tennessee. Writing in *Next Step Magazine*, a magazine for graduating high school students and their parents, he encouraged readers to study Spanish not only because of its current status as one of the most commonly spoken languages in the world, but because of its future growth. Copper pointed out that most Spanish-speaking countries are experiencing high rates of population growth.

Ironically, Spain, like the rest of Europe, is shrinking demographically. Spain currently has an annual population growth rate of only 0.15%. However, Spanish-speaking countries in the Americas are among the fastest growing in the world, and these nations are increasing the global importance of Spanish. Mexico's population growth rate is 1.17% — almost eight times the growth rate of Spain, and four times the rate of the United Kingdom.

Portuguese-speaking Brazil is the fifth-largest nation in the world, with a population of more than 186 million (more than triple the population of Great Britain). And Brazil is experiencing fast growth in both economic and human terms. The country's gross domestic product grew by 5.1% in

2004 (the U.S. economy grew by about 4% in 2004); and Brazil's annual rate of population growth is above 1%. These factors make Portuguese a major language today—and in the future, as well. (It should also be noted that Brazil is not the only country in the developing world where Portuguese is spoken.)

The Growth of Arabic

The populations of the Arabic-speaking world are growing even faster than those of the Spanish- and Portuguese-speaking countries. Egypt already has more than 77 million people and a growth rate of 1.78%. In Iraq, the growth rate is now 2.7%. Saudi Arabia's population is also growing by more than 2% a year; and Arabic-speaking Yemen's population is swelling at 3.45% per year.

Population Growth Rates in Perspective

Ideally, a country's population growth rate should avoid either extreme. On one hand, many European countries face uncertain economic futures because the numbers of people entering the workforce are not high enough to sustain economic growth and social benefits. On the other hand, the excessively high population growth rates of the Arabic-speaking world are tied to rigidly patriarchal social structures, and limited opportunities for women.

Nonetheless, birth rates do have a significant impact on the future of a language. If more native speakers of a particular language are being born today, then there will be more adult speakers of that language twenty years from now. Likewise, a decline in the birthrate of the speakers of a particular language will result in fewer adults speaking that language in the coming decades.

TREND 3: LINGUISTIC GROUPS ARE INCREASINGLY BORDERLESS.

The notion of a global community of speakers is an old idea. For centuries, French, English, Spanish, and a handful of other languages have been widely spoken in numerous countries. Now modern technology and travel are increasing the "borderlessness" of other languages as well. At the same time, the distinctly modern phenomenon of nonpermanent immigration is creating ambivalent attitudes about linguistic assimilation.

On average, immigrants lose their native language within two generations. (In the melting pot environment of the United States, the native language is often abandoned by the first generation born and raised here.) The permanent immigrant makes a multigenerational investment in a new country, while simultaneously breaking ties with the country of her birth. Nineteenth-century immigrants to the United States saw little practical benefit in retaining the Italian, Polish, and Gaelic of their homelands. American English would become the language of their children, and their children's children.

Residency abroad is increasingly a temporary situation. There are growing numbers of people who complete extended stays in a foreign country without the intention of becoming permanent residents. In most cases, these extended visits are the result of overseas posting by multinational corporations, or the desire of individuals to take advantage of economic opportunities abroad. In addition, the global nature of modern business creates many serial travelers, who spend large amounts of time in a foreign country without ever establishing a permanent residence.

These short-term immigrants and frequent visitors have different attitudes about the languages of their host countries. There is no sense of forsaking the homeland. The visitor/nonpermanent immigrant will almost certainly want to take her language with her while abroad. This creates a demand for a foreign-language media in the host country, and an infrastructure that speaks the visitor's language.

Telenovelas in Mexico—and in the United States

In the United States, the increase in temporary workers from Mexico has heightened the demand for Spanish-language broadcasting in recent years. Advertising on Spanish-language networks in the U.S. will reach $1.41 billion in 2005—more than double the amount six years earlier. The presence of Spanish-speakers and Spanish-language media in the United States is nothing new; but the recent upsurge in temporary workers has given the media a distinctly borderless quality. As more Mexicans spend part of the year in the United States and part of the year in their native Mexico, there is a growing market incentive to create Spanish-language media that can cross the U.S.-Mexican border with visitors.

Azteca América is a Spanish-language broadcasting company that primarily serves Spanish-speakers living in the United States. The company recently announced plans to launch *telenovelas*—soap operas—simultaneously in the U.S. and Mexican markets. The move was specifically motivated by a desire to take advantage of the borderless nature of their market. According to one industry analyst, "There's a lot of movement between the two countries. The Azteca viewer is in constant communication with their homeland so they're hearing and talking about the *novelas* at home."

Japanese as a Business Language in Ohio

The U.S. received a substantial influx of Japanese immigrants from the 1880s through the 1930s. These permanent immigrants followed the typical assimilation pattern. Their children grew up in an English-speaking environment, largely abandoning the Japanese language. Therefore, few Japanese-language media institutions were created to serve these early twentieth century immigrants from Japan—and those that did exist quickly folded after the first generation passed from the scene.

In the late 1980s, the U.S. had another influx of people from Japan, as Japanese companies like Honda and Toyota expanded their operations in the United States. This time, however, the "immigrants" consisted of businesspersons and their families who were posted in America for three- to five-year assignments.

I met many of these families during my own time in the Japanese automotive industry. While Japanese company employees posted overseas studied English enthusiastically, their spouses often existed in microcosms consisting of Japanese-speaking friends and transplanted Japanese media. These families had no intention of settling in the United States, so their need to "assimilate" was temporary, and did not include an abandonment of their native language.

Columbus, Ohio is a long way from traditional international hubs like Los Angeles and New York. Surrounded by farmland and small towns, Columbus is a city that still has a quasi-rural feel. Columbus is also home to Honda of America (in nearby Marysville), and dozens of smaller Japanese firms that exist to serve the American division of Japan's second largest automaker. The Columbus suburb of Dublin is home to scores of Japanese-speaking travel agencies, bookstores, and restaurants. Many of these media and service outlets are Japanese transplants that followed Honda to Ohio; and all of them rely heavily on business from Honda employees.

Ohio is also home to a fair number of Japanese-language schools. The Japanese school system subjects students a series of rigorous examinations, which is often called 試験地獄(*shiken-jigoku*), or "examination hell." Preparation for these tests is a fulltime job for all school-age children. Japanese students prepare for tests in school, and also in after school "cram schools" known as 塾(*juku*). If a student neglects her preparations while living overseas, it may be impossible for her to catch up with her peers when she returns to Japan. This potential dilemma for parents and students has led to numerous Japanese-language schools not only in Ohio, but throughout the world wherever there are sizeable numbers of Japanese transplant companies.

English-Speaking Islands Abroad

The above descriptions are accounts of foreign-language cultures that have made inroads into the United States. We English-speakers also create pockets of media and infrastructure abroad that cater to our needs. Most foreign countries have English-speaking schools that educate the children of American, British, and Canadian expatriates. Many large cities overseas also have English-language bookstores that cater to the English-speaking client who cannot yet read the local language.

Appearances, however, can be deceiving. On one of my business trips to Mexico, my colleague suffered the misfortune of losing his luggage and wallet. We spent an afternoon driving around to various department stores and financial institutions to address this minor crisis. When we entered the office of well-known American credit card company, there was no one on duty who spoke English. This struck me as odd given the fact that this company aggressively markets its services to Americans who are stranded abroad with no wallet or identification. The irony was compounded when we visited the local branch of Banamex. Banamex is a thoroughly Mexican institution, but we were greeted by a man who happened to have spent five years in the United States—and he spoke excellent English.

CHAPTER 3 APPENDIX: THE MANY ORIGINS OF ENGLISH

If you elect to study a Western European language, you will often encounter cognates—words that are similar or identical across English and another language. You can mostly thank long-dead invaders for these conveniences. English has been extensively influenced by the languages brought to the British Isles through ancient conquests.

The earliest inhabitants of Britain spoke a variety of languages, including various Celtic tongues. However, no Celtic language would help you order a cup of coffee in Heathrow Airport today. Ancient Britain's language and culture were quickly sullied by foreign influences.

In the mid-5th century, three Germanic tribes, the Angles, the Saxons, and the Jutes, invaded Britain. Their invasion was linguistic as well as military; the languages spoken by the Germanic tribes soon overwhelmed the Celtic ones. But the Celtic past of England persists in some words of Celtic origin that are still used in modern English, such as: *gravel*, *bard*, *bother*, *clan* and *slogan*. (The latter is an adaptation of the Celtic word *sluagh-ghairm*, or "battle cry".)

As the Germanic tribes thrived in Britain, English became infused with a vast Germanic vocabulary. You can thank these tribes if you ever decide to learn modern German. Many German words, like *der Apfel* ("the apple"), *die Mutter* ("the mother") and *der Vater* ("the father") will be immediately recognizable to you.

The word "English" came into common usage in the area of Britain lying between the Thames and the southern frontier of Scotland. This portion of modern-day England was settled by the Angles, who came from the wedge of land, or "angle" which comprises the region presently known as Schleswig-Holstein. Over the next few centuries, several dialects of English evolved. These dialects did not converge until the 14th century.

The alphabet that we English speakers use today has its roots in Rome. The invading Germanic tribes originally had a system of writing that used runes. In this period, European writing techniques were still crude. Letters had to be carved into wood or stone surfaces. Runes therefore consisted of straight lines and angles. (If you have ever read any of the Tolkien works, then you have an idea of what these characters looked like.) As Roman invaders, and later Christian missionaries, brought Latin to

British shores, the runes were gradually replaced by the Latin alphabet. Latin vocabulary also made deeps inroads into the English language, although English is not a derivative of Latin to the extent that French, Spanish, and Portuguese are.

In the northern section of England, Viking invasions brought an early Scandinavian language known as Old Norse. We still speak fragments of Old Norse today. *Sky, egg, skin, window,* and *ugly* are all Old Norse words. We can also give a nod of thanks to the Vikings for the personal pronouns *they, their,* and *them.*

The evolving English language suffered a temporary setback in 1066 when England was conquered by a new group of invaders—the Normans. The ruling Normans spoke an early version of French, which became the language of the English nobility for several hundred years. The Norman invaders repaid the subjugated Britons with a vast array of new French-based vocabulary. Most of this vocabulary exists today in the form of synonyms of older English words. Norman French added depth and variety to the English language.

For example, if you want to say that an event happens once per year, you can use the English word *yearly,* or the French word *annual.* If you note that the door to your office is *shut,* you are connecting with your English roots; if you say that the door is *closed,* you are using a remnant of Norman French. And don't forget to thank the Normans the next time you order a meat entree in a restaurant; *beef, veal,* and *pork* are all derived from French.

French is itself Latin-based; so many Latin words that originally entered English through Latin itself later arrived through the medium of French. In many cases, scholars are uncertain of whether a modern English word can be authentically traced to purely Latin influences, Latin-French influences, or both. Consider the English word "sententious," which means "pithy" or "abounding in aphorisms and moralizing." The Latin word *sententiōsus* means "full of meaning." But there is also an Old French equivalent: *sententieux.* Whether sententious is truly derived from French or Latin is a matter of some speculation.

During the Middle Ages, loanwords from other languages reached English, often via the conduit of French. *Marmalade* is of Portuguese origin. *Sable* is derived from a Russian word. Many readers will be surprised to learn that English also contains scores of Arabic loanwords: *cotton, hazard, mosque, algebra, zenith, sugar,* etc.

CHAPTER 4

HOW LINGUA FRANCAS BECOME LINGUA FRANCAS

The following rule has been demonstrated again and again throughout the linguistic history of the world: *If your society possesses disproportionate cultural, military, or economic strength, then your language will achieve dominance over neighboring languages.* A language does not succeed because of its own qualities; a language becomes dominant because the people who speak it have been extraordinarily successful.

This chapter examines the processes by which a handful of major languages ascended to lingua franca status. We will also take a look at the empires, kings, and peoples who gave these languages their power.

THE RISE OF ARAMAIC

Many readers will remember Aramaic from Mel Gibson's 2004 film, *The Passion of the Christ*. Aramaic was the primary language of New Testament-era Palestine, and much of the Middle East. Aramaic's star has since fallen. Less than a million people speak the language today; and most of them live in areas that current geopolitics have made unsuitable for Western travelers: Syria, Iran, Lebanon, and a few other corners of the Middle East. Aramaic exists in the twenty-first century mostly in the form of Syriac—a minority tongue that is used primarily for liturgical purposes.

Aramaic has its roots in distant Mesopotamia, the so-called "cradle of civilization" between the Tigris and Euphrates rivers in modern-day Iraq. It became the dominant language in Mesopotamia after supplanting two earlier languages, Sumerian and Akkadian, which subsequently passed into history.

Aramaic, like Arabic and Hebrew, is a Semitic language. Unlike Sumerian and Akkadian, which were written in cuneiform symbols, Aramaic looks vaguely "modern," if a bit exotic. Aramaic script closely resembles the written form of modern Arabic.

The Assyrians, the Babylonians, and the Persians

In its heyday, Aramaic had influential sponsors. The Aramaic language was propelled to world-class status by three ancient powers: Assyria, Persia, and Babylonia. Each of these three nations played a role in making Aramaic the language of New Testament-era Palestine.

The Assyrians were the early ancient world's most aggressive empire-builders. The Assyrians practiced systematic terror; they were known to behead entire villages, and impale prisoners on sharpened poles that had been driven into the earth. These practices gave them a fearsome reputation, even by the standards of the ancient world. The Assyrians ruled a vast swath of the Middle East with an iron fist from 900 to 612 BCE. At its height, the Assyrian Empire included western Iran, Iraq, Palestine, and Syria. For about half of this period, Aramaic was the official language of the Assyrian Empire. The Assyrians were more often feared than emulated; but their empire made Aramaic the language of power in the Middle East.

In 626 BCE, another Aramaic-speaking nation, Babylonia, rebelled against the Assyrians. The Babylonians finally sacked the Assyrian capitol of Nineveh in 612. But the Babylonians weren't given much time to build their own empire. The Babylonians were absorbed by the mighty Persian Empire in 540.

The Persian Empire grew to extend as far east as India, and as far west as Libya. (This area included Palestine.) King Darius I of Persia made Aramaic the official language of the western half of the Persian Empire in 500 BCE. The Persians continued to rule the region for several hundred years, during which the Aramaic language flourished and became further entrenched as the prestige language of the Middle East.

There is more to the story of Aramaic than armies and empires. Aramaic was also the language of settlers. Aramaic-speaking nomads, farmers, and merchants dispersed throughout the Middle East during Old Testament times. Although their names are not recorded in history books, these common people also contributed significantly to the spread of Aramaic.

What about Hebrew?

Hebrew developed in the land known as Canaan (present-day Israel, Jordan, Syria, and Lebanon). Hebrew closely resembles ancient Phoenician and Moabite, two other Canaanite languages which are now extinct. The first five books of the Old Testament, known collectively as the Torah (תורה), are written in Hebrew.

As a spoken language, Hebrew declined as Aramaic flourished, and several books of the Old Testament (including Ezra and Daniel) were composed in Aramaic. By the time Jesus was born, Aramaic was firmly established as the language of daily life in Palestine. Hebrew was still studied by religious scholars; but few Jews of the period would have been able to hold a conversation in the language.

The Romans sacked Jerusalem in 70 CE following the Bar Kokhba revolt against Imperial rule. Jerusalem was renamed as a pagan city, *Aelia Capitolina*, and Jews were forbidden live there. The Jewish nation subsequently dispersed from the region to a variety of countries in Europe and the Middle East. Hebrew was now completely abandoned as a language of daily life, but it was retained for liturgical purposes for the next 1800 years.

Hebrew was revived as a "living language" in the late nineteenth century. Eliezer Ben-Yehuda was a Russian Jew who immigrated to Palestine in 1881. He began the movement to revitalize Hebrew as a language for Jews living in the old lands of ancient Israel. The idea initially met with skepticism. (Imagine a Catholic movement to revive Latin as a language of daily life.) However, the Hebrew language movement gained momentum in the early twentieth century, when Jewish immigration to Palestine increased.

Modern Hebrew is based on ancient Biblical Hebrew; but the influence of the diaspora years is apparent in the language that Israelis speak today. Some characteristics of Modern Hebrew can be traced to Russian, German, and English.

WHEN EVERYONE ASPIRED TO SPEAK GREEK

Another force rolled into the Middle East in 332 BCE. This time, the invaders spoke Greek. Israel, Palestine, and Syria became part of the vast Hellenistic empire of Alexander the Great. Alexander was originally from the northern Greek kingdom of Macedon, and his empire spread Greek language and culture as far away as India.

During the period of Greek domination, the Greek language became the official administrative language of the Holy Land. Aramaic persisted as the lingua franca of daily life, but many local residents also learned to speak Greek. The drive toward Hellenization was aided by the founding of Greek colonies in the area. Some Jews eagerly embraced Greek culture. Violence erupted when particularly zealous advocates of Hellenization tried to establish the cult of Zeus in the Jerusalem temple.

Historical trivia buffs were quick to point out that Mel Gibson's *The Passion of the Christ* contained no Greek. If you saw the aforementioned film, you likely remember the scenes in which the Roman and Jewish characters communicated in Aramaic. There was also a scene in which Jesus briefly spoke in Latin.

No one can say for sure which languages Jesus spoke, but we can make some guesses based on historical language trends. He almost certainly spoke Aramaic, bits of Hebrew, and some Greek. Few Jews in New Testament-era Palestine spoke Latin.

The Roman soldiers who occupied Palestine of course spoke Latin. Some of them may have learned to speak the local Aramaic. However, Greek would have been the natural "link language" between the Roman occupiers and the Jewish residents of Palestine.

Rome supplanted the empire of Alexander as the new power in the Holy Land by the first century BCE. The Romans made no attempt to de-Hellenize the lands they inherited from the Greeks. On the contrary, the Romans were enthusiastic students of Greek language and culture; and Greek—not Latin—became the language of administration in the eastern portion of the Roman Empire.

The Greek language was a towering lingua franca of the ancient world. The ancient world's reliance on Greek had nothing to do with the ease of learning Greek, or the innate suitability of Greek as a common language. The currency of the Greek language was a result of the universal respect for Greek culture. Greek achievements in philosophy, art, and literature inspired admiration and imitation in neighboring societies.

The Romans admired Greek culture much as nineteenth century Americans admired European culture. The Romans borrowed from Greek architecture, sculpture, and urban planning techniques. Even the Roman religion had its roots in Greece: the Roman god Jupiter was patterned after the Greek god Zeus. Minerva was a Latin version of the Greek goddess Athena. Neptune was a Romanized Poseidon.

A command of the Greek language was considered to be a mark of refinement for an ancient Roman. The Roman Emperor Marcus Aurelius wrote his famous *Meditations* in Greek—not Latin. When the Roman Senate passed a decree that needed to be conveyed to other parts of the Empire, it was most often translated into Greek, because Greek was the language shared by educated people throughout the Empire. In the early days of Roman Christianity, most of the gospels were recorded in Greek—rather than the Latin that would later become the language of the Catholic Church, or the Aramaic in which Jesus actually preached.

The Greek influence on world languages

Although Greek is no longer the world langage that is once was, its influence lives on in numerous Western European languages—including English. Modern English contains numerous Greek prefixes and suffixes. For example, the Greek prefix *mega-* ("great") is the basis of the English words *megadose, megalomoania,* and *megahertz.* (The Greek term Μέγας Ἀλέξανδρος (*Megas Alexandros*) means "Alexander the Great.")

THE RISE OF LATIN

When viewed through the retrospective lens of history, the Roman obsession with the Greek language seems a bit ironic. Rome itself would leave an even more significant linguistic legacy on Western Civilization with its own Latin. In the western portion of the Roman Empire, Latin became the lingua franca. Local versions of Latin would eventually develop into the modern Romance languages. Spanish, French, Portuguese, Italian, and Romanian are all modified versions of Roman Latin.

The Roman view of the Celtic west contrasted starkly with their view of the Greek east. When the Romans arrived, the eastern portion of the empire was already dominated by advanced cultures with Hellenistic influences; and the Greek language was an established lingua franca. In these areas, Roman rule was comparatively lenient, and the local languages outlived the Roman Empire.

The Greek culture that was so celebrated in the Mediterranean made only minor inroads into ancient Western Europe. Pre-Roman Europe was dominated by the Celts, a tribal people who were fierce warriors. Alexander the Great encountered the Celts in 335 BCE and was impressed at their capacity for making war. At the height of Celtic power (about 400 B.C.), the Celts controlled an area stretching from Ireland to the northwestern corner of Turkey.

The Celts spoke a variety of languages. When the Roman Empire expanded into Western Europe, Latin became the official language of much of the Celtic world. This would eventually lead to the death of a handful of Celtic languages—mostly notably Celtiberian (spoken in ancient Spain) and Gaulish (spoken in France).

To Roman eyes, ancient Western Europe was a remote, uncultured hinterland. The Romans regarded Celtic culture as inferior to their own. If the Greeks were worthy of imitation, the Celts were "barbarians" who had to be "civilized." Historians have since pointed out that Roman biases overlooked the richness of Celtic art, literature, etc. On the whole, however, Celtic culture lacked the monolithic quality of Greek civilization. There was no Celtic Plato or Socrates; nor was there a Celtic equivalent of the Athenian Acropolis.

The Celts also resisted Roman rule with a ferocity rarely seen in the eastern portions of the Empire. The Romans battled some Celtic tribes for generations, and both sides endured heavy casualties. During the reign of Julius Caesar, for example, an independent tribe of Gallic Celts known as the *Carnutes* slaughtered all the inhabitants of the Roman town of *Cenabum* (modern-day Orléans), and staged violent raids on other Roman settlements in occupied Gaul. The Romans encountered similar resistance throughout Western Europe. In Britain, Rome was finally forced to abandon the conquest of large areas of Celtic territory—opting instead to keep the barbarians out with fortified walls.

Celtic intransigence likely contributed to the more aggressive assimilation policies that the Romans adopted in Europe. The invading Romans would have had a desire to stamp out all vestiges of the enemy culture—including its language. In some cases, the demise of local languages can even be linked to specific rebellions. The decline of the aforementioned Celtiberean language accelerated sharply following the locals' defeat in the Numantine War, a particularly bitter conflict that hardened Roman attitudes toward the native population of Spain.

> **The Gauls were good at learning Latin.**
>
> The Gaulish language spoken in pre-Roman France was remarkably similar to Latin. Historians have speculated that this similarity may have contributed to the rapid demise of the Gaulish language in ancient France. In other words, the Gauls had minimal resistance to adopting the Roman language because Latin was relatively easy for them to learn.

LATIN AND CHRISTIANITY

The Roman Emperor Constantine legalized Christianity following his own conversion in 312 A.D., and the Emperor Theodosius made it the official religion of the Empire in 380 A.D. The Roman Empire in Western Europe collapsed around 476 A.D.; but a new force was now spreading the Latin language in Europe—the Christian Church.

> **When God spoke to the Roman Emperor, He spoke in Greek.**
>
> Constantine legalized Christianity in Rome following a prophetic dream that resulted in a military victory. The night before a battle, the emperor dreamt of a blazing cross suspended in the sky. Beneath the cross were the words, "By this conquer." History records that the words were written in Greek—rather than the Latin of Rome.

During the Middle Ages, the Christian Church was the dominant institution of European culture, education, and politics. Latin was therefore the European language of learning and administration. Latin retained its position of power even in later years, when Church power had been largely ceded to national governments, and other languages were on the rise. In 1726, Sir Isaac Newton—an Englishman—published *The Mathematical Principles of Natural Philosophy*. Newton wrote not in his native English, but in Latin. (This work is now in the public domain, and a copy of the original Latin text, *Philosophiae Naturalis Principia Mathematica,* is available on the Internet.)

Although no one uses Latin for practical purposes today, the language lives on in the fields of medicine and science. The scientific names of plants and animals are based on Latin (and Greek). It is impossible to earn a law degree without becoming something of an expert in the language of the Caesars. Legal terms such as *habeas corpus, caveat emptor, de facto, de jure, locus delicti, pro bono publico*, and many others are pure Latin.

Latin also left its mark on much terminology that is uniquely American. The quarter in your pocket bears the Latin slogan, *E Pluribus Unum*—"One from many." The motto of the Marine Corps—*Semper Fidelis*—is also Latin. When troops went into battle in the American Civil War, their regimental flags were often adorned with Latin phrases.

Latin remained the language of catechism for millions of Catholics until the mid-1960s. Catholics no longer conduct mass in Latin, but they continue to hold on to remnants of the language. When I learned the popular Christmas hymn, *Ave Maria*, during my 1970s-era Catholic grade school days, I learned the words in Latin (though I did not understand what the words meant.) Some Catholic traditionalists still cling to the language. When Cardinal Joseph Ratzinger gave his first homily as Pope Benedict XVI in April 2005, he notably addressed his congregation in Latin.

Even Shakespeare studied Latin.

The ability to speak Latin carried considerable prestige in Elizabethan England. (Queen Elizabeth herself spoke the language.) A thousand years after the fall of Rome, many educational institutions in 16th century England were focused entirely on teaching their students Latin. In fact, William Shakespeare is thought to have attended a Latin school in Stratford-upon-Avon during the 1570s.

PARLE VOUS FRANCAIS?

What was the language of power in 12th century Britain? Hint: It wasn't English.

In 1066 William the Conqueror, the Duke of the French region known as Normandy, successfully invaded England. This was the beginning of a period of French rule over England, during which the cultural and political spheres of France and England would be closely intertwined.

The Norman victory in England also made Norman French the language of power in England. William deposed the English-speaking nobility (some of whom were sold into slavery in Muslim Spain), and installed French-speaking nobility. Church positions and commercial posts were also doled out to French-speakers.

For about 300 years, England was a nation of three languages: Norman French, Latin, and English. English was clearly at the bottom of the hierarchy. French was the language of government and wealth; Latin was the language of the Church and scholars. English, meanwhile, was the language of day laborers, peasants, and the town market.

The decline of a distinct, French-speaking ruling class would not occur until the mid-1300s, when the devastation of the Black Death pandemic reconfigured the power structure of English society. The French-speaking nobles, who were always a minority, were killed in such numbers by the plague that it was no longer practical for them to maintain themselves as a distinct class. In the years following the plague, they were effectively forced to assimilate with the English-speaking majority.

THE RISE OF PARISIAN FRENCH

As Norman French was declining in England, another variant of French—Parisian French—was gaining momentum throughout Europe. Parisian French was based on the language spoken in the educated circles of Paris. During the 1400s, this variant of French began to distinguish itself as the global language of choice. Latin was still used by the Church, but French was now preferred by many diplomats and merchants in Europe.

Over the next several hundred years, French became especially entrenched within the European nobility. A nineteenth century Prussian nobleman once remarked that he only spoke German—his native language—to his horse. French was especially popular among the pre-Bolshevik Russian nobility. Russian aristocrats were often heard speaking French rather than Russian among themselves.

The legacy of French linguistic power persists today in international institutions. Although a relatively small percentage of United Nations representatives can actually speak French, most of the signs in the UN building are in French as well as English. French is also the second most common language (after English) on international documents like visas and passports.

THE AGE OF ENGLISH

In the early twentieth century, the phrase, "the sun never sets on the British Empire" was no empty boast. Great Britain's imperial possessions prior to World War II included (among other countries): Nigeria, India, Pakistan, Malaysia, Singapore, Hong Kong, Uganda, and Kenya. Three self-governing "dominions" were also nominally part of the Empire: Canada, Australia, and New Zealand.

Britain's rise as an imperial power began during the reign of Henry VIII (1509 - 1547), who established the modern British navy. From the late 1600s until World War II, the British Royal Navy was the most powerful navy in the world. The Royal Navy allowed Britain to secure colonial possessions in the Americas, Asia, Africa, Antarctica, Europe, and the South Pacific.

Britain's imperial expansion was based on a clever fusion of economic and military institutions. While the Royal Navy ruled the seas, quasi-governmental commercial institutions like the Massachusetts Bay Company and the British East India Company exploited economic opportunities in the colonies. England soon developed a vibrant mercantile economy based on carefully administered trade with its far-flung possessions throughout the world.

The British Empire was inevitably challenged by resistance from within the colonies. The Empire suffered a few major setbacks prior to the mid-20th century—the most significant being the loss of the American colonies in 1789. It began to unravel more rapidly in the wake of World War II, as nationalist movements gained momentum throughout the world. Britain was commercially and militarily exhausted from the war, and there was no national will to hold the Empire together by force. India became an independent nation in 1947, and numerous secessions followed throughout the 1950s and 1960s. In 1997, the last major overseas colony, Hong Kong, was returned to the People's Republic of China.

The British Empire lives on in the English language that is still spoken in many former colonies. In most of the Empire, English coexisted with local languages; and it continues to enjoy associate status in some former Asian colonies. In Hong Kong, both Cantonese and English are official (although Mandarin is growing in importance.) In Singapore, English shares official status with Tamil, Chinese, and Malay.

India was Britain's most populous colony. There is considerable debate about what percentage of the Indian population is proficient in English. Most estimates cite figures between five and ten percent. India is somewhat of an anomaly among nations: hundreds of regional languages are spoken within its borders; and the Indian constitution recognizes eighteen languages. Although less than one percent of the population speaks English as its primary language, English is an important "link language" between regions that speak different tongues. English is also a prestige language in India—much as French was a prestige language in nineteenth century Europe. However, the indigenous Hindi (the primary "official" language of India) is more important in daily life. Hindi is the first language of about 300 million Indians; and 500 million more have at least basic proficiency in the language.

ENGLISH AND AMERICA'S RISE AS A POLITICAL AND CULTURAL SUPERPOWER

Late in 1941, the government of Adolf Hitler was concerned that American culture was becoming too popular in Germany. The Nazis had declared war on America a few days after the Japanese attack on Pearl Harbor, and it was necessary to paint Germany's new enemy in a negative light.

The Nazis responded to the challenge with a propaganda film. The documentary *Rund um die Freiheitsstatue* (Round the Statue of Liberty) highlighted American "decadences" such as swing, jazz, and risqué fashions. Both Joseph Goebbels (Hitler's Minister of Propaganda) and Adolf Hitler himself personally screened the film before its release.

The film backfired as a propaganda piece. Young people in Germany's big cities flocked to *Rund um die Freiheitsstatue*, and emerged from theaters even more enthralled with American culture. Hitler's attempt to persuade young people to abandon popular American music, movies, and fashions was a complete failure. American swing and Dixieland music was illegal in Nazi Germany, but record sales thrived on the German black market throughout the war. (Ironically, many of the records were obtained from German soldiers who looted private collections in occupied Europe.)

Since the early twentieth century, American popular culture has had an almost universal appeal. Every American musical trend—swing, jazz, rock-and-roll, disco, rap—has swept the planet. Hollywood blockbusters become international blockbusters. The world's consumers may have a preference for Chinese-made microwaves and Japanese cars, but they still have a clear preference for American culture.

Why is American culture so successful in the global marketplace? With few exceptions, American artists have been able to work with unprecedented freedoms. The American systems of free enterprise and intellectual property rights protection have enabled not only artistic expression, but also the marketing infrastructures that transform a film, a book, or a piece of music into a product for mass consumption.

History has proven that when a culture spreads, the language of that culture spreads along with it. When a young person in Vietnam or Bulgaria greets a foreign visitor with a few words of English, he is able to co-opt a bit of American culture for himself.

THE ROLE OF RUSSIAN DURING THE ERA OF SOVIET COMMUNISM

During the Cold War era that lasted from the late 1940s through the late 1980s, the world was bipolar, linguistically as well politically. The United States not only had economic power, but we were also the bulwark against the spread of Marxism. This distinction greatly increased the significance of our language in the countries that feared the Soviet Union and Communist China.

If American English was emerging as the language of the free world, then Russian was emerging as the language of global communism. In the Warsaw Pact countries, Russian was often the only widely available second language option. For a while, even the Chinese were enthusiastically learning it; many Chinese who attended school in the 1950s and 1960s can converse in Russian.

For a brief period during the late 1950s, Americans seriously considered integrating Russian language courses into mainstream educational institutions. In October of 1957, the Soviet Union launched the Спутник (Sputnik) Satellite into orbit around the earth. Although one prominent U.S. rear admiral dismissed the 184-pound device as "a hunk of metal that almost anyone could launch," other experts drew more dire conclusions. The Soviets had beaten the United States into space. Elmer Hutchisson, then the director of the American Institute of Physics, predicted that the American way of life was "doomed to rapid extinction." *Life* magazine likened Sputnik to the first shots fired by the British at Lexington and Concord.

One of the Eisenhower Administration's many responses to Sputnik was to propose an overhaul of the American educational system. The National Defense Education Act of 1958 appropriated $1 billion of emergency educational aid. Most of the money was earmarked for increasing the number of teachers in key subjects—*including foreign language*.

In the aftermath of Sputnik, there were reports that Soviet schoolchildren were reading Shakespeare in the original English. (This was probably a gross exaggeration, given the comparatively low level of English skills in Russia and Eastern Europe today). The Eisenhower Administration reasoned that American strategic interests would therefore be served if American children developed an equal level of attainment in Russian. Some Russian-language programs were successfully piloted at a handful of U.S. high schools. These efforts soon fizzled out, however; and widespread American proficiency in Russian never materialized.

CHAPTER 4 APPENDIX:
LEARNING LANGUAGES IN RESPONSE TO GLOBAL EVENTS

After terrorists attacked the United States on September 11, 2001, enrollment in college-level Arabic courses dramatically increased. A similar upsurge in enrollment occurred ten years earlier, during the first Gulf War of 1990-1991. Unfortunately, our awareness of the importance of Arabic during the first Middle Eastern conflict did not create a sustained national interest in the language. At the time of this writing, we are still dependent on native speakers for our Arabic translation needs.

Older Americans often remark that Japan's attack on Pearl Harbor was the 9/11 of the mid-twentieth century. Since few Americans spoke Japanese in 1941, there was a shortage of people who could serve as interrogators and battlefield interpreters. During the early days of World War II, the American government hurriedly established the Army Specialized Training Program (ASTP) for Japanese Studies at the University of Michigan. The program was abandoned once Japan's defeat became inevitable.

Economic reasons can also motivate an urgent desire to learn a language. Japan's economic boom of the late 1980s inspired a brief boom in Japanese language studies in the United States. Political changes in Europe—the fall of the Soviet Union, the implementation of the European Union's Single Market, and the unification of Germany—inspired a renewed interest in certain European languages. But most of these trends were limited in scope and short-lived.

Will history repeat itself again? No one can say for certain. Hopefully the renewed sense of urgency about learning Arabic will result in more Americans being able to wield this strategically important language in the coming decades.

CHAPTER 5

LANGUAGE AND THE LIMITS OF GLOBALIZATION

"A language is a dialect with an army and a navy."
—Uriel Weinreich

The notion of English as a global language is closely tied to the wider concept of globalization itself. But what exactly is "globalization?"

Globalization is not a specifically codified doctrine. Nor is globalization an inherently right-wing or left-wing ideology. Globalization includes the following elements and outcomes:

- Unlimited free trade
- Borderless labor markets
- An increased role for supranational governmental bodies like the United Nations and the European Union.

Evangelists for globalization are enthusiastic about Global English for several reasons. A single world language would make the world more homogenous. Homogenized consumers who speak the same language could be reached through a single marketing message rather than multiple diverse ones. If all the world's workers spoke English, then a corporation in London or Chicago could hire engineers in China or Brazil just as easily (and much more cheaply) than they could hire them at home. A single world language would also make diverse populations less diverse, and therefore more accepting of international governmental entities.

The advocates of globalization have succeeded in implementing English as an administrative language in settings where it has no logical connection to the population it theoretically serves. For example:

- In Europe, English has become the language of instruction in some university programs in countries where English is not spoken as a native language.
- English is often used as a working language in the meetings of international governing bodies like the Association of Southeast Asian Nations (ASEAN) and the European Union, even when a minority of the delegates present actually speak the language.

There are also examples from the private sector. English has been forced into some European corporate environments where neither the customers nor the organizational staff speak English. (As you will recall from Chapter 2, the functional value of English in situations where no native speakers are present is minimal.) However, English is now a doctrinaire aspect of "going global." Many European managers have therefore hastened to introduce it into their organizations, without considering how the language is actually going to be *used*. Recall the rank-and-file Spanish engineer from Chapter 2 who described "the descent into babble" which accompanies the forced usage of English in the European workplace.

This has been fundamentally a top-down process rather than a grassroots movement. Globalization (and the accompanying emphasis on Global English) is led by management consulting firms, multinational corporations, and the cultural elite.

Predictably, there has been a grassroots backlash. In 1430, Joan of Arc energized her countrymen with the cry of "France for the French." Today, the cry is more likely to be "French for France," "German for Germany," or "Spanish for Spain." No one wants to see his language and culture swallowed by a "global standard." When European elites propose implementing English as the language of university-level instruction in countries where it is not the national language, the man and woman on the street understandably take umbrage. What is wrong with French, Danish, German, etc?

In 2003 a group of Japanese academics and media elites proposed granting English a secondary official status in the country. The result was a huge outcry on the Internet and in the letters-to-the-editor columns of every major newspaper. Common citizens were adamant: Japanese was the national language of Japan.

I can understand this attitude because I have a strong attachment to my own language. If French were to somehow recoup its position of international prestige, Americans would become more protective of English. We would bristle at the idea that we should conduct university classes in French, or make French the language of our corporations—just because people were speaking French in some classrooms and boardrooms on the other side of the world.

LINGUISTIC DIVERSITY IN EUROPE

The concept of "linguistic diversity" is a strong component of European identity. The EU recognizes twenty-one "official" languages. (The primary eleven are Spanish, Danish, German, Greek, English, French, Italian, Dutch, Portuguese, Finnish and Swedish.) Maintaining equal status for each of these languages is a highly politicized issue:

> *"In practice, French, English, and German are the most commonly used languages at EU meetings, and German, the mother tongue of about 24% of all EU residents, is the most common native language in Europe. But the Europeans seem dedicated to maintaining linguistic diversity. Said one German EU representative, 'It would be cultural suicide for the EU if we tried to go to only one language.'"* -Helsinki Sanomat, 5/4/2001

Europe, like the former Soviet Union, has seen the rebirth of once marginalized languages. Irish schools now teach Irish Gaelic; and minority languages like Welsh and Cornish have seen a revival in Great Britain. In France, speakers of Provençal have begun to reassert themselves. Minority languages are also resurgent in Spain and Italy.

A EUROPEAN LINGUA FRANCA?

The scope of the linguistic diversity in Europe makes the case for a European lingua franca. One (or two) common languages are needed as a mode of communication on the Continent. But which one makes the most sense? Some European leaders want to make English the European lingua franca, in imitation of the multinational corporations that have experimented with making English their official administrative business language.

There are practical reasons which make English an awkward common language for the EU. To begin with, English is not the native language of a single country in Continental Europe. (Imagine if Canada, Mexico, and the United States tried to use Chinese as the common diplomatic and business language among our three nations.) English is more difficult to pronounce than most European languages, and English grammar is more difficult than Italian, Spanish, or Portuguese grammar.

In Europe, the weight of raw numbers makes the case for German. Germany is the most populous country in the EU; the German economy accounts for a full one third of the European Union's GDP. And a third of the EU's population are already speakers of German.

The only real lingua franca of Europe is Latin—a language which forms the basis of most European languages. While Latin—a dead language that is difficult to master—is an impractical choice, Spanish, Italian, (or even French) would be far easier for the average European than English.

LINGUISTIC NATIONALISM IN EUROPE

The two most powerful countries in continental Western Europe are France and Germany. Both of these nations have launched recent campaigns to reassert the international usage of their languages. Germany's *Goethe-Institut* maintains offices throughout the world. The organization's mission is "the promotion of the German language and culture." The French government has launched similar initiatives for furthering the spread of French. While these efforts have so far met with limited interest in the United States, interest in French and German is on the rise throughout the present EU member countries, as well as in Eastern Europe.

The French have become legendary for their love of their own language, but they are not alone. In 1999, representatives from Germany and Austria threatened to boycott ministerial meetings held in Finland upon learning that only English, French and Finnish would be translated. The Finnish relented, triggering protests from the Italians and the Spanish, who then claimed that their languages should also be given equal treatment.

The image of European diplomats threatening to boycott meetings if their language is snubbed contains an element of pettiness that would quickly exhaust the patience of private sector professionals. Nonetheless, such attitudes are indicative of a Europe that may be less patient in future years with businesspersons who don't bother to learn the local language. The trend will be especially pronounced in France and Germany, whose languages are gaining popularity as second languages in Europe.

In late 2004, Greece joined the OIF (*Organisation Internationale de la Francophonie*), a European organization dedicated to the promotion of French as a language of global communications and commerce. Austria, Slovenia, Poland, the Czech Republic, and a number of other European nations are also affiliated with the group. A Greek official had this to say about his county's entry into the OIF:

> *"[The goal is to] reinforce the plurality of languages within the EU. We safeguard our own language by making room for more languages to be spoken".*
> Source: www.euractiv.com

The subtext of the above quote is clear: The Greeks wanted to encourage the spread of French as a counterbalance to English. Despite the importance of German, many Europeans consider French to be a more significant world language. French already has a wide global following, with native speakers in Europe, Africa, the Americas, and Asia.

BACKLASHES IN FORMER COLONIES

Europe is not the only place where a reappraisal is taking place. The conflict between Global English and local languages has special significance in countries where English was once forced on a population through colonial rule. In former British colonies, English is a force which creates two classes: an English-speaking one and a non-English-speaking one. The problem is particularly acute in India and Malaysia, where English continues to exist beside local languages. The groups that speak English are typically a disproportionately powerful minority, and are psychologically tied to the old colonial system.

Efforts to convince local populations that English has somehow become a "neutral language" inevitably lead to the question: but why *English*—and why *here*? There is no linguistic justification for English as a lingua franca in India—where most of the population speaks non-European languages. Going by the numbers, either Hindi (366 million speakers), Bengali (70 million speakers), or another indigenous Indian language would make more sense.

Some Filipinos have also questioned the appropriateness of English as a domestic mode of communications. The people of the Philippines have had two European languages forced on them in the past 500 years. Today the Philippines is a country where English exists alongside a dominant national language—Tagalog (also called Filipino), and a plethora of minority tongues.

The Philippines initially became a Spanish colony in the 1500s. Spain forced her language on the Philippines to varying degrees; but indigenous languages continued to thrive during the Spanish imperial era. After America defeated Spain in the Spanish-American War of 1898, the Philippines became an American commonwealth, and English became a major linguistic influence.

The Philippines was granted independence from the United States in 1946, although a U.S. military presence continued during the postwar era. Following the eruption of Mount Pinatubo in June 1991 and a rejection of a new lease agreement by the Philippine Senate, the American military abandoned Clark Air Base and Subic Bay Naval Station in December 1991.

The Philippines remains a key U.S. ally; but the new sense of independence has brought about a resurgent enthusiasm for the Tagalog language. The popular media has embraced Tagalog; and there has been a movement to reassert Tagalog as the language of government and education in the country. Several government leaders have noted that the connection between English and economic advancement is by no means axiomatic— citing the long list of prosperous countries in which English exists only as a foreign language.

ALL POLITICS ARE STILL LOCAL

People around the world are not just reappraising Global English. They are also reappraising of the appropriate goals, form, and extent of globalization. This process is taking place in the United States as well as abroad.

Writing in *The European Dream: How Europe's Vision of the Future Is Quietly Eclipsing the American Dream* (Jeremy P. Tarcher, 2004), author Jeremy Rifkin suggests that the "conventional nation-state political model" is being replaced by "the vanguard of a new global consciousness." Rifkin suggests that nationalism is outdated, and that this "new global consciousness" will change basic attitudes about everything from foreign peacekeeping operations to private property rights.

On the contrary, most of the organized national polities that exist today have existed for centuries. They are unlikely to dissolve themselves in the foreseeable future. National polities share common goals, a common culture, and *a common language*. Despite the aspirations of the internationalists, common citizens have continued to demonstrate their ongoing commitment to the old-fashioned nation-state.

In June 2005 French voters said *Non!* to the draft constitution of the European Union. The constitution was rejected by a large margin, with opposition coming from the political left, right and center. The *non* vote represented a grass-roots protest against Europe's established leaders. French citizens did not want to compromise their country's sovereignty to EU bureaucrats in Brussels. Voters opposed measures that would have given the European Union powers to regulate domestic issues like housing and immigration policy. As one twenty-eight-year-old French engineer said: *"I voted no out of a concern for democracy. For me, the decisions should not be made by Europe, but by each nation. I want France to make decisions for herself."*

French citizens were also concerned about proposed integration with Turkey and Ukraine—countries that are economically and culturally dissimilar to the nations of Western Europe. French taxpayers bristled at the idea of sending more money to Brussels for the EU to redistribute to poorer nations elsewhere in Europe. They also rejected the notion of opening up their borders to cheap labor from former communist nations. A nursing student in Paris summed the decision up as follows: *"They are already taking money from our paychecks. These changes are going to affect my generation more than others."*

The *non* vote proved that—despite the wishes of Europe's political and media elite—French voters placed a higher priority on the welfare of their own families than on visions of a fully integrated, homogenous Europe. A few days later, Dutch voters also rejected the EU constitution.

Later that month, EU leaders held a summit in Brussels, and yet another disagreement erupted. Britain did not want to disburse more funds to the EU until the French reformed their agricultural subsidies programs. Once again, there were protests at the grass-roots level: this time, it was British taxpayers who did not want to subsidize French farmers.

Even within the United States, there are bitter disagreements over spending bills that promise benefits for some states while increasing the economic burden on others. Imagine the practical difficulties involved in reaching a consensus across disparate nations in which some populations will see a portion of their income transferred to others.

STATELESS CORPORATIONS, BORDERLESS LABOR MARKETS

What happens when American managers have a vested interest in hedging against the U.S. economy in favor of India or China? The stateless multinational corporation has eroded the sense of economic nationalism that once characterized the managerial class of corporate America. In extreme cases, executives at U.S. multinationals have suggested that their companies are not "American" firms—but supranational economic entities whose loyalties are no longer exclusively tied to any one nation.

Companies like Motorola and IBM have transferred many of their core operations to distant locations in the developing world. Thanks largely to the influx of American high-tech firms, R&D spending in China is surpassed only by spending in the United States and Japan. Motorola, for example, has more than twenty research centers in China, and a staff of 1,800.

Why conduct R&D in China? A primary motive is cost. In pursuit of the global bottom line, large multinational corporations have sought to make capital and labor markets completely borderless. Recruitment in the developing world often enables companies to reduce their personnel costs by as much as a half to two thirds—even when additional administrative costs are factored in.

It is therefore not surprising that many professionals in the developing world are learning English. India—a former British colony—has built much of its economy on the offshoring plans of U.S. companies. In China as well, a job with a (usually American) multinational is currently viewed as the best path to a prosperous professional life for technical specialists and MBAs. And a job with an American company usually requires skills in the English language.

GAINS FROM MULTINATIONAL EMPLOYERS ARE SHORT-LIVED

Many professionals in the developing world are now landing jobs simply by accepting less pay than their American counterparts. This is certainly beneficial for multinational companies—and detrimental (at least in the short term) for Americans who are replaced by cheap foreign labor. *But what about the overseas workers themselves, and the societies in which they live?*

Poor nations become rich nations when development is homegrown, not when it is driven by distant multinational corporations. The postwar example of Japan is particularly illustrative. In the post-World War II era, the Japanese automotive industry rose to rival Detroit. This occurred through homegrown entrepreneurial efforts; Ford and General Motors did not lay off their American workers to take advantage of cheap Japanese labor in the 1950s. Toyota, Nissan, and Honda were all Japanese creations.

There was no H1-B visa program that enabled Japanese engineers to come to America as high-tech guest workers. (In fact, it was difficult for Japanese to even leave the country during the immediate postwar years.) Talented Japanese managers and technicians stayed home, rolled up their sleeves, and built up their nation's industries. And today Japan is one of the most prosperous nations on earth.

Conversely, employment based on ultra-low wages is short-term in nature. The Latin American countries that attracted textile and industrial manufacturing employment in the 1990s are already loosing ground to still cheaper labor in Asia. In Mexico, the jobs provided by U.S. companies seeking to take advantage of NAFTA have not delivered as much economic growth as promised. In hindsight, this result was predictable: Ford and Wal-Mart can only hire a tiny percentage of Mexico's total population. What Mexico needs is homegrown entrepreneurship on a large scale—and this will not occur until the nation revamps its antiquated commercial credit system. (Mexico's banking laws make it difficult for lenders to seize collateral when loans default, so there is little incentive for them to extend credit at affordable rates.)

Developing nations benefit when talent stays at home. A borderless labor market lowers costs for large corporations; but it ultimately undermines the countries that need to retain their best and brightest. Eastern Europe, India, and China are all suffering from a brain-drain, as H1-B visas and other "guest worker" programs lure talent to the West. It is in everyone's best interest for these countries to develop into thriving, prosperous nations—rather than ultra-cheap labor sources that simply export their populations.

In order for this situation to change, there will have to be a change of attitude in countries like the United States, which encourage poor countries to become overly reliant on multinational corporations and guest worker programs. There is evidence that such change is on the way.

THE AMERICAN ANTI-GLOBALIZATION BACKLASH

The anti-globalization backlash in the United States has made strange bedfellows on the Right and the Left. During the 2004 U.S. Presidential campaign, Democratic candidate John Kerry repeatedly used the term "Benedict Arnold CEOs" to refer to corporate executives who outsource American jobs to low-wage workers in the developing world. Pat Buchanan, an ultra-conservative former Presidential candidate, made a case for reexamining free trade agreements in *Where the Right Went Wrong: How Neoconservatives Subverted the Reagan Revolution and Hijacked the Bush Presidency* (Thomas Dunne Books, 2004). In the political center, CNN commentator Lou Dobbs regularly "outs" American outsourcers by maintaining a running list of companies who ship American jobs overseas. Dobbs has also written a book on the subject: *Exporting America : Why Corporate Greed Is Shipping American Jobs Overseas* (Warner Business Books, 2004)

In all camps, there is a particular concern over the transfer of U.S. industrial might and high technology to China. China, after all, is still a potential military rival of the United States. When American corporations transfer advanced technology to Chinese partners, this technology inevitably ends up in the hands of the Chinese military. This means that U.S. taxpayers will eventually be forced to spend more on defense. The net result is a U.S. taxpayer subsidization of the multinationals' China spending spree.

Attitudes about economic globalization are changing among Americans of all political stripes. A May 2004 Associated Press poll found that 69% of Americans believe that outsourcing hurts the U.S. economy. Among affluent Americans (those earning over $100,000 per year) support for free trade deals fell from 57 percent to 28 percent between 1999 and 2004.

A RATIONAL MODEL FOR GLOBALIZATION

Globalization will, without a doubt, continue—but it will likely move forward at a more measured pace in the coming decades, as the long-term interests of national economies are balanced against corporate and internationalist agendas. Developing nations will eventually grow weary of competing to supply the global bottom wage, and focus more on domestic enterprises. Meanwhile, voters and consumers in the developed world are waking up to the long-term costs of unlimited offshoring.

Nations must be realistic about their differences. Economic globalization assumes a consensus regarding laws and standards—the so-called "level playing field." But no such level playing field exists. The nations of the world disagree about the fundamental nature of capitalism. Americans prefer a laissez-faire model based on personal responsibility and individual initiative. Europeans prefer a more collective model, in which competitive forces are balanced against larger social concerns. In China, the government is still a major force at the macroeconomic level, manipulating currency levels and restricting the activities of labor unions.

The result is "free competition" in a global marketplace that is anything but free. In Europe, American firms must compete with quasi-public firms like Airbus that receive EU government subsidies. Government subsidies for private firms are consistent with the European model of public capitalism. Such subsidies are decried as "barriers to free competition" and "corporate welfare" in the more laissez-faire United States.

In China the playing field is even more tilted. Chinese firms enjoy the advantages of an artificially low Renminbi (the Chinese national currency). Chinese companies do not have to pay for health care benefits, or adhere to the same environmental standards as U.S. companies. Moreover, they can rely on China's central government to resolve labor disputes by force.

This is not the free market model that Adam Smith delineated in *The Wealth of Nations*. While resolving these differences is theoretically possible, the process will take decades. In the meantime, the objective should be fair, mutually beneficial trade rather than a totally borderless economic integration.

IMPLICATIONS FOR LANGUAGE

The emphasis on globalization has created some dramatically skewed attitudes about language. Many overseas institutions vainly believe that English is a panacea for all their national ills, while giving short shrift to more fundamental economic and social issues. Meanwhile, most English-

65

speakers anticipate that the worldwide adoption of their language is just a few short years away, so they see no advantage in learning the languages of others. Both sides have set expectations for English that are unrealistically high.

The reappraisal of economic globalization will have an inevitable effect on the worldwide enthusiasm for English, as the developing world focuses more on homegrown entrepreneurship, and the developed world reassesses the consequences of exporting its industrial infrastructure. At the grassroots level, this will mean more employment by locally owned companies who speak the local language—and less employment with multinational corporations whose representatives and customers speak only English. This does not mean that all professionals in the non-English-speaking world will suddenly stop learning English. However, the attitude that English skills are a precondition for success—and a guarantee of employment with an American-owned corporation—is likely to wane.

As noted in Chapter 3, there has been a dramatic increase in regional economic activity in which the United States is not a partner. This will lead to a greater emphasis on region-specific lingua francas. Within Asia, for example, Chinese may assume a preeminent role for businesspersons, with English becoming a language limited to certain specialized fields. This turn of events would not be unprecedented: A similar outcome has already taken place in Latin America, where Spanish is more important than English on the multilingual South American continent.

REAPPRAISING THE "ONE-WORLD" CONCEPT

In addition to being unrealistic, the "one-worldism" preached by many would make a hopelessly uniform and boring planet. We can love English without seeking to universalize it. Consider a world without Chaucer, Shakespeare, or Robert Burns. Now consider that Chinese, Spanish, Japanese, French and other languages have equally rich cultural heritages to offer the world.

In 1979, my sixth grade science teacher predicted that within ten years, America would abandon the English measurement system of inches, gallons, and pounds, and switch to the metric system, because the metric system was the "global system" of weights and measurements. "By 1988 or 1989," he predicted, "You won't think about your bodyweight in terms of pounds—you'll think about your bodyweight in kilograms. It will also be

66

more natural for you to think of distances in kilometers. Miles will become a thing of the past."

Even at the age of eleven, this notion struck me as counterintuitive. Of course we Americans should be able to cope with the metric system when necessary, but why should we abandon our pounds, miles, and inches just because the metric system was used in Europe and Japan? What relationship did my bodyweight, or the distance from my house to school, have with the way people measured things in Japan or Europe?

Twenty-six years later, I still think of my bodyweight as 170 lbs—not the 77.110708 kilograms that I calculated using the conversion tool on the Metric-Conversion.org website. I suspect that most of my fellow Americans are also more comfortable with miles, pounds, and gallons than they are with meters, grams, and liters. I can use these metric measurements when the need arises; but they have little relevance to my daily life—which is thoroughly grounded in the English system of measurement.

In the same way, the daily lives of people throughout the world are grounded in a variety of languages: French, Chinese, Japanese, Russian, etc. Why *should* they want to give them up, or subordinate them to another language? (Consider again the notion of Americans abandoning English for French.)

We should establish international standards on the fundamentals: basic human freedoms, racial/gender equality, and representative government. Where language is concerned, however, there is plenty of room for diversity; and the world that our grandchildren inherit will be far more interesting if no single language dominates the earth.

CHAPTER 5 APPENDIX: THE CONSOLIDATION OF LANGUAGES AT THE NATION-STATE LEVEL

Each modern-day European nation was once a tapestry of different languages. During the feudal era, life in Europe was centered around small localities—each of which had a distinct language. Language consolidation occurred gradually in Europe, and was driven by the formation and growth of national governments. But local languages persist.

In Great Britain, for example, the Welsh language has recently garnered a great deal of attention. Welsh is a Celtic language that was once the dominant language of Wales, an area of western Britain. Today only about 20% of the population of Wales speaks Welsh. Nonetheless, Welsh is more than just a cultural curiosity. While there are few monolingual speakers of Welsh, Welsh is an active, living language. There are some residents of Wales who consider Welsh to be their first, and most articulately spoken language. There is a Welsh television channel, and Microsoft recently began offering Welsh versions of *Office®* and *Windows XP®*.

Cornish is also a Celtic language. Cornish was once the main language of the Cornwall area. (Cornwall is a county on the southwestern tip of England.) Practically everyone living in Cornwall in 1200 spoke the language. As England's central government became more powerful, the Cornwall region became increasingly Anglicized. The last monolingual Cornish speaker died in 1777. Bilingual (Cornish and English) speakers were common through the late 1800s, but were rare by the 1930s.

A movement to revive Cornish began in the 1970s. Today there are about four hundred fluent speakers of Cornish, and many more Cornish enthusiasts who possess lesser degrees of fluency in the language. A group called *Kowethas an Yeth Kernewek* (The Cornish Language Fellowship) sponsors Cornish language immersion meetings. You can find out more about the Cornish language by visiting the website www.cornish-language.org.

Across the English Channel, France was once home to a patchwork of diverse languages. In fact, less than half of the country spoke Parisian French before the 1789 French Revolution. The government began actively repressing minority languages following the revolution, as these were seen as threats to national unity.

Occitan, the language of the troubadours, was originally the language of culture in southern France. Michael Crichton brought Occitan to the attention of English-speakers in his novel *Timeline* (Knopf, 1999). *Timeline* is the story of a group of graduate students who are transported back in time to 14th century France. One of the students is a medieval history aficionado who has taught himself Occitan—along with several other languages that would have come in handy in Europe during the Middle Ages.

Until the 19th century, standard German, or *Hochdeutsch*, existed primarily as a written language that most Germans learned as a foreign tongue. Germany was divided into many states, each of which spoke a slightly different version of the German language. Consolidation of the German language was accelerated with the founding of the German nation-state in 1871. Dialectical differences persist to this day; the Bavarian dialect of German in particular remains distinct and recognizable to native German-speakers.

If it's good enough for Arnold...

Arnold Schwarzenegger, a native of Austria, speaks German with a Bavarian accent.

Before the 1861 unification of Italy, only a small percentage of Italians spoke standard Italian. Renaissance Italy was a collection of distinct, powerful city-states. Venice, for example, was once a significant independent power in Europe. Venice had a powerful navy; and the Republic of Venice negotiated trade agreements with other European countries. Venice also had its own language—a derivative of Latin known as Venetian.

Although every Italian citizen alive today can speak the language known throughout the world as "Italian," the regional dialects associated with the Italian city states can still be heard in Italy. Venetian is spoken by more than one million Italians. Other minority languages in Italy include Neapolitan, Piemontese, and Cimbrian. And don't forget Sicilian—the language made famous by the *Godfather* film trilogy.

CHAPTER 6

LANGUAGES AND THE BUSINESS WORLD

"Buy from the world in your language, sell to them in theirs…"
-German government official

Most business organizations in the English-speaking world are only beginning to wake up to the realities described in the preceding chapters. In the corporate environment, the embrace of imprecise globalized English has been preceded by declining standards of the language used among English-speakers themselves. Articulate language has given way to bullet points and vague buzzwords like *proactive*, *re-purpose*, and *actionable*. The unclear "management-speak" described by author Don Watson in *Death Sentences : How Cliches, Weasel Words and Management-Speak Are Strangling Public Language* (Gotham, 2005) is arguably one step removed from the stripped down, globalized versions of English that one frequently encounters in international business situations.

I once attended a seminar on international business negotiations. Noting that the instructor had completely ignored the topic, I asked him what he thought about the role of language skills. Should an English-speaker always insist on using English? He laughed and asked me what language I would prefer: should business negotiations take place in Indonesian?

My answer—as explained in this chapter and the next one —is that *yes, there are definitely times when you should conduct your business in Indonesian!*

But don't take my word for it. One English-speaking CEO recognized the need to do business in a language that very few of us in the Western world have mastered: *Korean.*

THE BRITISH CEO WHO SPOKE TO KOREAN
CONSUMERS—*IN KOREAN*

In November 2003, struggling Korean automaker GM Daewoo launched a series of television commercials aimed at boosting its sales in Korea. Among other challenges, the company was fighting a public perception problem. Its two main competitors in the Korean market, Hyundai Motor and Kia Motors, were homegrown Korean firms. GM Daewoo, on the other hand, was owned mostly by U.S. automaker General Motors. Polls revealed that the average Korean consumer viewed the company as an outsider with a questionable commitment to the Korean market. The company needed a publicity campaign to establish itself as a "real" Korean firm.

Nick Reilly, the company's British-born CEO, took the GM Daewoo message to the Korean public. His appearance in Korean television commercials made national news in Korea, and reverberated throughout the global automotive industry. He was, of course, not the first automotive CEO to appear on TV. Jacques Nasser, Lee Iacocca, and several members of the Ford clan have also stepped down from the CEO's pedestal to directly pitch their company's wares to consumers.

Nick Reilly's television appearances made news because the CEO addressed viewers *in Korean*. Using their own language, Reilly expressed the company's commitment to Korea, and its desire to be accepted as a truly "Korean" automaker.

Japanese executives from Toyota and Honda regularly address American audiences in English (and Mexican audiences Spanish, etc.) –but this doesn't make the news. Korean is an especially challenging language; but the reporters who showered so much attention on Reilly's publicity campaign did not focus on the relative difficulty of the Korean language. The commercials made the news because a high-ranking manager from the English-speaking world was displaying real competency in a foreign language. The Korean-language commercials would likely have been deemed less newsworthy if the GM Daewoo CEO would have been a German or a Japanese national.

Nick Reilly's Korean television commercials prove that a native English-speaker need not be a professional linguist in order to competently handle a foreign language. Moreover, there is clear evidence that the corporate world values foreign language skills. (Otherwise, U.S. multinationals would not hire so many of the foreign-born educated elite.) Therefore, the next logical question is: Why don't more American businesspersons learn a foreign language?

"BUT A LANGUAGE ISN'T A BUSINESS SKILL."

I recall from my undergraduate days a subtle sense of competition that existed between the liberal arts colleges and the business/technical schools. My friends who were liberal arts majors regarded subjects like accounting as hopelessly dry and uninspiring. Business and technical students, meanwhile, dismissed liberal arts courses as impractical annoyances—useful only for fulfilling general studies requirements.

American managers who resist learning languages often assert that "a foreign language isn't really a business skill." The irony is that they are right—*and profoundly wrong*—at the same time. A foreign language *isn't* a technical business skill—like calculating present value or deciphering an income statement. A foreign language is a *basic* competence—more akin to literacy or arithmetic skills than to advanced financial analysis.

Here is another way to look at it: If your work involves the Mexican market and you don't speak Spanish, then your inability to speak the language prevents you from performing basic tasks. Spanish proficiency, as a skill, is arguably distinct from the skills acquired in an MBA program. But this distinction is irrelevant in the real world. A person working at a professional level in the Mexican market *should* be able to speak Spanish. This is especially true if the job involves extensive communication and cooperation with others.

HEARTS AND MINDS

Although Nick Reilly's training in the Korean language might be a story in itself, the important question is: *why did the company choose to have Reilly address the Korean public in Korean?* From a purely utilitarian standpoint, this wasn't necessary—and certainly not efficient. Nick Reilly could have appeared in the commercial speaking English, and they could have dubbed a voiceover by a native Korean-speaker. Subtitles could have been used. For that matter, the company could have allowed one of their Korean executives to appear in the commercial, thereby avoiding any tinge of "foreignness."

Nick Reilly appeared in the commercial because a British CEO who speaks Korean symbolized the company's commitment to the Korean market more effectively than Korean subtitles, voiceovers, or a Korean-born representative. As is often the case where language is concerned, it was much more than a simple matter of translation.

Foreign language skills allow you to identify more closely with others. The link between language and identity continues to be strong, even in the globalized 21st century. Polls in Russia indicate that businesspersons resent foreigners who want to do business in Russia but refuse to learn the language. (In Chapter 8, we read about a young American who refused to stand for the Pledge of Allegiance when it was delivered in a language other than English.) Two of the world's main religions—Judaism and Islam—maintain a strong link between their faith and specific languages (Hebrew and Arabic, respectively).

While a language does not guarantee personal rapport, it can often be the first step to identifying with your audience. When we Americans meet a person abroad who speaks our language, we often assume that they have a knowledge of and appreciation for the United States. When we go to the trouble of learning another language, non-English-speakers give us the same benefit of the doubt.

READING AND LISTENING BETWEEN THE LINES

Knowledge of a language is sometimes necessary in order to really understand what a person means (as opposed to a translation, which merely tells you what the person has *said*.) Consider the following phrase in Japanese:

ちょっと難しいです。

The above (pronounced *chotto muzukashii desu*) translates into English as "it's a little difficult." However, when a native Japanese-speaker tells you that your proposal is "a little difficult," she really means, "It's not going to happen. Forget about it." But you may not get this insight from a translator, or a member of a Japanese delegation who happens to speak English.

Subtleties like the above are not unique to Japanese. They exist in every language, including English. Examine the following three statements:

I'm annoyed at what you did.
I am incensed at your actions in this matter.
You've really pissed me off.

A basic translation of each of the above three sentences will tell you that the speaker is displeased. The particular choice of words in each sentence contains insights about the speaker's degree of anger, her level of education, and the relationship between the speaker and the listener. In order to read between these lines, you have to understand English. Likewise, grasping a person's true feelings, intentions, or motivations often requires an understanding of Spanish, French, Chinese, etc.

THE POWER OF TAKING THE INITIATIVE

I am on the mailing list of a number of language textbook publishers. I recently received an advance copy of a business Chinese textbook that proposed the following scenario: "Suppose you are representing an American company in Shenzhen, opening discussions with a prospective Chinese client. The first words out of your mouth include an idiomatic Chinese expression that perfectly fits the situation. You even have a draft copy of the contract in your attaché case—written in correct, formal Chinese."

In many contexts, we recognize the value of being able to "master another person's game" or "score points on the other team's home turf." Linguistically, this is the power of taking the initiative—of entering another person's world and persuading her using her own idiomatic paradigms.

Without foreign language skills, English-speakers are unable to take the initiative as described above. Instead, we are forever at the mercy of the other side's abilities in English. Moreover, since it is always the other side that is meeting us halfway by speaking our language, we are hobbled by a need to defer to the fact that they are speaking English. In this regard, the global status of English in the business world is a constraint rather than a source of power for native English-speakers—because those who learn English are always free to score points on *our* home turf.

THE COSTS OF RELYING ON THE LANGUAGE SKILLS OF OTHERS

The costs of this relying on the language skills of others are many: untapped market opportunities, increased personnel costs, and the surrender of managerial autonomy—just to name a few.

I once met an American manager who was sent to Japan on a five-year assignment. When I asked him if he learned Japanese, he nonchalantly informed me that he had no need for the language. "I had a bilingual administrative assistant," he said. "She served as my eyes and ears."

With all due respect to the administrative assistants of the world, there is a problem when a manager relies on administrative staff to function as his or her "eyes and ears." This manager was in charge of a marketing division of a large consumer products firm; but he could not even read the local consumer press, or comprehend the television commercials that his company produced for Japanese television. His perceptions of the Japanese market—and indeed of his own workplace—were created by others.

One of the primary costs of our reliance on Global English is that American businesspersons resign themselves to experiencing the non-English-speaking world secondhand. Rather than just diving in and reading the local business press or talking to key employees on the plant floor, American expatriate managers must wait for an intermediary—for someone who speaks English.

Chapter 7 explores a scenario in which one of these intermediaries is actively duplicitous. But even when the intermediaries are honest, there is always a loss of certain nuances. Time and efficiency are also lost, because waiting for a translation takes time, and a willing translator will not always be at hand.

TALK TO EVERYONE

When you restrict yourself to speaking only English, you restrict the number of people whose hearts and minds you can reach. This is true not only in business, but in international relations as well. When Yasser Arafat was the leader of the PLO, Israeli leaders consistently complained that his professed desire for peace was meaningless when it was said in English. What was important, the Israelis stressed, was what Arafat said in Arabic, since this message reached an entirely different audience.

You may never have any involvement in international diplomacy. If your job involves the non-English-speaking world, though, there will be numerous occasions when you will need to communicate with someone who speaks little or no English. English skills cannot be taken for granted overseas outside the circle of the educated elite.

It is one thing to rely on English when contacting the central headquarters of a Fortune 500 company. However, suppose that your job takes you to the office of a small distributor in Brazil, a factory in France, or a branch office that serves the local market in Japan. In these situations, English will never be enough.

In one of my previous positions in the automotive industry, I spent many hours on the plant floor of Nissan Mexicana, talking to quality control inspectors, machinists, shipping personnel, and other staff whose duties were internally oriented. Spanish proved indispensable in this environment. If your company is involved in overseas manufacturing, you will likely encounter a similar situation. You will be able to gather plant-side information, make department-level contacts, and represent your company much more effectively if you can speak the local language.

MASTER MULTILINGUAL MEETINGS

In theory, business meetings that involve people who speak multiple languages should be held in English. In my experience, these English-language meetings usually break down after about ten minutes, as attendees inevitably branch into side conversations in the languages in which they are most comfortable.

I will refer again to my experience in Mexico: In meetings, there were usually three nationalities present: Americans, Japanese, and Mexicans. Some of the Japanese in attendance spoke fluent Spanish but could not speak English. Some of the Mexicans were fluent in English, and others could barely speak English. Although the intention was to conduct business in English, the meetings would inevitably split into separate English-, Japanese-, and Spanish-language conversations.

I was thankful on these occasions that I could speak all three languages. Sometimes it would be necessary for me to join a side conversation in Spanish or Japanese. The time that I had invested in learning these languages frequently enabled me to gain valuable information, or to convince a key participant regarding my own company's position.

TAKE YOUR SHARE OF THE LINGUISTIC BURDEN

Throughout most of my business activities in Mexico, my main contact was a man named Miguel. Miguel had a good working knowledge of English, and I never encountered a situation in which I felt that he was trying to be dishonest or manipulative. I sensed early on that Miguel rather enjoyed practicing his English with me, so I never addressed him in Spanish. Miguel wasn't even aware that I could speak Spanish until I visited Mexico and met with his manager, who spoke only Spanish.

After Miguel realized that I could speak Spanish, he began to speak in Spanish to me during about one out of every three telephone calls. Once, when he complimented me on my Spanish, I assured him that his English was quite good, and that he could feel free to address me in English. (At this time, I was spending one week out of every month in Mexico—so I was getting plenty of Spanish practice.)

"It's just that I get tired of speaking English all the time," Miguel said. "You know—there are times when it is just easier if I can telephone you in Spanish."

Even if you primarily use English for business purposes, your counterparts will be appreciative if you don't require them to make the effort all of the time. Speaking in another language for hours on end is a mentally taxing process—as you may soon discover.

I once worked with a South African man named Martin who told me an interesting story about the give-and-take that accompanied his own multilingual environment. Martin served a stint in the South African army, and his comrades were a mixture of native English speakers and Afrikaans speakers. Both groups were more or less fully bilingual, but it was obviously more taxing for the English speakers to use Afrikaans all day, and English was a burden for the Afrikaans speakers. They therefore developed the custom of making English the "official" language one week, and Afrikaans the primary mode of communication the next week. This way, no one was unfairly forced to speak a foreign language one hundred percent of the time.

READ ANYTHING, ANYTIME

Overseas companies and governments produce plenty of documentation in English—when there is an economic incentive for them to do so. Most of the translations produced abroad are created with one purpose in mind: to sell something to the English-speaking world. Hyundai, for example, does not force American consumers to learn Korean in order to learn about the cars that the company manufactures.

Beyond the consumer level, though, translations become more difficult to find. There is no economic incentive for translating many of the materials that American businesses could employ to research overseas markets. Trade magazines and other periodicals written for a specific local market will be available only in the local language. The same is true for many government reports, industry websites, and consumer surveys.

Translations can always be purchased. When doing market research, however, it is often necessary to survey a wide range of materials—much of which ultimately turns out to be useless. Hiring out this volume of translations would be prohibitively expensive in many cases. (Imagine having to use a translator to execute a hundred or so searches on the Internet.) Purchased translations are only cost-effective when a small, finite amount of material is needed.

TRADE SHOWS

Overseas trade shows and industry exhibitions can provide excellent opportunities to conduct research about a foreign market—*if* you can communicate. You will not be able to take full advantage of these situations unless you are able to talk to any person on the exhibition floor. If you are limited by the language barrier, then you will likely wander around looking for someone who happens to speak English. If you speak the local language, on the other hand, then you can confidently walk up to anyone and begin a conversation.

Total Market Research Skills

The impact of language skills becomes clear when applied to a comprehensive business objective. Suppose that you want to research the market for your company's products in Mexico. There are several methods that you could employ. You could:

1. Search for information on the Internet
2. Contact local chambers of commerce in Mexico
3. Make exploratory calls to potential customers by telephone
4. Attend trade shows in Mexico.

The above list is by no means exhaustive. However, all of these activities would require the ability to read and/or speak Spanish.

MOVING BEYOND "THE TINY SUPERSTAR SUBSET"

Up to this point, the educated elite from Asia, South America, Europe, and elsewhere have had a virtual monopoly on the bilingual liaison positions that are so necessary in the global business environment. When an American multinational corporation hires a German-speaking accountant or a Chinese-speaking lawyer, the person who fills the position is almost always a foreign national who was educated in the United States. This is not the result of some vast conspiracy. Few native English-speakers even compete for these jobs, because so few can fulfill the bilingual requirements. The result is that Americans, Britons, Canadians, and Australians have voluntarily chosen to disqualify themselves from thousands of lucrative positions in the global job market.

A 2001 article in CareerJournal.com described the competition for bilingual positions in Europe as almost exclusively European. European professionals are focused on the global marketplace, and actively study foreign languages, so they claim most of the more desirable management-track positions on the Continent:

> "....your competition will be primarily Europeans -- not other Americans. Many European managers now are focused on building international careers and willing to cross borders for a good

opportunity…. A number have been educated in the U.S. or outside their home country, and most speak English, in addition to three or more European languages… The most desirable candidates, say recruiters, are Americanized Europeans, a tiny superstar subset. " (Source: "Execs Looking to Europe Face Several Challenges" by Sharon Voros, careerjournal.com, 2001)

The above article refers to the job market in Europe, but very similar lines could have been written about the many globalized segments of the job market in the United States. American professionals cannot even compete effectively for the bilingual positions that exist in our own country—much less the ones that exist abroad.

In fact, jobs for bilingual professionals in the United States are often written with the assumption that the person who fills the job will be a non-American. The bilingual positions advertised on Monster.com often list visa and green card requirements.

The situation has become so bad that many managers in the United States believe that it would be a waste of time to even look for an American with language skills. I recently had a conversation with a professor of foreign languages who teaches at a university in the Midwest. When she found out that the CEO of a local company was planning a recruiting session on campus, she was enthusiastic: she is especially interested in the applicability of languages in the business world. Then she heard the details: the CEO planned to focus his recruiting efforts on foreign exchange students. He apparently did not believe that any American candidates would possess the language skills he needed.

This "foreigners first" approach to recruiting language talent has become an accepted practice in the United States. In Japan, however, it would strike everyone as counterintuitive. Japanese companies do hire foreigners who speak Japanese, but their first instinct is to hire Japanese nationals who speak other languages.

HIRE THE BEST CANDIDATE—NOT THE BEST ENGLISH-SPEAKER

Writing in an article posted on Careerjournal.com, Sharon Voros mentioned the *"tendency [of U.S. companies] to hire the best English speaker – rather than the best manager – for a foreign management post."* I have dubbed this tendency the "English blindfold."

Many American companies wear the "English blindfold" when selecting key staff and partner firms in overseas markets. In one case that I am familiar with, an American machine tool company was recruiting technical sales staff in Mexico. Since the sales job was for the Spanish-speaking Mexican market, English capabilities should have been a negligible consideration. But no one on the U.S. side spoke Spanish. As a result, the company limited its consideration to candidates who spoke English.

The result was disastrous; the company ended up hiring three individuals who knew English—but not machine tools. I later found out that the company summarily rejected the Spanish-language résumés of more than a dozen candidates who could have performed competently in the Mexican machine tool market.

This situation is not isolated. American multinational companies frequently assume that the overseas staff member who speaks the best English also possesses the strongest business and technical skills. This is not surprising. Few American managers speak foreign languages, so they must rely on their overseas employees who do speak English. The flip side of this situation is that American managers are often unaware of business and technical talent residing in the non-English-speaking ranks.

TIME FOR A NEW ATTITUDE

The American attitude that foreign languages are "artsy" pursuits that have no applicability in the business world is outdated and self-defeating. Our foreign competitors who learn English have proved just how practical a foreign language can be.

In the 1920s, U.S. Secretary of State Henry L. Stimson shut down the American cryptanalytic (code-breaking) service on the grounds that "gentlemen don't read each other's mail." We Americans often rejoice that so much of the world reads our mail—while remaining unable to read *their* mail. This has obvious implications in the arena of foreign intelligence; but it also has significant implications for our long-term commercial competitiveness.

I sometimes hear American businesspersons express relief when overseas suppliers, customers, employees, and partners can speak English. This relief should be tempered with the realization that these bilingual foreigners hold a trump card over the heads of their monolingual American counterparts—a trump card which is explored in depth in the next chapter.

CHAPTER 6 APPENDIX: ESTABLISHING A CORPORATE LANGUAGE PROGRAM

This book primarily examines language study as an individual endeavor. Managers and company owners will naturally speculate about the feasibility of applying the ideas in this book to the organization as a whole. Some managers may want to establish a companywide language study program. Others will prefer to focus their efforts on functional areas that interface frequently with non-English-speaking customers—such as the export sales department.

Company-sponsored learning can be broken down into two broad categories. First, there is onsite learning, in which the company hires instructors who conduct classes in a meeting room or in the company cafeteria. Secondly, there is offsite learning, in which the company subsidizes scholarship that employees pursue in their own spare time.

Onsite learning is best suited to subjects that can be neatly packaged into one- or two-day seminars. The mastery of a foreign language requires a lot of time and effort, and it is doubtful that any organization would be willing to dedicate the time and resources that would be needed in order to conduct effective language instruction onsite.

The advantages of learning English have been apparent to the Japanese for years, and companies often assist employees by providing in-house English language instruction. These classes are usually offered once or twice per week after work hours, and attendance is voluntary.

However, among the Japanese I have met who are competent in English, very few give much credit to these company-sponsored programs.

Most attribute their skills to some individual factor: outside private classes, dedicated self-study, or time spent abroad.

On the other side of the Pacific, the results have been dismal. In the lifetime of every Japanese company in the United States, there is a moment when someone on the American side says, "Hey, let's all learn Japanese." The company then either hires an outside teacher, or persuades one of the translators to hold classes one or two evenings per week.

The first night of class, it is standing room only. By the third class, the number of students is reduced by half. After the fourth class, the audience has dwindled to a small handful of people. The tenth class (if it is held at all) will be attended by one or two students.

Most employees attend the first class with a sincere desire to learn a new language, only to emerge overwhelmed at the scope of their new undertaking. A weekly language class will provide employees with a start in learning a language—but significant individual efforts (i.e., homework) will be required. Even employees who have a solid work ethic have probably not done "homework" since they were in high school or college. Therefore, they expect that *the class alone* will be sufficient to build their skills in a new language. This inevitably leads to a perception of slow progress—and then feelings of discouragement. In the absence of outside study, it would take ten years of weekly classes before any real proficiency could be reached. Individual initiative will always be the key factor in the acquisition of language skills.

This does not mean that employers can take no effective actions to encourage and facilitate language study. The company can make sure that university language courses are covered under its tuition reimbursement policy. The company may also elect to offer partial reimbursement of language study materials, with certain restrictions. A good example would be a 50% reimbursement of language study materials up to $500, for languages that are relevant to the employer.

Most importantly, managers can promulgate the fact that language skills are a valued commodity within the organization. This can be done formally as well as informally. Some Japanese companies make the attainment of applicable language skills an element of the employee performance review. Another effective measure is to make language skills a prerequisite for positions that deal with outside divisions and customers who speak other languages.

CHAPTER 7

LEARN THE OTHER SIDE'S LANGUAGE—EVEN IF THEY *DO* SPEAK YOURS

At some point, every American who works in the international business arena asks the following question:

> *"I know that the overseas firm our company works with has appointed a representative who speaks English, so why should I bother to learn their language?"*

The question is reasonable. Why not rely on this person's language skills?

Let's consider a typical international project scenario. Suppose that your company is working on a long-term project with a Korean firm. You have been given the responsibility of serving as the main contact to the Korean company. Over the next four to five years, you will be working extensively with the Korean partner, and you will be traveling to Korea on a bimonthly basis.

It turns out that one of your counterparts, Mr. Kim, excelled in English during his school days, and has kept up with the language since graduation. When you talk to him on the phone, he particularly impresses you with his ability to understand everything you say, and his mastery of English vocabulary. He even throws in little bits of English slang, like "cool" and "sure thing."

However, you have another counterpart in the Korean company, Ms. Lee. Ms. Lee also studied English in school, but she was more interested in subjects like math and computer science. Although she has thought about brushing up on the English she learned as a student, she is too busy with other tasks. And besides—she never really *liked* English as a field of study.

When Ms. Lee and Mr. Kim visit your company's headquarters, you are able to establish a rapport with Mr. Kim, but it is difficult to talk to Ms. Lee because of her limited grasp of English. And establishing a rapport with

Ms. Lee is important; you discover that Ms. Lee—not Mr. Kim—is the real decision-maker on the Korean side.

Several weeks later, you make your first trip to Korea. You are relieved to note that the signs in Kimp'o International Airport are in English as well as Korean. Otherwise, you would not be able to find your way to the baggage claim area.

Mr. Kim is waiting for you on the other side of customs. As he drives you to his company's office, he points out the sights in downtown Seoul, and tells you many interesting facts about Korean culture—in nearly impeccable English.

When you arrive at the Korean firm's headquarters, Mr. Kim takes you to the office of an older gentleman named Mr. Park, who is the president of the company. Mr. Park says, "I'm glad to meet you," in faltering but understandable English. You respond in kind, and add that you have full confidence in the project's success. Mr. Park stares at you blankly, fidgets uncomfortably, and then turns to Mr. Kim. Mr. Kim faithfully (you assume) translates what you have just said. Mr. Park smiles, nods, and adds a remark in Korean which Mr. Kim neglects to translate. Before you can ask Mr. Kim to translate, he ushers you out of the president's office, and Mr. Park returns to his work.

"I missed Mr. Park's last comment," you mention casually, as Mr. Kim is escorting you past rows of desks, ringing phones, and computers.

"Oh, I'm sorry," Mr. Kim says. "He just said that he also hopes the project will overcome whatever difficulties there are to reach success."

Wait a minute, you think. *I said that I am sure the project will be a success, not that I* hope *the project will be a success. Does Mr. Park now think that we're having second thoughts about our abilities to pull it off? And what did Mr. Park mean by "difficulties?"*

You start to ask Mr. Kim for a clarification, but he is obviously in too much of a hurry. He asks you to have a seat in a chair by his desk while he locates Ms. Lee. While you are waiting, a woman working at a nearby computer station strikes up a conversation with you. She introduces herself as Miyung Hong. You compliment her on her skilled command of English, and she mentions that she lived in the United States for six years while her father was stationed in Los Angeles as a manager at Samsung. As you are talking to Ms. Hong, you notice that two women working at adjacent computers cast occasional glances in your direction. You acknowledge them with a smile and ask them how they are, but they look at Ms. Hong.

Ms. Hong speaks to the women in a flurry of incomprehensible speech. They speak back to her, and she translates for you:

"They said they are fine, and how are you?" She adds apologetically, "I'm sorry, but they don't speak English very well."

You begin to reply to the women but decide to cut the conversation short with a smile and a nod. Talking to the office workers through Ms. Hong doesn't seem worth the effort. Besides, Mr. Kim has just returned with Ms. Lee.

"Let's go to a meeting room," Mr. Kim says.

When the three of you arrive in the meeting room, another man is waiting for you. He is introduced as Mr. Kang, the engineer assigned to the project. The four of you take your seats at a table in the center of the meeting room, and Mr. Kang unfolds a large blueprint. You recognize it immediately as the blueprint of the product which your company and the Korean firm are jointly developing. Mr. Kang begins pointing to the various points on the blueprint, while Mr. Kim translates.

Everything is going fine until Mr. Kang informs you (speaking through Mr. Kim) that the Korean company has decided to eliminate a key product feature. Your heart skips a beat. Your company's management team had emphasized this feature when explaining the future product to distributors.

"Wait a minute, please," you interrupt. "Why were the blueprints changed?"

"Oh, this will enable us to sell the product at a 5% lower price," Mr. Kim explains. "Our engineering department suggested the change, and we thought that your company was in favor of eliminating excess costs where possible. And this is just a cosmetic feature."

"No, no," you protest. "This feature is a key selling point. Mr. Kim, please explain that our side cannot agree to eliminate this feature, because it adds to the functionality of the product—it is *not* just cosmetic."

Mr. Kim pauses, and reluctantly turns to Ms. Lee and Mr. Kang. He says something in Korean—but of course you are not sure exactly what he has said.

Ms. Lee and Mr. Kang shake their heads and respond in Korean to Mr. Kim. "My colleagues are in agreement in this matter," Mr. Kim says. "There is no need to include this feature in the product. The most important thing is to keep the cost down."

You begin to sense that Mr. Kim may have a hidden agenda. Perhaps it was originally his suggestion to change the blueprint. Your head is full of customer data, case histories, etc., which could bolster your argument. But in order to make your point, you will have to rely on Mr. Kim, whom you fear may subtly sabotage your cause. You look forlornly at Ms. Lee and Mr. Kang. If only you could speak to them directly.....

The above story, which is a composite of several real incidents that I have either witnessed or heard secondhand, illustrates an important fact of international business: when you rely solely on the linguistic abilities of your foreign counterparts, you are also forced to rely on their willingness to use these abilities. This means that if the other party doesn't want you to understand the contents of a conversation or document—then you probably won't. If your message to the other side could ruffle feathers, then it may be watered down or artfully modified when it is translated.

It would be wrong, however, to blame such predicaments solely on the scheming of wily foreigners. In international business situations, native English-speakers routinely assume that their counterparts owe them a prompt and unabridged translation. For some, this becomes almost a sense of entitlement—a belief that as English-speakers they are exempt from the responsibility to handle information in other languages.

This mindset is ultimately self-defeating. If you are only able to understand half of the communications, then you are effectively giving the other side an advantage which they may or may not choose to use against you.

87

CHAPTER 8

FOREIGN LANGUAGES, PATRIOTISM, AND AMERICAN VALUES

"To know your enemy, you must become your enemy...Keep your friends close and your enemies closer." –Sun Tzu, The Art of War

To celebrate Foreign Language Week in 2005, Maryland's Old Mill High School broadcast the Pledge of Allegiance in a variety of languages, including Spanish, Latin, French, and Russian. The English-language version of the Pledge was also broadcast for the student body. One fifteen-year-old student protested the Foreign Language Week observance, and refused to stand for the pledge. When asked to explain himself, the ninth-grader said:

> *"This is America, and we've got soldiers at war. When you're saying the Pledge in a different language which nobody understands, that's not OK."*

The boy's father supported his son's protest, and compared the reading of the Pledge of Allegiance in a foreign language to "wearing a cross upside down in a church."

Now let's examine a far more serious story that made the news about three years before the Maryland teen staged his protest. Shortly after the 9/11 attacks, it was revealed that our national security apparatus suffered from a lack of FBI agents and CIA operatives who speak Arabic, Farsi, and Pashtu. On June 7th, 2002, ABC News even reported that U.S. government officials were unable to complete a timely translation of "at least one conversation in Arabic before the Sept. 11 attacks in which the participants spoke about something big that was going to happen on that day... " By the time the relevant materials were translated, the attacks had already occurred. (Source: ABCNEWS.com, 06/07/02)

In *The Art of War*, Sun Tzu suggested that we should know our opponents even more intimately than we know our allies. In this light, studying other languages and cultures provides strategic advantages. However, as long as the study of language is a one-sided endeavor, the advantages of bilingualism will only function for our commercial and strategic rivals.

Like other nationalities, Americans have often felt an urge to expel the language of the enemy. During the First World War, German language schools in my native Cincinnati were shut down. Throughout the more recent Cold War, Russian Studies professors were frequently the target of McCarthyist persecutions. To learn the language of the enemy is sometimes seen as a sign of surrender. Hypothetical defeats are often alluded to in linguistic terms: *"If the war had been lost, we would all be speaking German/Russian/etc."*

The Navajo Language and World War II

In war, linguistic insularity has been the difference between victory and defeat. In recent history, the best known example is the story of the "code talkers" of World War II. The code talkers were Native Americans of the Navajo tribe whom the American government recruited to relay sensitive messages in the Pacific combat theater. The Navajo language was unknown outside the American Southwest, so there was no way that the Japanese military could decipher intercepted radio messages broadcast in Navajo. This weakness ultimately contributed to their defeat in the South Pacific.

Opponents of the United States and Western values don't see any contradiction in learning English. A report from Saudi Arabia provides a striking example. On November 17th, 2002, CNN aired "Inside Saudi Arabia", a documentary about the reclusive Middle Eastern kingdom that has occupied the headlines so much since the terrorist incidents of 2001. While acknowledging the negative aspects of Saudi society, the program also attempted to shed light on some reforms that are being made within the country.

Traditionally, Saudi Arabia's school system has placed an excessive emphasis on religious studies. Students spend large amounts of time memorizing the Koran and other religious texts. Some reformers inside the country have noted that Saudi schools should teach more subjects that are relevant to technology and international commerce. One of these subjects, of course, is English.

The CNN camera crew entered an elite Saudi school that had placed a special emphasis on English. The scene was a modern, immaculately clean classroom, where the sons (no daughters) of Saudi Arabia's millionaires received top-notch English language instruction. The private educational institution had even hired a teacher from the United States, so that authentic, accent-free English would be taught.

Several of the young men in the classroom were interviewed by the CNN reporter. (Ironically, one of these youths was the nephew of Osama Bin Laden.) To their credit, the young men spoke English fairly well—certainly much better than the average American high school student speaks Spanish or French, let alone Arabic.

In the context of the "Global English" discussion, these Saudi youths might seem to be yet another argument for Anglophone complacency. Such a conclusion would be short-sighted. Never mind that the sons of Saudi millionaires are not representative of the entire country, or the Arab world in general. There is another, far more important reason why we should not throw away our Arabic textbooks just because some wealthy young Saudis are learning English.

Saudi Arabia is a nominal U.S. ally, but no one can doubt that there are many elements within the country that mean us harm. Saudi Arabia is, after all, the home of radical Wahhabi Islam, and the country of origin of fifteen of the nineteen September 11th hijackers. If a large number of Saudis can speak English, but practically no Americans can understand Arabic, then who has an advantage on the intelligence front? Who can gather information the most easily? Who can casually read the news and opinions available on the other side's Internet?

Following the publication of the first edition of *Why You Need a Foreign Language & How to Learn One*, I was interviewed by the magazine *Transitions Abroad*. One of the interview questions concerned the shortage of U.S.-born Pashto, Farsi, and Arabic speakers, and the significance of this weakness in the wake of the 9/11 attacks. I responded as follows:

> *"There is an obvious problem when so few Americans can casually read what is written on a jihadi website, or the Arabic-language site of Al-Jazeera. We rely too heavily on foreign nationals for our translation needs in the Middle East. I'm not saying that every*

American should speak Arabic, but an imbalance exists when
almost no Americans can speak Arabic. The Middle East is an area
of long-term strategic importance to us, and the current struggle
against Al Qaeda is only one part of it. We also now have a long-
term commitment in Iraq. Our chances of success will be greater if
American soldiers, diplomats—and eventually, businesspersons—
can understand what average Iraqis are saying. "

It would be easy to dismiss American's lack of prowess in foreign
languages as simple xenophobia. An examination of the past reveals a more
complex picture. The United States—unlike the tightly clustered nations of
Europe—is a vast country with oceans on two of our major borders. For
most of our history, we were able to exist in relative isolation.

Moreover, America began its existence as a weak country amid
much stronger European powers. In the decades after the Revolutionary War,
threats from abroad were a constant source of anxiety. Even George
Washington was worried about foreigners meddling in the affairs of the
United States. In his Farewell Address of 1796, President Washington urged
Americans to avoid "passionate attachments" to other nations.

More than two hundred years before Americans ordered "Freedom
Fries," there was anxiety about the French. Alexander Hamilton once
derided Thomas Jefferson for his "womanish attachment to France." In 1814,
the White House and a series of national monuments were burned to the
ground—not by Islamic terrorists, but by invading British troops. And
American apprehensiveness about interference from Europe persisted well
into the 20th century, when public opinion was bitterly divided over U.S.
participation in two European land wars.

We still worry about the "insidious wiles of foreign influence" that
Washington described in 1796. The European threats of the 18th and 19th
centuries have been replaced today by fears of Middle Eastern terrorists, and
China's growing military and industrial power. However, the isolationism of
the past is completely untenable given the technology, geopolitics, and
globalized economy of the 21st century. We must engage both friend and foe
alike. In the coming years, this will mean that many more of us will need to
master foreign languages.

LANGUAGE AND DEMOCRACY

Some proponents of Global English have even suggested that the English language could—simply by virtue of being the English language—be a vehicle for political and social change. I have read a number of editorials that describe English as the "language of democracy." The producers of the aforementioned CNN documentary were similarly encouraged by the English classes in Saudi Arabia. They expressed hope that Saudi Arabia would become more liberal and Westernized through the study of our language.

While such hopes are appealing, there is no demonstrable link between English study and Western democratic values. Saudi Arabia and Kuwait—two wealthy oil states—boast especially high numbers of competent English speakers, due to a large and well-educated privileged class. Neither of these countries is "liberal" or "Westernized." (In fact, both countries severely restrict the rights of women, foreigners, and non-Muslims.)

In Pakistan, where English shares official status with Urdu, women are often murdered by male family members in "honor killings," as atonement for minor moral infractions. Radical Islamic parties are a major force in the country's government. Nor has English made Pakistan America's friend; according to a December, 2002 news report, the most popular toys for young Pakistanis at the end of the year were Osama Bin Laden theme toys. (CBS News.com, 12/05/02)

In contrast, there are comparatively few fluent English speakers in Spain, Italy and France. The French in particular are famous for their resistance to the "linguistic hegemony" of English. Yet these countries have well-developed democracies, and human rights are respected within their borders. While the language barrier is a serious factor when visiting Madrid, few would choose the repressive societies of Pakistan or Kuwait over monolingual Spain—just because there are greater numbers of Pakistanis and Kuwaitis who can chat in English. Language, as it turns out, is a communication tool—not a political philosophy.

92

LOCAL LANGUAGE CONFLICTS

The politics that surround language do not always involve global power shifts and international disputes. In fact, many of the more bitterly contested language controversies arise from conflicts *within* countries rather than conflicts *between* countries. Some of these battles are scarcely known outside the particular regions where they take place.

Consider the case of Spain's minority languages. Everyone knows that Spanish is spoken in Spain, but not everyone is aware that people in certain regions of Spain also speak Catalan, Basque, and Galician. The most numerically significant of these—Catalan—is actively spoken by about 7 million people. (The total population of Spain is about 43 million.)

General Francisco Franco, who was dictator of Spain from 1939 to 1975, banned Spain's minority regional languages. The minority languages were later legalized following the restoration of the constitutional monarchy and democracy in Spain. Legalization, however, did not depoliticize them. Politicians, journalists, and common citizens in the minority language areas continue to lament the state of their languages vis-à-vis the national one. Meanwhile, some Spaniards outside the minority language areas wonder aloud whether the minority language speakers have truly assimilated into the greater Spanish polity.

Similar worries have arisen perennially within the United States. In colonial times, Benjamin Franklin expressed concern that German immigrants were too slow to learn English and to assimilate into the culture of the United States. In the early 20th century, Teddy Roosevelt warned his fellow citizens not to let America become "a polyglot boarding house for the world." Many Americans hold the same concerns in the early 21st century. In states that have high numbers of immigrants, there have been ballot initiatives to restrict the public use of languages other than English.

U.S. English, a citizen's action group dedicated to the passage of official English legislation, describes itself as "*the nation's oldest, largest citizens' action group dedicated to preserving the unifying role of the English language in the United States.*" The U.S. English website (www.us-english.org) documents the group's state-by-state efforts to have English officially declared the language of the United States.

U.S. English correctly states that English is "the language of opportunity" in the United States. However, there is no evidence to indicate that immigrants, as a group, disagree with this point. Even The National Council of La Raza (an advocacy group for Hispanics and Spanish-speaking immigrants in the U.S.) acknowledges that *English competency is a necessity for success in the United States.*

At a more grassroots level, I would cite what I call "the grandparent test" as evidence that immigrants are assimilating linguistically into the United States. The grandparent test is simple: try to find a second-generation immigrant born in the United States who speaks her parents' language more fluently than she speaks English. Then try to find a third-generation immigrant born in America who can even manage a basic conversation in the language spoken by her grandparents.

I have met no second-generation immigrant who speaks Spanish or Swahili better than she speaks English. And the only third-generation immigrants I have met who can speak their grandparents' language at all learned it at school—not in the home. In either case, the results of the grandparent test make clear that the melting pot still functions in the United States. There are no multigenerational enclaves of immigrants in the United States who primarily speak Chinese, Russian, Spanish—or any other language besides English.

Most of the linguistic controversies within the United States involve Spanish. Spanish is the only language with enough speakers in the United States to create the perception that it is somehow competing with English. This is not, however, a problem of assimilation. The U.S.-born descendents of Spanish-speakers pass the "grandparent test" I describe above. In study after study, the children of Spanish-speaking immigrants to the United States express a clear preference for English.

There is, however, no denying a simple fact: we currently have a large number of first-generation Spanish-speaking immigrants in the United States—especially in border states like Texas, Arizona, and California. These people speak Spanish because it is the language they grew up with— outside the United States, in a Spanish-speaking country.

This issue is closely related to the topic of illegal immigration. While many of our immigrants arrive in the United States legally, many others arrive *illegally*. Our illegal immigration problem is often conflated into a "Spanish language problem." But the Spanish language isn't the problem. We need to control our borders—not pass official English laws.

When you probe beneath the surface of outcries about the presence of the Spanish language in the United States, you invariably find that the real concern is illegal immigration—not *español.* In April of 2005, California Governor Arnold Schwarzenegger publicly chided a Spanish-language television station for a billboard that it placed along a Los Angeles freeway. The words on the billboard were in Spanish, but the Governor's complaint did not concern the mere use of Spanish. At the top of the billboard, the abbreviation for California (CA) was crossed out and replaced with the word "Mexico," so that the sign read: "Los Angeles, ~~CA~~ Mexico" The effect was a strong suggestion that the city of Los Angeles is located in Mexico—rather than the U.S. State of California.

Schwarzenegger acknowledged that the billboard was probably intended as a slick marketing ploy rather than a political statement. However, he was concerned that the billboard promoted illegal immigration. The Governor urged the station to take the controversial billboard down.

California is home to 2.4 million illegal immigrants—half of whom come from Mexico. Illegal immigration costs California taxpayers about $10.5 billion annually. The chaotic situation along the U.S.-Mexico border has inordinately swelled the ranks of first generation immigrants in the United States. A secondary effect of this huge influx is an exaggerated fear that American English is threatened within our own borders. But the children of these Mexican immigrants will almost certainly become fluent native English-speakers if they grow up in the United States.

When immigration is properly controlled, the small-scale presence of a foreign language within our borders creates no negative impact on national unity, or practical communications on day-to-day matters. My own Cincinnati, Ohio provides a persuasive example. Cincinnati is home to a substantial but reasonable number of immigrants from around the world. We have Spanish-language radio stations, Chinese-language newspapers, and a smattering of local media in other languages. None of these is seen as an effort to compete with the English language; and the local immigrant who cannot hold at least a basic conversation in English is rare.

CHAPTER 8 APPENDIX: MORE NON-HISPANIC AMERICANS SPEAKING ESPAÑOL

I recently upgraded my cable TV package to include several Spanish-language channels. While those of you who live in New York or L.A. have had access to Spanish-language TV and radio channels for decades, finding live broadcasts *en español* was very difficult here in Ohio until just a few years ago.

My favorite Spanish-language channel is *CNN en Español*. Although the Spanish-language version of CNN has a slight focus on Latin American news, the content is more or less the same as its English-language counterpart. Thanks to *CNN en Español*, I have been able to discipline myself to consume most of my news in Spanish, which of course helps me to improve my skills in the language.

The more I watch *CNN en Español*, the more evidence I see of a growing interest in the Spanish language among non-Hispanic Americans. The other day, I was surprised to see New York Governor George Pataki chatting volubly with a reporter in Spanish. President George W. Bush can only manage snippets of the language; but his brother Jeb (the Governor of Florida) has excellent Spanish skills. And lesser known non-Hispanic Americans appear on *CNN en Español* seemingly every other day. Some of them struggle a bit—but I have yet to see any of them totally blow an interview because their Spanish skills weren't up to the task.

In fact, I have noticed that Spanish-speakers in the United States are no longer terribly surprised to meet a non-Hispanic American who is comfortable in their language. More often than not, they don't even suggest that the American who speaks Spanish is doing something out of the ordinary. They simply reply in Spanish and continue the conversation in Spanish—their reaction no different than that of an American abroad who is addressed in English.

The experts agree that non-Hispanic Spanish proficiency is becoming less unusual in the United States. Cristina Gómez, a professor in the Hispanic Studies department of the University of Chicago, commented on this issue in a recent article appearing in the online version of *CNN en Español*.

> *"El número de personas bilingües ha aumentado y no sólo es de origen hispano, sino de otras razas porque entienden que el español es ahora el segundo idioma en la nación"*

("The number of [Spanish-English] bilinguals has increased, and this group is not only of Hispanic origin. It also includes people of other ethnicities, because they understand that Spanish is now the second language of the country.")

96

As I mention elsewhere in this book, Spanish is a solid choice for the American who knows that she wants to learn a foreign language, but remains undecided about which one. While there are scores of useful languages to choose from, you simply can't go wrong by starting with Spanish.

Part II

How to Learn a Foreign Language

CHAPTER 9

THE RELUCTANT LANGUAGE LEARNER

STUDYING SPANISH IN CINCINNATI

I was first exposed to foreign language study as a high school student in the 1980s. In retrospect, I must admit that at the time I really didn't see the point. My hometown of Cincinnati, Ohio had a negligible immigrant population. There was no Chinatown or Little Havana. The two major non-English-speaking immigrant groups in the Cincinnati area—the Germans and the Italians—had arrived in the 19th century, and had long since assimilated into the general population. German language schools had once thrived in Cincinnati, but these fell out of favor amid the anti-German sentiments of World War I. The German schools were closed during the war, and never reopened.

As a teenager, my world was completely monolingual. About half of the kids at the school I attended had either German or Italian last names—but no one in their families had actually spoken these languages for generations. There was a minor trend for kids with German last names who had a strong sense of heritage to fulfill their high school language requirement with two years of German. My peers who had Italian last names did not have this option; only French, German, and Spanish were offered at my high school.

At this stage in my life, I had barely been out of Ohio; any chances for foreign travel were still light years in the future. I took First Year Spanish and received reasonably good grades. However, I considered Spanish to be a purely academic pursuit—somewhat similar to solving quadratic equations or learning to identify iambic pentameters.

The following year, I met someone who forever changed my fundamental ideas about foreign languages. My Second Year Spanish teacher was Miss Kramer, a no-nonsense educator who took her subject very seriously. To our surprise, she also took us seriously. Miss Kramer expected

14- to 17-year-olds to comport themselves like adults, and to learn like adults. (Most of us were still quite content to be kids.)

On the first day of class Ms. Kramer sized us up like a Marine drill sergeant looking over a barracks full of new recruits. She matter-of-factly informed us of her goal for the year: We were to become "functional in Spanish" by the following May. And Miss Kramer suggested that the easy ride we had enjoyed in First Year Spanish had come to an end. *"I will pace the class,"* she said. *"But I will not work at a pace that insults your intelligence."* Such words are Teacherese for "expect to work your tails off."

From the beginning, I knew that Miss Kramer's methodology was going to be radically different from that of the First Year Spanish teacher, whose lessons had kept us safely tethered to the textbook. Miss Kramer brought Spanish out of the textbook and into the real world. *"This is how they say it in Mexico versus in South America,"* Miss Kramer would explain... *"This word is only used in Spain."* For the first time, I became aware that Spanish was more than an academic subject—it was actually a tool that I could use to communicate with millions of people around the world.

Miss Kramer focused on the specific language needed to accomplish practical, everyday tasks. *"Here are the words you need to open a bank account in a Spanish-speaking country...This is what you would say if you wanted to exchange dollars for pesos..."* And she wanted us to be able to read the local newspapers in the Spanish-speaking world. Class would frequently open with an announcement like, *"Today we are going to analyze the language in an editorial from El Pais that discusses Latin American government."*

We were constantly tested on our ability to *function* in Spanish. Rather than rely solely on watered-down, fill-in-the-blank and multiple choice tests, Miss Kramer made us translate newspaper articles, decipher recordings of radio broadcasts, and write extensive essays in Spanish. I don't know if I was truly "functional" by the time Second Year Spanish broke for summer vacation, but I had absorbed a significant chunk of the language.

One day Miss Kramer said something that has stuck with me for the past twenty years. We were reading a Spanish newspaper article, and she asked a student for an on-the-spot translation of a particular sentence.

The student looked at the sentence, and shifted uncomfortably. He briefly gazed around the room for help, then threw himself on the mercy of Miss Kramer.

"I don't know what *se redactan los códigos* means," he admitted.

Miss Kramer smiled. "It means, 'the codes of laws are drawn up.'" She paused, and put her copy of the newspaper article down on her desk. She stepped to the front of the room.

"Now class, you'll remember the discussions we have had about vocabulary."

There were a few groans from the room. Ms. Kramer had a habit of assigning us copious amounts of vocabulary to learn.

"The reason that you have to learn so much vocabulary is simple: If you don't know the vocabulary, you'll never get past square one in the real world."

These words became one of my fundamental laws of language learning. Whenever I begin to learn a new language, I start with a heavy dose of vocabulary. But enough on that topic for now: we'll be talking a lot more about vocabulary a bit later.

Miss Kramer had a unique talent for motivating kids to learn Spanish. However, my progress came to a standstill after I left her classroom. I made a few desultory attempts at expanding my knowledge of the language, but these forays into independent study were short-lived. My enjoyment of Spanish could not overcome one overwhelming fact: a teenager living in the Cincinnati of the mid-1980s had no practical need to speak Spanish.

When I entered college, I took more Spanish to fulfill the undergraduate language requirement, and continued to make incremental progress. After I fulfilled my language requirement, I did not sign up for any more Spanish courses. That might have been the end of my career as a language learner. However, a series of incidents during my second and third years of college inspired me to make languages a lifelong pursuit.

HOW STEVEN SPIELBERG GOT ME INTERESTED IN JAPANESE

One evening in 1988, I was sitting in a movie theater with Donna L., watching Steven Spielberg's *Empire of the Sun*, a movie about the Japanese occupation of Shanghai during the early days of World War II. Earlier in the evening, Donna had been telling me about one of the classes she had enrolled in for the current semester: Japanese. Northern Kentucky University had long offered classes in Spanish, French, and German, but Japanese had been added only that year.

I was curious about the class, and Donna humored me by teaching me a few elementary Japanese phrases in the car as we drove to the theater. By the time the movie started, the only one I remembered was "*arigatoo*"— the Japanese word for "thank you."

At some point during movie, the hero—a young British boy separated from his family in the chaos of the Japanese invasion—used the phrase, "*arigatoo*"—and I—low and behold—understood what it meant.

Donna gleefully poked my arm. "You see," she said. "That means *'thank you.'*"

The movie contained a lot more Japanese which I could of course not even begin to understand, but the language nonetheless asserted a certain hold on me. Whereas French, Spanish, and German were plain vanilla subjects that could be acquired in a high school in Ohio, Japanese was exotic. Japanese was something that you learned to go off and have adventures in the distant capitals of the Far East.

With the whimsical approach to the future that is rarely possible past the age of twenty-three or so, I began to consider enrolling in Japanese classes during the following fall semester. At the same time, I started to investigate some other Asian languages. The first of these was Korean. My father had been stationed in Korea during the Vietnam War era. When I was a child, he had taught me a few Korean phrases that he had picked up during his stay, and the strange staccato words had stuck with me over the years. The pictures that he brought back of Korea's temples and hilly landscapes struck me as alien and irresistibly intriguing.

But before I settled on Korean or Japanese, I would have to find out about the most widely spoken Asian language, Chinese. (It also turns out that Chinese is the most widely spoken language in the world, as measured by the number of speakers.) A student in my Biology class happened to be from China. One day I struck up a conversation with her and mentioned that I was interested in learning more about the Chinese language. She was kind enough to draw a few Chinese characters for me on a piece of notebook paper.

The first character she drew looked like a parallelogram bisected by a vertical line. "This character means 'middle,'" She said. "You pronounce it as '*zhong*.'" Then she drew another, more complicated character. This one looked vaguely like a distorted square with a latticework grid placed inside it.

"This one means 'kingdom,' or 'country.' It's pronounced *guo*. Together they form the word for China—*Zhongguo*." I noticed that her voice was making a special pitch on each syllable, but I didn't think to ask her about it. I looked down at the word for "China," written authentically in Chinese. Could I really learn this stuff?

My desire to learn an Asian language had now reached critical mass. I continued to page through the materials available in the Asian languages section of the campus bookstore. I was still window-shopping at this point, but I was sure that I would learn an Asian language. This was at the height of the "Japanese management techniques" craze of the late 1980s. The Japanese language was a hot field of study at this time, and Japanese books occupied vast tracts of shelf space. There were also quite a few books for learning Chinese, and a smattering of materials for students of Korean and Vietnamese. I was like a honeymooner trying to decide between Hawaii, Rome, and the Bahamas.

As chance would have it, I had recently met an older undergraduate named Randy, who spent four years as a Chinese translator for the U.S. Navy before entering college. Prior to assuming his duty post, Randy had studied Chinese for more than a year at the Defense Language Institute in Monterrey, California.

"Chinese phonetics is based on a tonal system," Randy explained one morning in the university center. "If you vary your tone, the meaning of the word changes." As he demonstrated a few examples, it was difficult for me to even recognize that each word had a unique pronunciation. Randy's pitching, indistinct syllables were totally outside my paradigm of what language was supposed to be. Japanese, with its monotone pronunciation, and clearly identifiable words like *arigatoo* seemed far more within my reach.

Shortly after my conversation in the university center with Randy, I made the decision to tackle Japanese. The university did not yet offer Chinese classes, and the language seemed like too high of a hurdle without formal instruction. I passed on Korean and Vietnamese for the same reasons. There were no classes to be found in these more junior Asian languages, and the self-study offerings in the campus bookstore were too sparse.

103

GETTING HOOKED ON JAPANESE

I would not be eligible to take a Japanese language class through the university until the following September, when the next course sequence began. It was March, and I decided that I would not wait for the fall semester. I purchased *Hugo's Japanese in Three Months* from the bookstore. This book did not teach the Japanese written language, but it provided a solid introduction to Japanese grammar and basic vocabulary using a transliterated (Romanized) version of the language.

I knew that I would have to go back and learn the Japanese writing system later, but for the time being I was content to rely on the crutch of the Latin alphabet. I spent the next several months absorbing as much as I could from *Japanese in Three Months*. I also bought a tourist-oriented Japanese cassette course. This did not teach much grammar, but it gave me an idea of how Japanese was pronounced. So far, I had not had any contact with a real live person who actually spoke Japanese.

Then, in the summer of that year, I had an opportunity to visit Los Angeles. Compared to Cincinnati, L.A. was a language lover's paradise. Entire sections of the city were dominated by shop signs and billboards written in Spanish, Korean, Chinese, and languages that I could not even recognize. There were foreign-language radio stations. Every shopping mall and restaurant was occupied by at least one group of people who were speaking something other than English.

I was waiting for my companions to arrive in the hotel lobby one evening when a tour group walked in. The labels on their suitcases—JTB— "Japan Travel Bureau"—identified them as visitors from Japan. The group of about thirty tourists began milling about the lobby, some queuing at the check-in counter. I listened intently to the bits of conversation that I could hear. I could understand a portion of what I overheard, but most of it was incomprehensible. However, I was certain that the tourists were speaking Japanese.

A woman of about thirty-five years of age plopped down on the sofa beside me. She looked over and smiled, as if to apologize for disturbing me. On an impulse, I smiled back and blurted out, "*Konbanwa*"—"Good Evening."

"*Konbanwa*," she replied. She looked at me wide-eyed, as if I had just recited her name, birth date, and passport number. But I knew that greetings were easy. I was determined to leverage the little Japanese I knew into a halfway respectable conversation.

"*Nihon no doko kara kimashita ka?*" I asked unevenly, taking my Japanese for its first test drive. I wondered if she would understand me.

"*Tookyoo kara kimashita.*" She said—"I come from Tokyo". Apparently I had strung my words together correctly, or at least close enough to get the point across.

I had successfully used a foreign language for the first time in the real world, and I was determined to keep going. We fumbled through another ten minutes or so of conversation, limited by my minimal grasp of Japanese. The woman—whose name turned out to be Fumiko—apparently recognized that I was a beginner in her language, and therefore spoke slowly and simply. However, two or three times she departed from the small confines of my vocabulary. I could only shrug and smile apologetically. As Miss Kramer had said, *You can't get past square one in the real world if you don't know the vocabulary.*

The first time you successfully use a foreign language in a spontaneous situation is a major milestone. This provides a peculiar sense of satisfaction—similar to what you felt as a child the first time you rode a bike without the training wheels. Your first experience—like mine—will probably be short and simple. However, you need that first small shred of empirical evidence to prove to yourself that you really can learn to communicate in a foreign language.

After the trip to Los Angeles, I was hooked. Before the end of the summer, *Japanese in Three Months* had become dog-eared, and some of the pages were starting to fall out. But when I enrolled in Japanese 101 in September, I had a significant head start over the other students.

I attended Japanese language classes during my last two years of college. Then I graduated, and I was forced to continue my studies without the aid of a structured classroom environment. Although I learned a lot of Japanese in the two years of classes, I actually learned a lot *more* Japanese during my first two years as a working adult. As we cover language learning strategies in the subsequent chapters, I will give you the laundry list of self-teaching techniques that I have used over the years, and some suggestions regarding how these methods can complement each other.

CHAPTER 10

WHICH LANGUAGE SHOULD YOU LEARN?

A VERY BRIEF INTRODUCTION TO THE LANGUAGES OF THE WORLD

Which language do you want to learn? Perhaps you have already picked one out—or perhaps you are just window-shopping at this point. Your selection of a language is analogous to your choice of an undergraduate major. You have to determine your goals.

Do you want to learn a difficult language (like Korean) or a relatively easy language (like Spanish)? Would you be interested in a language that you could use extensively in the Western Hemisphere (Spanish or Portuguese), or are you looking for a language that would involve opportunities in exotic, faraway countries (Chinese, Vietnamese, etc.)? Is there a particular region of the world that has always interested you? Does your heart race at the thought of strolling down the streets of a stately European capital, or are you drawn to the high-tech factories of Japan?

You should consider the difficulty of the language. As a general rule, Western European languages—Spanish, French, German, Italian, etc.—are easier for native English speakers to learn than Asian, Eastern European, or Middle Eastern languages.

A LOOK AT LANGUAGE FAMILIES

Most languages share common elements with at least one or two other languages. A *language family* is a group of languages that share common characteristics. Some of the most important language families are indicated below:

- *Western Germanic:* German, English, Yiddish, Dutch, Afrikaans, Flemish
- *Scandinavian:* Swedish, Norwegian, Danish, Icelandic
- *Romance:* Portuguese, Spanish, French, Romanian, Italian
- *Slavic:* Russian, Ukrainian, Belorussian, Polish, Slovak, Czech, Slovenian, Bulgarian, Serbo-Croatian, Macedonian
- *Sino-Tibetan:* Chinese, Thai, Lao, Burmese
- *Semitic:* Hebrew, Arabic

These close relationships between languages result from a variety of historical and geographic circumstances. (You probably noticed that many of the languages within the same family are spoken in neighboring countries.) In many cases, similar languages represent divergent branches of the same linguistic origin. At one point, a group of people were speaking essentially the same language, but one branch of the tribe migrated to another area. As a result, two mutually unintelligible but closely related languages developed. If you decide to specialize in the languages of a particular region, you may be able to take advantage of such similarities. For example, the languages of Scandinavia, which include Norwegian and Swedish, are substantially alike due to their common roots. If you learn Norwegian, then it will be fairly easy for you to learn Swedish later on.

A LOOK AT SOME SPECIFIC LANGUAGES

As mentioned earlier, each language has its own special challenges and rewards. Some languages are easier than others. Given the current trends in international business, some languages are guaranteed to be useful in the business world, while the commercial value of other languages is more speculative.

What follows are my observations about some specific languages that you might choose to learn. I have concluded this section with some concrete recommendations for those who are still undecided.

SPANISH

If you are living in the United States and you are undecided about which language to learn, then you can't go wrong by choosing Spanish. Spanish is the "unofficial second language" of the United States, and it is widely used in public life in California, Texas, and other states near the Mexican border. Moreover, Spanish is a solid choice for the career-oriented language learner: *español* is the foreign language that is most commonly requested by employers on job sites like Monster.com.

The 1994 enactment of the North American Free Trade Agreement has made Spanish extremely important to U.S. businesses. All major U.S. companies have a presence in Mexico, and the country is becoming a growing force in the manufacturing sector. The Mexican economy has encountered some bumps along the way—such as the peso crisis of the mid-1990s—but the country seems dedicated to achieving prosperity as a free market democracy. With a population of over 100 million, and a surging economy, Mexico alone makes Spanish a key language for businesspeople.

Spanish is also the language of most of Central and South America. (Worldwide, more than twenty countries use Spanish as an official language.) The economic development of the other Spanish-speaking American countries has so far been irregular, and plagued with banking crises, guerilla insurgencies, and other calamities. However, significant progress has been made. Both politically as well as economically, Latin America is far better off today than it was twenty years ago. Dictatorships have been replaced by democratic governments in Argentina, Chile, and Nicaragua. (Cuba is still a Marxist dictatorship; but Castro is nearly eighty years old at the time of this writing.)

Of course, Spanish is also the language of Spain. Spain was once considered an economic basket case, but Spanish industries have rebounded in recent years. I have been particularly surprised at the extent of the Spanish presence in the automotive and machine tool sectors.

As foreign languages go, Spanish is relatively easy to learn. As a Latin-based language, Spanish shares numerous cognates with English. Even if you have never studied the language, you can probably guess the meaning of the following words: *nación, importante, mucho, fotografía, fortuna*. Of course, there are some aspects of Spanish that are tricky; but the language is nonetheless far easier for English speakers to learn than Japanese, Russian, or even French.

There are innumerable books and self-teaching programs to assist you in learning Spanish. The Spanish area usually occupies the most shelf space of the foreign language section in any bookstore. Spanish is taught at nearly every institution of higher learning in the United States, including community colleges. If you live in a major U.S. city, then you can find newspapers, television channels, and radio stations that use the language.

Spanish-speakers as a group are extremely generous with foreigners who attempt to speak their language. If you let on to a Spanish speaker that you are learning her language, you will receive encouragement, help, and lots of patient practice.

JAPANESE

Japanese is spoken by about 130 million people, most of who live in the Japanese islands. Japanese is not a global language like Spanish, French, or English, but the language is understood in a number of locations outside Japan. During an extended business trip to São Paulo, Brazil, I was surprised to discover that many of the second-, third-, and fourth-generation Japanese living in the area still understood the language. In fact, a number of Japanese-language newspapers and radio stations continue to thrive in the São Paulo area, although the influx of Japanese immigrants tapered off more than half a century ago.

During the Great Depression, Japan's economy was thoroughly battered, prompting an outpouring of economic refugees. American laws to limit Asian immigration had recently made the U.S. a less than friendly destination. Brazil, conversely, had liberal immigration laws, and millions of acres of cheap farmland. The Japanese came by the thousands, and the region surrounding São Paulo, Brazil, today hosts the largest Japanese population outside the home islands. The Japantown, or *Nihonmachi* district of São Paulo is a bustling mixture of Japanese restaurants, bookstores, and other interesting businesses. The area might easily be mistaken for one of the smaller cities in Japan, were it not for a few excessively quaint touches that are obviously designed for tourists, such as streetlights shaped like traditional Japanese lanterns.

Ironically, the Brazilian-born children and grandchildren of many of the original economic immigrants from Japan themselves became guest workers in the land of their forebears. In the late 1980s and early 1990s,

Japan's factories were operating at full capacity, and the country experienced a severe labor shortage. Although Japan had always had tight immigration controls, guest workers from abroad were granted temporary work visas. These guest workers came from a variety of countries, but Brazilians of Japanese descent comprised a singularly large percentage.

The Japanese immigrants to the United States settled mostly in California and Hawaii. In the American tradition of the Melting Pot, the language was preserved for superficial ceremonial purposes, but mostly vanished from everyday communications. Although remnants of Japanese culture persisted in cities like Los Angeles and San Francisco, these lacked the linguistic authenticity of São Paulo's *Nihonmachi*.

Then, in the 1980s, the Japanese language began to receive widespread attention in the United States. Japanese citizens suddenly had money, and their favorite tourist destination was America. Japanese businesses were also coming to the United States. A new influx of Japanese came to Southern California as expatriate managers for companies like Sony, Ricoh, and Toshiba. Service companies like the Japan Travel Bureau followed.

Local companies vied for a share the *nouveau riche* yen, often using the Japanese language as a sales and marketing tool. At the height of the Japanese investment boom in the United States during the early 1990s, Japanese-speaking tour guides, interpreters, and real estate agents enjoyed a lucrative seller's market.

The existence of so many Japan-related jobs, and the rise of Japan as a major industrial power caught the attention of educators. The Japanese language, which had previously been relegated to the academic backwater of Far Eastern Studies, suddenly became a sought-after skill for engineers, MBAs, and others in the "mainstream." Every university seemed to be starting a Japanese-language program, or looking for a qualified instructor to start such a program. Prior to 1987, self-instruction books and courses for learning Japanese were as sparse as hen's teeth. By 1992, the Japanese instructional market was outpacing that of practically every other language.

Japan's economy hit the skids in the mid-1990s, and world events have since propelled a number of other languages to greater prominence. NAFTA revived Americans' flagging interest in the Spanish language, and the emergence of a unified Europe renewed interest in old favorites like French and German. In more recent years, the economic boom in China, and problems in the Middle East have perhaps made Chinese and Arabic the new "cutting edge" languages. The Japanese language has lost some of the luster that it had back in 1990 or so, when "Japanese-style management techniques" were all the rage, and the press heralded the coming of *Pax Nipponica*.

Nonetheless, there are still plenty of good reasons for learning Japanese. While Chinese and Arabic may become more significant to the United States in future decades, Japanese is more commercially advantageous at the present time. Japanese is spoken in the boardrooms of Toyota, Honda, and other universally recognized corporations. Moreover, you do not have to travel to Japan to take advantage of all this Japan-related work. Japanese speakers are frequently sought by automotive component manufacturers in the Detroit area—about as far away from the streets of Tokyo as one can possibly get. Japan is a major player not only in automobiles, but also in consumer electronics, machine tools, and steel.

Japanese is an agglutinative language. This means that most words are formed by combining one morpheme (the smallest meaningful unit of a language) with other morphemes. True competency in Japanese is reached by learning how the various pieces of the language are used in combination. Example sentences are a key aspect of learning any language—but they are especially important when learning Japanese.

Japanese is classified as one of the most difficult languages for English speakers to learn. Learning Japanese requires you to enter an entirely new language paradigm. Although the language has borrowed a small number of words from English, German, and other Western languages, you will be mostly unaided by cognates. Japanese grammar does not resemble anything that you learned in English, Spanish, or German class. Sentences can exist without subjects, adjectives often behave like verbs, and the passive verb tense is used extensively. Japanese word order seems to have been deliberately designed to be the diametric opposite of English grammatical rules. Verbs typically fall at the end of the sentence. When you say, "I went to the office" in Japanese, you literally say, "*I to office went.*"

Politeness, humility, familiarity and disdain are conveyed in Japanese through subtle distinctions in the parts of speech. You can insult or complement someone by your choice of a verb. There are several polite endings that can be added to a person's name, such as the suffix *–san*. When you are first learning Japanese, you may occasionally make a mistake and say something that is insulting or overly familiar. However, the Japanese are usually patient with foreigners who make such gaffes.

111

The most intimidating aspect of Japanese is the writing system. Japanese is written with two syllabaries—which are similar to alphabets— and about 2,000 Chinese characters known as *kanji*. However, Japanese instructional texts often make use of *rōmaji*—Japanese transliterated into the Latin alphabet. Therefore, you can learn grammar, vocabulary, etc., while you are still getting up to speed in the written language.

FRENCH

Next to English, French is the most popular second language in the world. Until the mid-20th Century, French was the international language of diplomacy. The language has since ceded this distinction to English, but French continues to be used along with English on international documents such as passports and visas. In educated circles, French has retained its status as a language of high culture.

French is a major European language. It is spoken by the 60 million residents of France, by about 5 million Belgians, and around 2 million Swiss. French is also the official language of a number of African countries that were once under French or Belgian rule. In Canada, French is the primary language in the province of Quebec, and it shares official language status with English nationwide. French is also understood in Haiti, Martinique, French Guyana, and Guadeloupe.

If you learned French and you live in the United States, don't focus solely on job opportunities that involve Europe. There are millions of French speakers just across our northern border. Any company that has a significant customer base in Canada could potentially use a salesperson who can speak French.

The presence of two major European languages in Canada (English and French) is the result of the global ambitions of two former colonial powers. In the 1700s, Canada was a common flashpoint for the Anglo-French contest over North America. In fact, from 1754 through 1763, the British and the French fought an 18th century version of the world war, fighting each other across the Caribbean, the Americas, and Europe. Canada was only one of the prizes up for grabs—but it was an important one, given its close proximity to the British colonies along the Atlantic seaboard.

The British ultimately gained control of North America, but a large population of French-speakers remained in Canada. Although the profile of

Queen Elizabeth appears on Canadian currency, Canada is today officially bilingual; public services are offered throughout the country in both English and French.

The influence of the French language on daily life is strongest in the former French stronghold of Quebec. Most Quebecois have at least passable skills in English, but French is by far the preferred method of communication. As a result, a French-speaking sales representative can open doors in Quebec that will remain shut for a monolingual English speaker.

Although French is a Western European language that shares common roots with English, it is the most difficult of the Romance languages. Vocabulary acquisition is relatively easy, as there are many shared cognates between French and English: *riche, signer, entrer,* etc. However, French phonetics present an initial challenge for English speakers. If you decide to learn French, you will have to spend a lot of time listening to tapes to hone your pronunciation.

Since French is a very popular language, there is no shortage of French study materials. Nor will you have trouble finding French newspapers, websites, or magazines.

CHINESE

This is the language spoken by about 1.3 billion people in China, about 23 million in Taiwan, and an unknown number of Chinese living abroad. The Chinese diaspora has carried the language to practically every corner of the globe. Wherever there is a major population center, there is almost certainly someone who speaks Chinese. I have used the Chinese that I know in such unlikely places as Hopkinsville, Kentucky and Mexico City, Mexico.

You may have heard that Chinese is impossibly difficult because there are scores of dialects, or local versions of the language. Although there are many dialects of Chinese, the Mandarin dialect has become nearly universal in the Chinese-speaking world. This is the version of Chinese that is used in schools throughout China and Taiwan, and it is also the version of Chinese that is taught to foreigners. If you buy a cassette course for learning the "Chinese" language, you have actually bought a cassette course for learning the Mandarin dialect.

The only real competition for Mandarin comes from Cantonese, which is spoken in an area of southern China, including Hong Kong.

However, even the Hong Kong Chinese are now learning Mandarin, since the island reverted to Chinese control in 1997. Some speakers of the Cantonese dialect might be inclined to disagree with this statement—but the future of the Chinese language belongs to Mandarin, hands down.

Chinese is quite difficult, but there is an increasing number of books and instructional programs on the market to help you rise to the challenge. You can get started with some of the mass market programs available on Amazon and Barnes & Noble.com. Once you've mastered the basics, then visit specialty stores like Cheng & Tsui and Chinabooks for some more advanced materials. (See Chapter 19.)

A mere generation ago, the Chinese language would have been of interest only to academics and foreign policy strategists. Today, however, Chinese is increasingly important for businesspersons. China currently has the fastest growing economy, ranked at number two or three in the world by some measurements.

China is still nominally Communist, but the nation has shed most of the purely Marxist ideology that ruled in the 1950s, when Mao Zedong was forcing people into communes and agricultural collectives. In the early 1980s, Deng Xiao Ping, an economic reformer, came to power and instituted a wide range of market reforms. These began as "special economic zones"— areas in which capitalism was permitted on a provisional basis. These experiments with the free market gradually expanded. In fact, China now even has its own stock market—what would Mao Zedong say?

As capitalism has become increasingly entrenched throughout the country, China's politicians have begun to abandon the "class struggle" rhetoric that prevailed through the mid-1970s. In November, 2002, China's leaders met in Beijing for the 16th Communist Party Congress. The following principles, known as "The Three Represents" were written into the party's constitution:

1. *Represent the most advanced productive forces, including private business.*
2. *Represent the most advanced culture.*
3. *Represent the fundamental interests of the broad masses (i.e. not merely a "revolutionary party" but one that stands for all Chinese.)*
   Source: CNN.com November 15th, 2002

In March, 2003, the Chinese legislature passed another round of sweeping changes designed to bring the country closer in line with global free market ideals. New mechanisms were implemented to bolster bank profitability, consumer safety, and more liberalized foreign trade. The legislature also decided to reform China's strict population control program, which has been the object of much international criticism.

Of course, not all of the news about the Middle Kingdom is good. China still has a number of obstacles to confront before it fully joins the community of free, prosperous nations. There is a vast disparity between the standards of living found in China's booming coastal cities, and the largely agrarian interior regions. Moreover, while China has embraced a variant of free-market capitalism, the Beijing government still maintains a monopoly on the political front. (In other words, *capitalism* is one thing, *democracy* is another.) Basic freedoms of speech, assembly, and the press are often subject to severe curtailments in China that would be unacceptable in the United States, Europe, or Japan. The transition to a true representative democracy will probably take at least another decade.

Mainland Mandarin vs. Taiwanese Mandarin

One remnant of the Communist revolution of 1949 is that there are effectively two Chinas: the *People's Republic of China* (Mainland China) and Taiwan, or the *Republic of China*. When Mao Zedong's army took over the mainland in 1949, the remnants of the Nationalist forces fled to the small island of Taiwan and set up a national government.

Today, Taiwan is a modern, free-market economy, but the nation clearly exists in the shadow of its behemoth Communist rival. There has been sporadic saber-rattling between the two Chinas since the 1950s. China claims Taiwan as a "renegade province" of itself, while Taiwan asserts its right to nationhood.

However, the two Chinas are pursuing economic integration even as they continue to squabble over political issues. As of September, 2002, Taiwanese investments in the People's Republic surpassed the $100 billion mark. During the first half of 2002, Taiwanese investments in China grew by 47%. (Taipei Times, 2002) In early 2003, the Chinese government called for a massive easing of restrictions in commercial flights between Taiwan and the Mainland.

115

Mandarin is the dialect of Chinese used officially in both the People's Republic of China and Taiwan. However, the writing system varies slightly between the two countries. The Communist government in Beijing has simplified the complex Chinese writing system in an effort to make it more accessible for Chinese nationals and foreign students alike. The simplified system of writing Chinese characters that is used in China is called *jiantizi* ("simplified characters"). The system used in Taiwan is called *fantizi* ("traditional characters"). The two writing systems do have significant differences, but most educated readers can switch between the *jiantizi* and *fantizi* with minimal difficulty.

In both countries, there has historically been a bias against using the character system of the other. The Mainland Chinese once viewed the *fantizi* as a vestige of the "old" China, whereas the Taiwanese viewed the *jiantizi* as a corruption of the traditional beauty of the Chinese language. However, this seems to be becoming less of an issue as economic ties between the Mainland and Taiwan increase. Most Chinese textbooks written for non-Chinese defer to the *jiantizi*, given their relative simplicity, and the fact that the People's Republic is so much larger than Taiwan.

The differences in the spoken languages of the two Chinas are more subtle, and might be likened to the differences between the English spoken in London and the English spoken in Alabama. In China, the Mandarin dialect is referred to as *putonghua* ("common speech"), while the Taiwanese use the term *gouyu* ("national language"). In Taiwan, you refer to a tomato as *fanqie*, while in most of China, you would use the word *xihongshi*. There are China- and Taiwan-specific terms for most words which refer to technology that has been developed since 1949. For example, the Chinese and Taiwanese use different words to indicate answering machines, computers, and electronic pagers.

The radically different political histories of Taiwan and the People's Republic have also left their mark on the language. In China, it is common to speak of the establishment of the Communist government in 1949 as "liberation," or *jiefang*. People often use this historic event to mark time, just as Americans use the term "postwar" to designate World War II as a chronological marker. Newspapers in China speak of events occurring "before liberation", or "after liberation." These terms have come into such wide usage in China that they have lost much of their political significance. But be careful not to use this term if you travel to Taiwan. Needless to say, a reference to the 1949 Communist victory as "liberation" will not earn you any points with your business partners in Taipei.

In the immediate post-revolutionary period, the mainland Chinese largely discarded traditional forms of address like "Miss" (*xiaojie*) and Mr. (*xiansheng*) in favor of the universal and egalitarian form of address, *tongzhi*, which means "comrade." As a foreigner, you will not be expected to use or answer to *tongzhi*, and the Chinese use this word less and less among themselves. It is once again acceptable to use traditional forms of address in China, so do not hesitate to refer to your counterparts as "Mr. Wang," "Miss Li," etc.

Grappling with the Tones of Chinese

Next to the writing system, the tonal system of Chinese is probably the greatest challenge for students of the language. Every Chinese syllable is pronounced with one of four distinctive tonal pitches, or a flat "neutral" tone. For example, the syllable pronounced "*shu*" can alternatively mean "book," "tree," or "cottage" depending on the tone.

The only way to learn the tones is through repeated listening. They are difficult to master, and there are foreign speakers of Chinese who have been using the language for years and still haven't completely mastered the tonal system. This brings us to another important point: although you should strive for mastery of the tones, a few mistakes in this area won't hinder your daily communications. Chinese listeners can understand your meaning through the overall context of what you say. In practice, you will usually be understood even if your tones are largely incorrect.

GERMAN

Along with French and Spanish, German is one of the "big three" foreign languages that are taught in American schools. Therefore, some readers may already have been exposed to the language in high school or college.

Germany is the economic powerhouse of continental Europe; and the language is also spoken in Austria and Switzerland. Smaller pockets of German speakers can be found in northern Italy, eastern France, Argentina, eastern Belgium, Luxembourg, and the principality of Liechtenstein.

117

There is a strong demand for German language skills in banking, finance, and throughout the industrial sectors. German companies have been actively locating branch offices in the United States for years. Based on the job data available on Monster.com, many of them value German language skills on a résumé.

I would classify the German language as lying within the intermediate range of difficulty. German grammar is perhaps the most difficult among the Western European languages. There are many details that take a long time to fully master.

German and English have common roots. There are aspects of modern German grammar which are strikingly similar to Old English. For example, the verb forms "thou hast," "thou comest," "he hath," and "he cometh" are not used in modern English. But German speakers continue to use these equivalents: *du hast*, *du kommst*, *er hat*, and *er kommt*, etc.

The shared lineage of German and English means that there are numerous cognates. Words such as *Winter*, *lernen*, *Garten*, and *Onkel* will be familiar to English speakers from the beginning.

PORTUGUESE

As the language of the South American nation of Brazil, Portuguese is the logical choice after Spanish for the aspiring Latin American area specialist. Although there is of course no rule which says that you must study Spanish before you study Portuguese, this seems to be the universal practice.

The similarities of Spanish and Portuguese originate from the geographic proximity of Spain and Portugal. If you dive into Portuguese after you have first achieved competency in Spanish, you will already be acquainted with vast amounts of Portuguese vocabulary. Many Portuguese words are identical to Spanish words, and many others are only slightly different. A person who knows Spanish well can comprehend the headlines of a Portuguese newspaper, and perhaps even the gist of each article.

But Spanish is by no means a free pass to fluency in Portuguese. Portuguese pronunciation and grammar are somewhat more difficult. Whereas the Spanish accent comes easily to the average English-speaking learner, the nasalized sounds of Portuguese require some more practice. The complexities of Portuguese grammar, while not insurmountable, will make the rules of Spanish seem generously lenient.

Portugal itself is a small country, with a population of around 10 million. (To put this in perspective, the population of Germany is 83 million.) Economically, Portugal has yet to realize the same level of prosperity enjoyed by many of its neighbors. The country's GDP per capita is about 25% below the Western European average. As a low-cost producer, Portugal has recently faced stiff competition from the new capitalist economies of Eastern and Central Europe. Portugal is also plagued by an ailing educational system and a high national deficit. As a result of these factors, Portugal is not currently a major player on the global economic stage.

Nonetheless, Portuguese is truly a global language, on par with heavyweights like French. (In fact, native speakers of Portuguese actually outnumber native speakers of French.) Portuguese is spoken across a number of continents, and in a diverse array of countries. This is all the result of Portugal's seafaring past. Like England, France, and Spain, Portugal was once a major colonial power. In the 1500s and 1600s, Portuguese sailors, soldiers, and settlers carried their language throughout the world.

Today, Brazil is the largest Portuguese-speaking country, with a population of more than 186 million. It is also the largest country in South America: in population, GDP, and land mass. People who are not acquainted with South America often assume that Brazilians, like most of their neighbors, speak Spanish. Many Brazilians can understand Spanish, but relatively few are truly comfortable holding a conversation in Spanish.

Brazilians speak Portuguese rather than Spanish because of an agreement made between Portugal and Spain in 1493. The two European countries decided to divide the New World along an imaginary north-south line just west of the Cape Verde Islands. Under the agreement, Spain laid claim to the lands located west of the line, and Portugal acquired rights to the lands located to the east. Brazil occupies the portion of South America which lies to the east of that demarcation line. Therefore, Brazil is today a Portuguese-speaking country in the middle of a Spanish-speaking region.

The Brazilian economy has well developed agricultural, industrial and service sectors. Over the past decade, Brazil's fortunes have fluctuated with broader global trends. After a boom in the mid-1990s, the country was hit by the Asian and Russian financial crises of 1997 and 1998. Moderate growth resumed in 1999, only to be slowed again by the global recession of 2001. Growth has resumed in recent years as the global economy has improved.

Brazil's own economy is consistently ranked as one of the ten largest in the world. For the past ten years or so, American, European, and Japanese companies have been moving into Brazil in large numbers. The nation has the potential to become a major economic force in the future. Of equal long-term significance is the fact that many world leaders are now beginning to view Brazil as an ascending political power.

Although Brazil is the prime destination for students of Portuguese, the language is also spoken in a handful of African nations: Mozambique, Angola, Guine-Bissau, Cape Verde, and São Tomé e Principe. In Asia, you will find Portuguese speakers in the Chinese territory of Macau (next to Hong Kong), and in the newly independent Indonesian state of East Timor. Portuguese is also widely spoken in the Indian territory of Goa. There are additional pockets of Portuguese speakers in North America: in sections of New England, and in the Canadian province of Ontario.

KOREAN

This is the language of North and South Korea, as well as substantial overseas Korean communities in the United States and Japan. Korean is the third most commonly studied of the East Asian languages, after Chinese and Japanese.

The Korean alphabet, known as *Hangul*, is one of the most significant linguistic achievements in history. An initial version of Hangul, known as *Hunmin chong-um*, or, "correct sounds for common instruction" was invented the Korean King Sejong in 1446. At that time, there was no native Korean alphabet. The learned classes used Chinese characters for written communications, but these were beyond the grasp of commoners.

King Sejong wanted to create a writing system which was both uniquely Korean as well as easily accessible for common citizens. The king recognized that Chinese characters, being foreign, were an imperfect vehicle for the Korean language. Hangul, on the other hand, was created with Korean phonetics and grammar in mind. Although modern Korean makes limited use of Chinese characters, today most written Korean texts consist entirely of an evolved version of King Sejong's Hangul.

The Korean alphabet is logical and relatively consistent. It is much easier to learn to read and write Korean than Chinese or Japanese. Chinese and Japanese each employ thousands of complex characters. By contrast, a dedicated student can absorb the Hangul alphabet over a few weeks.

The above is not meant to imply that Korean is an easy language. In fact, Korean is one of the hardest languages for English speakers to learn. It shares many grammatical characteristics with Japanese—another language noted for its difficult grammar. Korean verbs are placed at the ends of sentences. There are dual counting systems, and multiple levels of politeness. There are no tones in Korean, but most English speakers struggle before achieving a correct pronunciation. Moreover, we get few breaks on vocabulary; Korean shares no common roots with English.

Korean is a worthwhile challenge. South Korea is surging forward in a number of industries, including automobiles and machine tools. The nation is a major trading partner of the United States, Britain and Canada. Like Japanese firms in the 1980s and 1990s, Korean companies are now building plants and locating offices in the United States and elsewhere.

While North Korea is currently an insular Stalinist state, it will become a new market when the communist regime inevitably falls or reforms. Until that time, the North Korean threat makes Korean one of the languages most in demand in the national defense and intelligence sectors.

Just as Portuguese is overshadowed among the Romance languages by Spanish, French and Italian, Korean is typically neglected for other major languages in the East Asian sphere. Most language students with an interest in Asia veer toward Chinese or Japanese. Korean is therefore a good choice for the learner who wishes to acquire a scarce yet marketable skill.

If you decide to study Korean, you should visit the Hollym (www.hollym.com) and the Cheng & Tsui (www.cheng-tsui.com) websites. Hollym specializes in Korean materials, and Cheng & Tsui includes many Korean language products among their Far Eastern languages selection.

RUSSIAN

The language of the former Soviet Union received a great deal of attention during the Gorbachev era. With the prospect of Russia being open for business, students filled Russian-language classes across the United States and Western Europe.

The reality of economic reforms in Russia has been more sobering. Since the dissolution of the Soviet Union, Russia has been battered by mafia turf wars, attempted coups, rampant drug abuse, and a declining population. In 1998, there was a run on the Russian ruble, creating even more chaos.

121

But Russia has been down in the past, only to bounce back in later years. In this century alone, Russia has survived catastrophic war casualties, dictatorship, and famine. And in the most recent few years, the news from Russia has brightened considerably. The banking system has recently recovered from the 1998 Ruble crisis. There have also been more broad-based economic improvements. In 2004, the major sectors of the economy posted a 4.1% improvement against the previous year. Russia has abundant natural resources, and a well-educated population that is struggling to ascend the learning curve of free enterprise.

Russian is not an easy language, but it is not nearly as difficult as Chinese, Arabic, or Korean. Although the Cyrillic alphabet looks intimidating at first, it is among the easiest of the non-Latin scripts. Russian grammar, however, is quite difficult.

NON-RUSSIAN CENTRAL AND EASTERN EUROPEAN LANGUAGES

Prior to the 1990s, countries like Poland and Bulgaria were the enemy. This is not the case anymore. I recently spoke with a colleague who is a buyer at a major automotive manufacturer in Great Britain. When I asked him, "Where are most of your suppliers located?" his answer—"Poland"—was a surprise. However, it is no longer unusual for a product to be manufactured in Poland, Romania, or the Czech Republic. The countries of the old Warsaw Pact are seeking greater integration with Western Europe (such as membership in the European Union), and they are aggressively pursuing capitalism.

The Central and Eastern European region is extremely diverse linguistically. The Slavic languages share significant amounts of vocabulary and grammar with Russian. About half of the Slavic languages—Polish, Czech, etc.—use the Latin alphabet, while the other half, which includes Bulgarian and Serbian, use the Cyrillic alphabet.

The Romanian language is thought to be descended from the Latin spoken by Romans who colonized the area near modern Transylvania in 106 A.D. The Roman colony, known as Dacia, dispersed around 275 A.D. due to repeated barbarian incursions. The Latin-speaking population dwindled to small settlements deep in the Carpathians. The legacy of the Dacian Romans is a close resemblance between Latin and modern Romanian. In addition to elements of Latin, the Romanian spoken today also reveals strong Slavic and Greek influences.

Hungarian is often described as a "linguistic island." Hungarian is a difficult language, with numerous verb and noun inflections. It is not similar to any of the Western European languages, nor is it similar to Russian. The only modern relatives of Hungarian are Finnish and Estonian, two languages with which you are unlikely to be familiar.

In the last ten years, there has been a marked increase in the number of Central and Eastern European language materials on the market. If you learn one of these languages, Audio Forum and Spoken Language Services should be your first stop. (See the Language Student's Buying Guide later in Chapter 19.)

VIETNAMESE

There aren't many Americans learning Vietnamese today, but that might change in the near future. For decades, the Vietnamese language, like everything else related to Vietnam, had only one association: the Vietnam War. Things changed in the 1990s, when President Clinton authorized the restoration of U.S.-Vietnamese diplomatic relations. It is now much easier for Americans to travel to Vietnam for business as well as pleasure. Moreover, in 1986 the Vietnamese government began the process of *doi moi*, or "reform and renovation". Incentive programs and private enterprise were gradually introduced. In 2000 a stock market was founded in Ho Chi Minh City

Vietnam is still a communist nation, and the country has a long way to go before it is a serious economic player. But there are reasons to be hopeful for the future. The Vietnamese people are known for their industriousness and thrift, and the literacy rate in the country is near 100%. Prior to the start of the Vietnam War, Vietnam had the strongest economy in Asia outside of Japan.

Vietnamese is a good language to learn if you want to corner a niche in the East Asian arena. In Western countries like the United States and Canada, Vietnamese speakers are limited to the refugees who fled Vietnam in the late 1970s and early 1980s. In fact, there are only a handful of non-Vietnamese who speak the language well.

Vietnamese might be a particularly strong choice for the East Asian specialist who has already mastered Chinese or Japanese.

INDONESIAN

Indonesian, or Bahasa Indonesia ("Indonesian language"), is the official language of the Republic of Indonesia. Bahasa Indonesia is the mother tongue of about 25 million people, but most of Indonesia's population of 200 million can speak and understand the language.

Indonesian has the reputation of being easy to learn in comparison to other major East Asian languages. Indonesian uses the Latin alphabet, and the grammar is simple and consistent. Among the Asian languages, Indonesian seems like a walk in the park if you have ever studied Chinese, Japanese, Korean, or Thai.

The approachability of Indonesian makes it an addicting language to study, and the huge population of Indonesia qualifies Bahasa Indonesia as a major world language. There are, however, a few caveats to consider. First of all, learning materials for Indonesian are not especially numerous. Many of the major language materials publishers do not even sell materials for learning Indonesian. In addition, native speakers and books written for them are difficult to find—at least in the United States. Although I am sure that one would have better luck in Los Angeles or Chicago, I have met exactly two native Indonesian speakers in Cincinnati—although I have met dozens of native speakers of Chinese, Spanish, Korean, and even Thai.

Moreover, Indonesia has recently undergone turmoil that threatens the country's economic development in the near future. Sectarian violence, terrorism against Western tourists, and governmental infighting all weaken the odds that Indonesia will emerge as a major economic power anytime soon. However, Indonesia's large population and past runs of strong economic performance make the language worthy of your long-term consideration.

ITALIAN

The aesthetically pleasing sounds of the Italian language have led many observers to describe the language as one of Italy's greatest national resources. Indeed, spoken Italian does have a melodic quality that few languages can rival. Italy itself is a country that enchants the senses. In fact, there is so much beauty to observe in Italy, that you may not get a chance to notice the language. Italy is the land of ancient Roman ruins, Venetian canals, and rugged Mediterranean landscapes.

Italy is also one of the middleweight economies of Europe. Italy's main industrial sectors include clothing, footwear, machine tools, and precision instruments. Italy is also the home of the automakers Fiat, Alpha Romeo and Ferrari.

Italian is a Romance language, and is acquired with minimal difficulty if you have previously learned Spanish or Portuguese. Once you learn Italian, you will find that the language is useful not only in Italy, but also in sections of Switzerland, and in limited areas within Argentina and Brazil.

ARABIC

Arabic a difficult, fascinating, and *potentially* useful language. There are about 245 million Arabic speakers in the world, most of who live in the Middle East. If the number of speakers alone were the primary criterion, Arabic would be an advantageous choice for the language student.

The problem, of course, is that political turmoil in the region, such as the Arab/Israeli conflict, the war in Iraq, terrorism, etc., have made the area far too unstable for companies to come in and start building factories. Add to this the fact that by severely restricting the rights of women, most Arabic-speaking countries have effectively disabled half of the participants in their economies. In the current climate, it is difficult to conceive of many career opportunities utilizing Arabic, outside of a few specialized areas such as petroleum and national security.

I recently read that Arab countries purchase less than 2% of U.S. export goods. When I searched the Internet for job postings related to the Arabic language, there was almost nothing outside of the CIA, FBI, etc.

But perhaps it is unnecessarily pessimistic to assume that the problems in the Middle East are permanent. I occasionally reflect on the irony that while my grandfather faced Imperial Japan in battle, I have benefited greatly from the peaceful ambitions of Japan, Inc. Today's foes can often become tomorrow's trading partners. Once the political problems in the Middle East are solved, there is no reason to believe that the region should not develop economically. Perhaps Americans will one day even purchase cars that are manufactured in a free, capitalist Iraq. (If this seems ludicrous, consider, from the perspective of 1942, the idea of Americans buying Japanese cars.)

Although Arabic is not currently one of the most useful languages for businesspeople, there is a long tradition of Arabic language studies at major U.S. and British universities. There are many materials on the market that can help you to learn this language.

STILL CAN'T MAKE UP YOUR MIND?

If you are completely undecided about which language you want to study, I would recommend that you select one of the following: Spanish, Japanese, German, French, or Chinese. My recommendations are based on two facts:

1. Each of these languages is spoken in one or more of the world's major economies. These languages will always have a place in the business world.
2. For each of these languages, there is a large body of published learning materials. Therefore, you can learn any one of these languages through independent study.

CHAPTER 10 APPENDIX: ARTIFICIAL LANGUAGES— AN ATTEMPT TO CREATE A LEVEL PLAYING FIELD

All the world's languages developed gradually over time, and often in ways which make them difficult for adult learners to grasp. With few exceptions, every language on earth has certain aspects which are intrinsically difficult—the tonal system of Chinese, the irregular verb and adjective forms of English, the case endings of Russian. As a result, when a particular language is used for communications purposes, the native speakers of the language have an obvious advantage. It is always the other, nonnative side which must do the heavy lifting.

In 1887, Dr. Lazarus Ludwig Zamenhof created a language which was supposed to put everyone on an equal linguistic footing. His invention—the language known as Esperanto—was designed to be easy to learn. Esperanto featured simple, consistent grammar, uncomplicated phonetics, and a small number of basic vocabulary elements that could be easily combined to create more complex terminology.

Esperanto failed to take off. Today, it is estimated that only about two or three million people actually speak Esperanto. Other artificial languages, such as Universalsprache and Kosmos, have also failed to attain a wide following. Lingua francas seem to be chosen by random, accidental market forces rather than by deliberate planning or design.

Despite this track record, there is no shortage of new artificial languages on the scene. One of the newest ones is Mondlango. Mondlango was created in China in 2002. Based on Esperanto, Mondlango is a phonetically accessible language with consistent grammar. Advocates of Mondlango claim that it can be learned in a tenth of the time required to learn any naturally evolved language.

CHAPTER 11

THE FIRST STEPS IN LEARNING A FOREIGN LANGUAGE

LANGUAGE LEARNING IS A PROCESS

In an academic setting, languages are typically grouped with the humanities. Most of these subjects—history, literature, sociology, etc.—involve the learning of broad concepts, or the memorization of facts.

From the learner's perspective, foreign language study actually has more in common with mathematics or computer programming. A language is a skill. While an accomplished historian certainly possesses a great deal of knowledge and insight that can be applied to various situations, history itself is not a skill.

As with any skill, your abilities in a foreign language can be measured by your capacity to solve problems. At first, the level of problems that you can solve will be extremely limited: You will be able to greet someone correctly at different times of the day ("good morning", "good afternoon", etc.), and you will be able to give and solicit basic personal information such as your name, age, and nationality.

After more study, you will be able to solve slightly more difficult problems. Whereas before you were relying entirely on memorized scripts, you will now be formulating your own questions and statements. You will understand simple questions and responses from native speakers. The range of topics that you can effectively handle at this point will still be restricted. For the most part, your conversations will be limited to basic factual information: what you ate for breakfast, does the other person like living in New York, whether or not food is expensive in Italy, and so on. At this stage, however, a discussion about a complex philosophical or technical issue will be beyond your grasp.

If you persevere, you will notice that the difficult problems gradually become less intimidating. One day, you will discover that you can actually explain your company's products in the other language. Someone will insist on drawing you into a political discussion, and you will be able to reasonably present and defend your opinions regarding America's latest foreign policy decisions. There will still be a lot of gaps in your abilities to express yourself, but you will begin to get the feeling that you "speak" the language.

With more study, you will refine your skills, and develop the ability to discuss practically any topic in the foreign language. Speaking in the foreign language will be somewhat more comfortable to you. Conscious effort will no longer be required each time you participate in a conversation. Although you will realize that you lack the accent and cultural perspectives of a native speaker, you will be confident dealing with native speakers in their own mode of communication.

It is important to understand from the outset that the learning of a foreign language is a process, with many small milestones along the way. One of the milestones in my Spanish language studies fell into my lap many years ago in the Mexico City airport. A man sitting next to me struck up a conversation in Spanish, and identified himself as a resident of Cuba. I wanted to confine our conversation to politically neutral topics, but he seemed intent on engaging the first American he had ever met in a political discussion. We had a long debate about the pros and cons of capitalism and communism, and the American opposition to Castro. We never did come to an agreement, but we exchanged contact information, and agreed to continue the discussion in the event that one of us ever had the opportunity to visit the other's country.

CLASSES VERSUS INDEPENDENT STUDY

We will assume that you are going to learn and utilize your foreign language in a non-academic setting. However, if you do have access to formal language instruction—then by all means take advantage of the opportunity. Traditional classroom instruction does not conflict with the self-instructional methods described below.

Universities are the most popular destination for language students who want to pursue the traditional learning route. Over the past ten years or so, the demographic profile of the "typical" university student has dramatically changed. Undergraduates (and even graduate students) were once comprised almost exclusively of the under-twenty-five, daytime student crowd. Non-traditional adult learners now make up the fastest growing segment of the university population. Universities are responding to this trend by offering more and more classes in the evenings—when working adults can attend.

Many employers offer tuition reimbursement to their employees. The content of these courses is usually subject to company approval. Therefore, if you want your employer to pay for your evening Spanish class, then you will have to build a case explaining why Spanish is relevant to your current position. (If your employer already has customers or facilities in a Spanish-speaking country, then you should be able to build a case.)

To find out whether or not the university in your area offers evening classes in the language of your choice, check their website—practically all universities now offer searchable online class schedules.

LEARNING A LANGUAGE ON YOUR OWN

If formal classes at a university or other institution don't happen to fit your lifestyle and budget, don't despair. If you can't go to classes, then you can bring the language instruction to you. On a modest budget, you can equip yourself with books, audio materials, and even multimedia computer programs designed for self-studying language students. An assortment of these items (plus supplemental exposure to the foreign language) is all you need to learn any language.

If you have never studied a foreign language independently, then you probably aren't aware of the specific books and audio courses that are on the market, and their relative strengths and weaknesses. To address this concern, I have included in this book a section entitled, "The Language Student's Buying Guide." This chapter is a roadmap for first-time shoppers.

As a prelude, though, it is worth mentioning a few of the broad categories of the materials that you will be using:

- *Full-length audio courses:* These are packaged programs that contain a course book, and a compliment of audio cassettes or CDs.
- *Supplemental audio programs:* These often consist of only an audio component. They focus on a particular aspect of language-learning, such as vocabulary, or verb conjugation.
- Textbooks, dictionaries, and flashcards

When you choose the self-study route, you don't have to designate fixed blocks of time (such as every Tuesday and Thursday night from 6:00 to 8:30) to learn a language. You will, of course, have to maintain your own study regimen, but you can blend language study into the normal routine of your life.

BEGIN WITH A REVIEW OF ENGLISH GRAMMAR

You have probably not formally studied English grammar since grade school or high school. Even if you are an articulate speaker and writer of English, you may not know off the top of your head what the pluperfect tense is, or the difference between a gerund and an infinitive. Once we become functional in our own language, these distinctions tend to fade quickly from the mind. It is safe to say that the average corporate CEO would not be able to produce an impromptu diagram of a sentence if his or her life depended on it.

While the terminology of grammar may have a negligible impact on the average adult professional life, there is a lot to be gained by reviewing fundamental grammatical concepts before you begin the study of a foreign language. This will enable you to more quickly identify the differences and similarities between English and a foreign language.

English grammar books are easy to obtain. You can buy one at any bookstore. Don't fret too much over the selection of this book; your only objective is a basic review. If you are the parent of an adolescent, then you may even be able to borrow your child's grammar text.

STRANGER IN A STRANGE LAND: LEARNING TO EAT WITH CHOPSTICKS

Despite all my years as a student of the languages and cultures of East Asia, I have never really mastered the art of eating with chopsticks. Although I have some degree of functionality with these implements, I usually throw in the towel and ask if a knife and fork are available. When I visit a traditional Asian restaurant at home or abroad, I cannot avoid the involuntary Euro-centric notion that Western eating utensils are more efficient than chopsticks. How can anyone eat with slivers of balsa wood?

131

Delving into a foreign language is kind of like being forced to eat with new utensils. You will observe that your new language accomplishes everything that English does, but it often employs different means—just as people in most Asian countries eat with chopsticks rather than knives and forks.

In Russian, if you are going to say, "I am an American," you would say, "*Ya Amerikanyitz.*" *Ya* means "I" and "*Amerikanyitz*" means "American." The verb "to be" is assumed, even though it is not specifically indicated by the speaker. In addition, you would only say *Amerikanyitz* if you are a man. A woman would use the feminine form, *Amerikanka*, to identify herself as an American.

How can Russians make sense of sentences that are missing verbs? Why do they need a masculine form and a feminine form of the word "American?" Can't they just use a single word, like we do?

This is a reaction that you will have any number of times as you dive into foreign languages. Western European languages have more in common with English than Asian, Middle Eastern, or Slavic languages; but every foreign language uses at least some unfamiliar means to accomplish familiar ends. Your target language will seem to be full of unpardonable omissions on one hand, and mountains of useless baggage on the other.

These preferences are merely the result of our lifelong familiarity with English. English, too, has a number of attributes which bedevil foreign students. Consider irregular spellings, such as *through*, *weigh*, and *vogue*— just to name a few.

I don't know what language you will be studying, but the following grammatical elements commonly vary across languages. As soon as you dive in, begin sorting out where your target language (the language that you want to learn) stands on these items:

GENDER

The concept of a "masculine noun" and a "feminine noun" is limited in English. Expressions of a noun's gender are primarily confined to words such as "actor" (masculine) or "actress" (feminine). Moreover, gender-specific nouns are an endangered species in English—especially American English. The trend over recent years has been to replace gender-specific words with a neutral equivalent. Rather than saying "salesman" or "saleswoman", the all-inclusive "salesperson" is now preferred. Instead of

132

saying "policeman" or "policewoman", it is recent custom to refer to both as simply "the police." (In fact, I have even heard that the word "actress" has fallen out of favor. Both men and women in the acting profession are now described as "actors.")

The concept of "feminine" and "masculine" words is pervasive throughout many languages, including French, Spanish, Arabic, Hebrew, and Italian. In the countries where these languages are spoken, this linguistic gender distinction is not a source of controversy, perhaps because the reference to "gender" does not have an automatic social implication.

For example, the Spanish word *máquina* ("machine") is feminine. The fact that *máquina* is grammatically feminine does not imply any associations between machines and women. Similarly, the fact that the Spanish word *horno* ("oven") is masculine does not suggest that men should stay home and bake bread while the womenfolk go to work as machinists. This distinction simply governs the way in which *horno* and *máquina* affect other parts of speech.

"Red machine" is *máquina roja*. However, "red oven" is *horno rojo*. Because *máquina* is feminine, the word for "red" becomes *roja*, the feminine version of the adjective. *Horno*, however, is masculine, so it takes the masculine *rojo*.

WORD ORDER

In the above section about gender, you may have noticed something strange about Spanish word order. If *máquina* means "machine," and *roja* means "red," then the phrase *máquina roja* literally means "machine red," not "red machine." Why place the adjective *after* the noun? That's not how we do it in English. We say "blue sky," "tall man," and "flexible material." The adjective *always* comes before the noun.

However, if you're speaking Spanish, the adjective always comes *after* the noun (with a few exceptions). Spanish speakers don't see anything strange about this. Neither do speakers of French, Portuguese, or Italian, who also place their adjectives after their nouns.

The rules governing word order are by no means uniform across languages. Perhaps the best examples of convoluted word order (from an English speaker's perspective) are Japanese and Korean, which place the verb at the end of a sentence.

ARTICLES

In English, these are the words "the," "an," and "a." Most Asian languages completely ignore these. There is no exact equivalent of "the" in Chinese or Japanese. Other languages use definite articles only under limited circumstances.

In most European languages, the article changes according to gender. In Spanish, "the house" is *la casa*. *Casa* is a feminine noun, so it takes the definite article *la*. On the other hand, the word for "car," *coche*, is masculine. Masculine nouns in Spanish take the direct article *el*, so "the car" is *el coche*. As noted below, the articles in many European languages also change if the noun happens to be plural.

PLURALS

Whenever there is more than one of something, a plural is involved. In English, plurals are generally formed by adding an –s to a word. We have "cats," "dogs," and "automobiles." (Of course, we also have our share of irregular plurals.)

The Romance languages (Spanish, French, etc.) are relatively well behaved in regard to plurals. (In fact, the plural forms in most Romance languages are more consistent than those of English.) An –s is added, and a consistent change is made to the definite article. In Spanish, for example, *el libro* ("the book") becomes *los libros* ("the books").

However, German—another commonly studied European language—has a complex system of plural formation that requires quite a bit of memorization. When a German plural is formed, the direct article and the ending of the original word both change. "The year" is *das Jahr*. However, "the years" is *die Jahre*. "The boy" is *der Knabe*; "the boys" is *die Knaben*.

Arabic is perhaps the most maddening of all—the plural version of a noun may take a form which looks like a completely different word. For instance "a house" is *bayt*. However, "houses" is *bayut*. There are several distinguishable patterns for plural formation in Arabic—but Arabic plurals are challenging, nonetheless.

In Japanese, explicit plural forms are seldom used. In most situations, context tells you whether you are talking about one armadillo, or a whole pack of armadillos. If you need to specify the exact number of armadillos, then you use a special auxiliary word, called a counter, which indicates quantity. Just to keep you on your toes, Japanese has different counters for different types of objects. There are unique counters for books, animals, people, cupfuls, etc.

Indonesian plurals are perhaps the easiest and most logical. An explicit Indonesian plural is formed by simply doubling up the noun. For example, the Indonesian word for "child" is *anak*. The word for "children" is *anak-anak*.

Plurals are one of the first aspects of grammar that you will have to learn. The difficulty that you will face in this area will largely depend on the language which you decide to study.

Counters in Asian Languages:

Chinese and Japanese do not have universal plural forms like we have in English. However, the *counters* employed by these languages enable you to be specific if you need to emphasize a particular quantity.

Suppose, for example, that I want to say "three books" in Chinese. The basic word for book in Chinese is 书 *shū*. Rather than modifying the noun itself to specify the plural, a speaker of Chinese would use the number three 三 *sān*, and the common counter for books 本 *běn* before the unmodified form of 书 *shū*. Therefore, "three books in Chinese becomes 三本书 *sān běn shū*.

VERBS

Mastering these "action words" is typically the most challenging aspect of learning any language. In most languages, the conjugation, or inflection, of the verb varies according to its tense, as well as the gender and the singular/plural status of the subject.

We are all already used to working with verb conjugations in English. For most of us, English verb conjugations are so deeply ingrained that they have now become second nature. Without any conscious effort, we distinguish between "I believe," "I believed," and "I have believed."

In each language, there is a set pattern for conjugating verbs. The past tense of English verbs is generally formed by adding *–ed*. The past perfect tense is formed with "have" + the *–ed* form of the verb. Similarly, an *–s* is added to the third person present tense of most English verbs. *I live* in Cincinnati, but *he lives* in Chicago.

These rules are especially useful when you encounter a new verb for the first time. Even if you don't know the meaning of the verb "actuate", you will know its conjugations based on your experience with English verbs: "*I actuate,*" "*she actuates,*" "*we have actuated.*" (By the way, *actuate* means "to put into mechanical action or motion".)

Foreign languages also have uniform rules for conjugating verbs. Consider the Spanish word for "to talk," *hablar*. This verb is conjugated as follows in the present tense (the pronouns are omitted): I talk = *hablo*; you talk = *hablas*; he/she talks = *habla*; we talk = *hablamos*; they talk = *hablan*.

Similar verbs are conjugated in the same way. The verb *fumar* ("to smoke") ends in an -*ar*, just like *hablar*, and its present tense conjugations are: I smoke = *fumo*; you smoke = *fumas*; he/she smokes = *fuma*; we smoke = *fumamos*; they smoke = *fuman*. You can probably detect the pattern: for the first person singular, the –*ar* ending is dropped, and an –o is added; for the second person singular, the ending becomes –*as*, and so on.

This is not the whole story on first person Spanish verb conjugations (there are actually three basic conjugation patterns, which vary according to the last two letters of the verb), but you get the idea. Once you learn the pattern, you can easily apply it across most of the verbs in the language.

Why do I say "most of the verbs?" Well, practically every language contains malevolent creatures known as "irregular verbs." Irregular verbs do not follow standard conjugation rules. They follow a unique conjugation pattern, and therefore must be memorized one at time.

There are many irregular verbs in English. Consider the verb "eat": Rather than say "I eated," or "I have eated," we say "I ate," and "I have eaten." Rather than saying "I goed," and "I have goed," we say "I went," and "I have gone."

Although most of us don't think of ourselves as being oppressed by irregular English verbs, they are a major stumbling block for foreigners who attempt to learn our language. Likewise, when you study a foreign language, irregular verb conjugations will bedevil you to a greater or lesser degree, depending on the language you select.

What are the best ways to learn verb conjugations? Although verb conjugations are covered in every textbook and instructional course worth its salt, you should also avail yourself of some special "verb tools" that are on the market.

The *Barron's* "501" verb book series is perhaps the best known. These thick books dedicate a single page to the conjugation of each verb. Another tool is the audio verb conjugation series produced by *Living Language*. These tapes, like the Barron's books, can be readily procured at any major bookstore.

Although verbs are difficult, they are the key to proficiency in your target language. Once you climb the mountain of verb mastery, you are well on your way to basic competency in the language.

137

COGNATES

Cognates are closely related words that are similar across different languages. Some good examples would be the Spanish words *presidente*, *resistencia*, and *invasión*. Even if you have no prior knowledge of the Spanish language, you can easily determine that the English translations for these words are "president," "resistance," and "invasion."

Cognates provide an obvious means of assistance when you are learning a foreign language. Since the foreign word is so similar to the English one, it is easy to memorize. Cognates are especially plentiful across the Western European languages. In addition to the Spanish examples mentioned above, there are numerous cognates in French (*technologie*, *imaginer*, etc.) and in German (*Studenten*, *Kameras*, etc.), as well as in Portuguese, Italian, and Dutch.

Cognates are often the result of common linguistic origins. In Western Europe, the pervasive influence of Latin throughout the centuries left a wide trail of common vocabulary across the present-day languages of this area. Many of the words that are now used daily by speakers of English, French, Spanish, and Italian were originally Latin vocabulary. The words were modified in a slightly different manner in each region of Europe, but they remain close enough to the original Latin to be recognizable as descending from common roots.

However, some cognates are "false friends." A false cognate resembles a common English word, but conveys a different meaning in the foreign language. Consider, for example, the Spanish words *asistir*, *carpeta*, and *actual*. At first glance, you might say, "Hey, I know the meanings of these words." And indeed, it would be easy to mistranslate these words as "assist," "carpet," and "actual." But the English definitions of these words are "attend," "folder," and "current."

While many cognates derive from ancient linguistic roots, others are the products of more recent cross-pollination between languages. In English, we commonly use foreign loanwords such as *tsunami* (Japanese), *amok* (Indonesian), and *kowtow* (Chinese). Similarly, numerous elements of English vocabulary have been adopted into other languages over the past hundred years. The French word *le weekend* is a European example; but more distant languages, like Japanese, contain English loanwords such as *nyuusu* ("news"), *aisu kuriimu* ("ice cream"), and *jaa* ("jar").

Chinese Cognates in East Asian Languages

As you increase your knowledge of languages, you will become aware of cognate systems that exist within groups of foreign languages. For example, Chinese is the Latin of the Far East: many East Asian languages have derivative Chinese words. Below are just two examples.

Chinese word/root : 茶 *chá* (tea) / Derivative (Japanese): 茶 *cha* (tea)
Chinese word/root : 国 guó (nation) / Derivative (Vietnamese): quốc (nation)

LEVELS OF POLITENESS

The English pronoun "you" can be used without distinction across hierarchical and social levels. You address your best friend, your next door neighbor, and your boss as "you." Outside of archaic terms like "your Majesty," and "your Grace," English speakers more or less make due with one second person personal pronoun.

Not so in German, Spanish, Chinese or Portuguese. In fact, most languages seem to have specific pronouns that are only used in polite company, while others that are used with friends and family. Japanese takes this principle to an extreme. In Japanese, there are about half a dozen ways of saying "I" and "you," depending on the level of politeness that one wants to convey.

Verbs also express politeness or familiarity. The Romance languages and German each have two levels of politeness. Japanese has crude, familiar, polite, humble, and honorific (extremely polite) verb forms.

Textbooks and other teaching materials tend to favor the polite forms of any language. It is a good idea to stick with polite language until you become very confident of your abilities, and your degree of familiarity with your audience.

In his book, *Japanese in Action*, Jack Seward skillfully sums up the politeness issue. In Japanese, there are various suffixes which can be attached to a person's name. The suffix –*san* is the standard polite form. Another suffix, –*kun*, is a familiar form. Seward advises nonnative speakers of Japanese to "err on the side of politeness" in regard to these name suffixes,

139

on the grounds that, "no one will really thing less of you for using *san* when a native Japanese would have used *kun*." The same advice might be applied to any language with different polite and familiar forms.

Demonstrating Courtesy through Verb Conjugations:

You can express either easy familiarity or reserved politeness in Spanish simply by your choice of a verb. Both of the following sentences mean, "Do you want to go?" in Spanish. But the second one is more polite, because it employs a more formal conjugation of the verb *querer* ("to want"). Note the *–ieres* vs. the *–iere* ending

Informal: ¿Quieres ir?
Formal:　¿Quiere ir?

WORKING WITH NON-ROMAN SCRIPTS

The language that you probably studied in high school—Spanish, French, or German—gave you a break that you perhaps never fully appreciated. These languages all employ the Latin, or Roman, alphabet. The same is true of all Western European languages, including Italian, Portuguese, Dutch, Swedish, and Norwegian.

Of course, we are not being completely honest here. Most Western European languages do contain a few letters that will be new to you. Spanish has the "n" with a tilde (ñ), as well as accented vowels (á,í,ó, etc.) German has the "u" with an umlaut (ü). Portuguese and French both contain the special "c" with a *cedilla*, which looks like a c with an upside down question mark attached (ç). But you can master all of these on the first day of class.

Consider the following: Even if you have never studied Italian, you could start reading a page of written Italian aloud, and others would understand at least part of what you were saying. You might not be completely comprehensible, and your accent would almost surely be atrocious. But at least some of what you read would convey a recognizable meaning to a speaker of Italian.

Now suppose that you pick up a page of written Arabic. All you would see is a mind-boggling swarm of squiggles. Your heartbeat would increase, and little beads of sweat would appear on your forehead. You wouldn't have the first idea of how to pronounce *anything*. After a while, your listeners would shake their heads, grumble, and disperse as you looked helplessly at the sea of squiggles, reminiscing about how wonderfully easy Spanish class was.

The same would be true of Chinese, Thai, Farsi, Greek, Russian, Hebrew, Bulgarian, Japanese, Ukrainian, Burmese, Hindi, Urdu, Korean and Serbian. These languages all use non-Latin writing systems. Some of the languages on this list are harder than others. You could probably master Serbian or Russian in about half the time it would take you to learn Chinese or Arabic. Nonetheless, each of these languages requires you to do something that Spanish, Italian and German will never require: learn to use a new writing system.

Therefore, if you have chosen one of the above languages, you will have to make an early decision about how you are going to handle the writing system. Most textbooks of Chinese, Japanese, Arabic etc., employ a method called *transliteration*. Transliteration is basically a representation of another writing system using the Roman alphabet. For example, the Japanese word for "car" is *kuruma*. A Japanese would actually write it using a specific kanji, or Chinese-style character (車). However, if you pronounce, "*kuruma*," your Japanese friends will know that you are talking about a car.

On your first exposure to the transliterated *kuruma*, you may experience what feels like an epiphany. You didn't have to learn the Japanese character that represents *kuruma* (車) in order to communicate the idea of "car" verbally. So why not just skip the Japanese writing system altogether? Why not just learn Japanese using transliterations?

This is the temptation to which you must not succumb if you have chosen one of the non-Roman languages. There is nothing wrong with using transliterations in the beginning, while you are still learning the other writing system. However, as soon as possible, you should learn the other writing system and begin using it to learn the language.

The notion of a phonetically oriented alphabet is nearly universal. Therefore, once you master the system, you will have few problems using the foreign writing system as a medium for learning. In fact, your study of Russian, Bulgarian, or Serbian would actually be impeded if you relied on transliterations beyond the first week or two of your studies. The Cyrillic alphabet employed by these Slavic languages is easy enough for most students to master. Moreover, some of the transliterated Cyrillic sounds are awkward to work with. For example, there is a single Cyrillic letter that is transliterated as *sh-sh*. Rather than grappling with this unwieldy combination, it's easier just to learn and use the corresponding Cyrillic letter (Щ).

The alphabets used in Korean and Thai are a bit more challenging; but once again, they are easier to work with over the long haul than transliterations. Even Japanese has a phonetically based alphabet. (Actually they have two, called *hiragana* and *katakana*. Although Japanese utilizes thousands of Chinese characters, most dictionaries contain a phonetic *hiragana* or *katakana* "spelling" of each word.)

The Middle Eastern languages, such as Arabic, are a bit trickier. These languages have alphabets, but short vowels are often omitted from texts written for adult readers. However, dictionaries and beginners' texts indicate all the vowels. In time, you will be able to anticipate the short vowels in a word, much as an Arabic- or Hebrew-speaker does.

Chinese is the one language for which a prolonged reliance on transliteration is necessary. In order to master the Chinese language, you will have to master thousands of Chinese characters, each of which has a distinct pronunciation and tonal designation. Since Chinese has no real alphabet, a system of Romanized transliteration known as *pinyin* has been developed to help nonnative speakers learn the language. Although *pinyin* is no substitute for learning the characters, you will probably use it for supplemental purposes for an indefinite period. When you learn a new Chinese character, you will have no way of knowing its pronunciation without seeing the *pinyin* version.

CHAPTER 12

DEVELOPING A LOVE FOR WORDS

FOCUS ON VOCABULARY

As Miss Kramer said, "You can't get past square one if you don't know the vocabulary." Words are the building blocks of any language. No matter how thoroughly you learn the grammar of a language, your ability to express yourself and understand others using the language will always be limited by your vocabulary. Therefore, the acquisition of vocabulary is one of your primary tasks when learning a new language.

In the Language Student's Buying Guide section of this book, I describe several commercially available tools that can help you build your vocabulary. (These are primarily the *VocabuLearn* audio recordings and the flashcards made by Visual Education.) As helpful as these products are, though, they are not sufficient by themselves for building a powerful vocabulary in a language. Early in your language studies, you must develop the habit of collecting words. Your desire for vocabulary should extend to the verge of gluttony. You must learn to look at every new word as a new tool in your arsenal, as an incremental expansion of your powers of comprehension and expression in the language.

There are four primary sources of new vocabulary: textbooks, authentic reading materials, conversations, and dictionaries.

When you momentarily encounter a new word in one of these sources, you may or may not retain it. Suppose that you come across the word 外交関係 *gaikoo-kankei* in a Japanese newspaper. Even if you stop to look the word up in dictionary, you probably won't remember a week or a year later that *gaikoo-kankei* means "diplomatic relations." Vocabulary retention requires repeated exposure. Therefore, you will need to cultivate the habit of extracting new words from the above sources and storing them for easy study.

There are many options for warehousing new vocabulary items. Many years ago, I used to keep new vocabulary lists in spiral-bound notebooks; but I found that the pages quickly became worn and fell out.

Computer technology offers better solutions. You might build a two-column table in a Microsoft Word® file, fill the left column with new words in the target language, and then type the English definitions in the right column. This will give you the choice of printing the pages or viewing them on your computer screen.

My favorite method of storing vocabulary is decidedly more low-tech. In my home, I maintain a constant supply of unruled 3" x 5" index cards, which can be cheaply purchased in any office supply store. I orient the cards vertically, so that they appear tall and thin rather than long and fat. Then I write my entries down one side of the card, turn the card over, and fill the other side of the card in the opposite direction. I can usually fit about five vocabulary words, (plus the English definitions) on each side of the card. For example, a side of one of my Spanish-language cards might contain the following:

estar (to be)

ver (to see)

el perro (the dog)

la casa (the house)

verde (green)

How many words is enough? The answer to this question depends upon your goals. It is estimated that William Shakespeare had a vocabulary of about 23,000 words. By contrast, a junior high school student might understand about 8,000 words in her own language.

While these numbers may seem daunting, vocabulary acquisition becomes much easier if you work on it a little every day. As the Japanese proverb says, 塵も積もれば、山と成る (*chiri mo tsumoreba, yama to naru*)— "Piled up grains of sand can make a mountain."

144

LEARNING VOCABULARY WITH A DICTIONARY

Most dictionaries have two sections: an English-to-foreign language section, and a foreign-language-to-English section. You use the English-to-foreign language section when you want to look up the translation of an English word in the foreign language. The foreign-language-to-English section is used to look up the English definitions of words you encounter in the foreign language.

Both sections of the dictionary are helpful for learning vocabulary. At least several times a week, flip through the pages of your dictionary. When you are in the English-to-foreign-language section, find a concept that you don't yet know how to express in the foreign language. If you happen to be studying Spanish, then you might notice that the word for "sidewalk café" in Spanish is *terraza*. You will certainly be able to use this one on your next trip to Mexico City. Write the word and its English definition on one of your vocabulary cards. Now page through the Spanish-to-English section. Suppose that you come across the word *matasellos*, which means "postmark." This is a word that you would like to add to your repertoire. Write it down on a card, and it can be yours.

USING WORD GAMES TO LEARN VOCABULARY

Imagine that you are just beginning to learn Japanese. You know that you will eventually learn thousands of Japanese words, but you want to start with the most high-frequency ones. It only makes sense to learn the words for "water," "eat," and "bathroom" before you learn how to say "root canal," "proselytize," and "vampire." But how can you make sure that you learn the most high-frequency words first?

The following system has served me well in every language I have studied. All you need is a notepad and a dictionary. Look around your house. What do you see? Perhaps you are in the kitchen—and you see a window, an oven, and a kettle. Write down "window," "oven," and "kettle" on your notepad. Are you hungry? Would you like to snack on an apple? Good— now write down "hungry," "snack," "apple," and "eat."

After you have finished your apple, pull out some blank index cards and an English-Japanese dictionary. Look up the Japanese words for "window," "oven," "kettle," "hungry," "snack," "apple," and "eat." Write them down beside their English definitions. These high-frequency words are now safely inscribed in your vocabulary card collection, and they will soon become part of your active vocabulary in Japanese.

The household examples were simple. Now let's play the same game at work. What is on your schedule for this morning? A meeting? Then write down "meeting." What is the topic of the meeting? The production schedule? You know what to do. Write down "production" and "schedule."

This technique will ensure that you learn the vocabulary that you need most before you learn the vocabulary that would merely be nice to have at your disposal. This may seem like a lot of trouble, but it will become second nature. You will soon be compulsively looking up the target language words for everything you do, see, hear, eat or touch. One evening you will be watching a documentary about the latest blood transfusion techniques, and you will be unable to go to bed before you look up the Portuguese words for "transfusion," "thrombosis," and "hematologist."

CHAPTER 13

TAKING YOUR NEW LANGUAGE FOR A TEST DRIVE

PRACTICE WITH NATIVE SPEAKERS

Although books, cassettes, and other study materials are all quite helpful, they are less demanding than active conversation. A conversation with a live human being requires you to simultaneously listen, process what you hear, and formulate responses. In order to become truly skilled at listening and responding "on the fly" in a foreign language, you will have to seek out live, unscripted conversation opportunities.

You should develop a network of native speakers of the language you are studying. These relationships might be structured as mutually beneficial "language exchanges." Perhaps you can meet a native speaker of your target language who is himself studying English. Suggest that the two of you work out a deal: you will help him improve his English, if he will serve as a sounding board for your Russian.

These informal study exchanges can provide an invaluable boost to your independent study efforts. During one summer in college, my Japanese language abilities improved by leaps and bounds thanks to two women named Yuka and Sakiko.

Yuka and Sakiko were the wives of two graduate students at the University of Cincinnati. I was introduced to them by Donna, my aforementioned American friend who was herself studying Japanese. Throughout that summer, Yuka, Sakiko, and I met in the University of Cincinnati library practically everyday. One day we spoke only English, and the next day we spoke only Japanese.

These sessions gave me my first experiences using the Japanese language for extended periods of time. Prior to that, my use of the language had been limited to mini-conversations that consisted of introductions and exchanges of simple information. By the time I left the library on one of our "Japanese days," my head would be aching, and I would have a notepad full

147

of new Japanese words, or words in English that I couldn't yet express in Japanese. Yuka and Sakiko gave me a tremendous incentive to advance in my Japanese studies. By the end of the summer, my Japanese skills were on par with their abilities in English.

If you recruit a native speaker who is already living in the United States, Canada, or Britain, she will likely speak English better than you speak her language. Therefore, your initial exchanges may consist of you answering detailed questions about English usage, while she struggles to understand your stumbling attempts at basic communication. Don't worry—you will erase this linguistic capability gap soon enough, *if* you are willing to hit the books (and the tapes, CDs, etc.) in between your practice meetings.

Although your practice meetings are informal study sessions, you should nonetheless introduce a bit of structure. Make sure that you don't spend all your time discussing linguistically lightweight topics such as what you each ate for breakfast. Prepare a list of reasonably challenging topics to discuss, and do your homework before the practice session. If you have decided that you are going to discuss currency trading on a given day, you should learn the words for "floating exchange rate," "monetary policy" etc. before the practice session.

Ask your practice partner to try to stump you (and do the same for her). It might be helpful for you to think of yourselves as athletes in training. When athletes train together, there is an element of friendly competition, and they thereby push each other to new levels of skill. You should each use language that you think might be just beyond the other person's current repertoire, without overwhelming him.

Conversations that are made deliberately difficult can benefit you even after you have reached advanced levels in the language. I recently participated in a Japanese language "benchmarking" activity that was conducted by several Japanese Studies professors in the United States. The professors interviewed various Americans who had studied Japanese, and rated their abilities to describe physical objects, convey abstract ideas, and respond to complex arguments.

Even though I had been studying Japanese for more than a decade by this time, I was surprised at how intense the language workout was. To cite one example, the professor who interviewed me asked me to give a synopsis of the American Revolution, and the respective British and American positions (in Japanese). Then she asked me to compare the American Revolution to at least one other political upheaval that had since occurred somewhere in the world. That would have been a fair challenge for me even in English!

TALK YOUR WAY THROUGH THE BUTTERFLIES

Although you will get a lot of benefit from conversing with a native speaker with whom you have entered into a mutual study arrangement, you will soon want to test your skills in an unstructured situation. This is especially true if you make regular visits to a country where the language is spoken.

The first time you address an unfamiliar native speaker in his or her own language, I can guarantee that you will be nervous. This is simply because it represents a new experience for you. For all your life, you have communicated from within the safety zone of your native language. It is only natural for you to feel jitters when you take your initial steps into another language.

You may fear that the other person won't understand you, or that you won't understand his response. If you are still a beginner, then this may indeed happen. Trust me, the world won't end. Learn whatever you can from the situation, and continue to study. The next time you visit Japan, the man working behind the ticket counter will probably understand when you ask about the train schedule in Japanese. In the meantime, let someone interpret for you so that you can get your train ticket, and move on.

You may even have fears that someone will laugh at your mistakes. This is rare, but not unheard of. After all, there are English speakers who make fun of foreigners' mistakes, so it is only reasonable to assume that there are a few bad apples on the other side of the fence. In all my years of language study, however, I can only remember one or two occasions when this has happened to me. If by chance someone is derisive when you attempt to speak in their language, don't let their reaction impede your progress. Most people you meet will be considerate and helpful.

Some people continue to experience butterflies even after they have developed a functional level of skill in another language. The duration of your nervousness will depend on your personality, your current capabilities, and the frequency of your opportunities to speak the language. As you gain experience, skill, and confidence, these feelings of anxiety will gradually diminish, and eventually disappear altogether.

149

Remember, this is a challenge that everyone who masters a foreign language goes through to some degree or another. Butterflies ultimately can't hurt you—so just talk your way through them.

LEARN YOUR "CRUTCH PHRASES" EARLY ON

The beginning language learner will occasionally need to ask her listeners to slow down, repeat themselves, and restate what they have just said in simpler language. Before you take your first trip to Mexico, it would be a good idea to make sure that you know how to say the following in Spanish:

> "Could you please speak more slowly?"
> "Would you mind saying it once more?"
> "Is there a simpler way to say it?"
> "I'm sorry. My Spanish is not very good yet."

Some people have more experience than others in using their own language with nonnative speakers. During my years in the international automotive industry, I noticed that some Americans have learned to filter their English for Japanese and German listeners. They stick to basic sentence structures, use slow pronunciations and clear enunciations, and restrict themselves to basic vocabulary. Americans who have less experience working with nonnative English-speakers typically talk too fast, use arcane vocabulary, and pepper every other sentence with slang.

I was once in a meeting at a Japanese automotive company in which half the Americans were veterans of the Japanese corporate environment, and the other half were from a company that had never before dealt with a Japanese firm. Also present in the meeting were two Japanese men who had been in the United States for about three years each.

The two Japanese spoke passable English, but they were used to interacting with Americans who used deliberately simplified language. Not surprisingly, the Americans from the visiting company constantly used words and cultural references that only a native speaker of American English would understand. As a result, the two Japanese businesspersons needed repeated clarifications and restatements of what the visitors said. One of the American coworkers of the Japanese finally resorted to "translating" everything the other Americans said into simplified English.

150

This incident illustrates the degree to which the linguistic habits and consideration of the other speaker can affect your ability to understand a foreign language. Most people—no matter what language they speak— realize that they need to deliberately choose their words when talking to non-natives so as to minimize confusion. If you encounter someone who is inexperienced in this regard, try one of the above crutch phrases.

Don't despair too much over fast talkers and the like. After a few years of regularly speaking the language, you will be able to handle even the most fast-mouthed, wordy, and roundabout speakers.

FACING UP TO THE TELEPHONE

The telephone is a device which strikes fear in the heart of every foreign language student. The telephone can be intimidating even after you have established a fair degree of confidence using the language in face-to-face situations.

Face-to-face encounters provide a lot of assistance to communication. You can watch a person's lips as they pronounce their words. The other person can read your facial cues, which might indicate that you are having trouble understanding. If a particular language is closely associated with a single ethnic group, then the other person may immediately realize that you are not a native speaker. (In Japan, for example, this would be true for anyone who is not of East Asian descent.)

The telephone, however, offers none of this helpful assistance. You cannot see the other person's face; and the other person may not realize that you aren't a native speaker until several complete verbal exchanges have transpired.

Conversations that take place over the telephone are perhaps intrinsically more prone to misunderstandings, regardless of the language factor. Nonetheless, the telephone is a mainstay of business communications. Despite all the new communications technologies of recent years—email, web conferencing, video conferencing, and phones with video screens— some version of the voice-only telephone will probably be with us for years to come. Therefore, you will have to overcome any aversion you may have to using your new language across Ma Bell's wires.

One preemptive measure is to practice speaking over the telephone in casual, non-business situations. This is an area in which your language

151

exchange partners can help you. You might consider conducting every third or fourth language practice session over the telephone.

Another technique is to use the double blindness of the telephone to your advantage. In face-to-face communications, you would lose credibility in a heartbeat if you pulled out a cheat sheet or a dictionary. When using the telephone, however, there is nothing to stop you from writing down key words and phrases on a notepad beforehand. This will help you if you should get stuck—and the other person will never know the difference.

BECOME AN ACTIVE EAVESDROPPER

In most situations, eavesdropping is considered to be impolite. However, if your motivation is language study, then you may permit yourself a bit of discreet monitoring of other people's conversations. In airports, restaurants, and other populated venues, you will have many occasions to discreetly intercept fragments of conversations.

I would encourage you to take advantage of these opportunities to intake doses of unscripted, realistic conversations. Since you will not be under pressure to respond to anyone, you can concentrate on listening. You can turn such a listening situation into a miniature self-quiz. See how much you can understand, and try to anticipate what one speaker will say in response to the other.

Be sure to capture any new or unfamiliar words or phrases that you hear in passing. You may be surprised to emerge from lunch in a crowded café with a long list of new words. For the proactive language learner, casually overheard speech can be a goldmine of linguistic information.

IF YOU DON'T KNOW—ASK, IF THE CIRCUMSTANCES ALLOW

In the beginning, you will be able to answer most of your own questions by referring to your dictionary or textbook. At this level, most of your inquiries will still be limited to straightforward items that can be easily answered, such as, "What's the Russian word for 'air compressor'?"

In time, though, your questions will become increasingly complex. Let's assume that you already know the Russian word for "air compressor." Now you want to know how you can delicately tell the Russian distributor of your company's air compressors that there will be a slight adjustment to the pricing arrangement—but it is really to the long-term advantage of both sides.

You could perhaps assemble your own version with the aid of a dictionary. For questions like this, however, a native speaker is really a better resource. A native speaker can help you with nuance, which is something that you won't get from most dictionaries.

ACCEPT CRITICISM WITH A SMILE

I remember reading once that when a jetliner flies from New York to Los Angeles, it is off-course about half of the time. However, the pilot makes countless navigational corrections during the trip, so most flights bound for Los Angeles don't end up in Seattle or Portland.

As you study and practice your new language, you will make innumerable little mistakes. Most of these errors will not irreparably damage the comprehensibility of your message. Nevertheless, mistakes are mistakes. Perfection is your goal, even if you never fully achieve it.

Some learners are content if they can just make themselves understood. Since their abilities in the target language are sufficiently advanced to allow them to "get by", they see no need to progress any further. I would advise you to resist this temptation.

Consider the opposite situation: You have probably struggled through at least one conversation with a foreign speaker of English who uniformly ignored certain rules of our language. You may recall that you understood the basic intent of what the speaker was saying, but there was something fundamentally unpleasant about the experience. It was rather like listening to a beginning musician practice with his instrument—you could not avoid an occasional involuntary cringe. (Many years ago, I studied guitar; but my performances *never* progressed beyond the level of mildly torturing my audience.)

In the beginning, such cringes are unavoidable, but you should be able to reduce these reactions as you gain knowledge and experience in the language. Persistent study is one method for honing your skills; deliberately exposing yourself to criticism is another.

Most speakers of your target language will be hesitant to correct you when you bungle a word or a grammatical rule. The vast majority of them will ignore the mistake, especially if it is not an impediment to comprehension. Every once in a while, though, you will meet a native speaker who takes it upon herself to correct even the most minor of mistakes. She will call you out on the carpet when you misuse a word, incorrectly conjugate a verb, or leave out an article.

Such individuals are worth their weight in gold.

When someone stops you in mid-sentence, points out your mistake, and then indicates what you should have said, she is handing you the language learner's equivalent of a five-dollar bill. The lessons that you learn in such moments will stick to you like superglue. The mistakes that you make when speaking usually involve elements of the language that you haven't fully grasped from study alone. Constructive critics therefore are like teachers who explain a chapter in a textbook to make sure that the class really understands the material.

When a person corrects you, don't let your ego get in the way, and complain that she should cut you some slack because you are, after all, a nonnative speaker of her language. Realize that the person is doing you a favor, and say in her language, "Thank you for making me aware of my error."

I have actually asked speakers of a foreign language that I was studying to make a point of indicating my mistakes. (It is usually better to make such requests of social acquaintances rather than of business contacts.) It is preferable to be criticized once for a mistake, rather than to allow the error to become a permanent habit.

IMPRESS YOUR LISTENERS WITH PROVERBS

In English, sayings like "The early bird gets the worm" have an air of triteness. But proverbs are a deeply respected element of some languages. In Japanese and Chinese, for example, nothing impresses listeners quite as much as an appropriate proverb casually delivered at exactly the right moment. Spanish, too, is rife with popular sayings that can be dispensed in a variety of situations.

For most languages, there are books available that are dedicated to proverbs. Most of these include explanations about the situations in which each proverb should be used, and the cultural subtleties involved. After you reach a basic level of communication skill in your target language, you should purchase one of these books, and memorize the proverbs that strike you as especially useful.

An additional advantage of learning proverbs is the insights that they provide into the culture in which a language is spoken. One of the most commonly circulated Japanese proverbs is *deru kugi wa utareru*—"the protruding nail will be hammered down." While an entire culture cannot be encapsulated in a single proverb, this adage does make a statement about the Japanese emphasis on conformity and social harmony.

Often you will discover proverbs in a foreign language that perfectly match the meaning of well-known English proverbs. In other cases, you will come across proverbs in the foreign language that are radically opposed to prevailing attitudes in the English-speaking world. These realizations often provide insight into behavior that doesn't outwardly make sense from an American or British perspective.

USE COLLOQUIALISMS APPROPRIATELY, USE SLANG SPARINGLY

In most languages, there are distinctions between the written and the spoken word. To use a familiar example from English, consider some of the expressions commonly used in written contracts and business documents. If you were to use a phrase like, "the aforesaid parties" in a conversation, most listeners would understand you. However, it would be far more natural to say, "the people whom I mentioned previously." When written language is employed in the conversational mode, the effect can be overly formal, and might even be interpreted as arrogance. The person who talks like a contract or a formal business letter will alienate many listeners.

In some languages, the use of written speech in a conversational setting can even render your message incomprehensible. Japanese is a good example in this regard. The language makes extensive use of Chinese characters. Although every word has its own pronunciation, there are many homonyms (words that have identical pronunciations but different meanings.) This abundance of homonyms is one of the more challenging aspects of Japanese.

When two homonyms are written down, they are easily distinguished by their Chinese characters. In speech, however, it may be more difficult to tell one homonym from the other. If you use a formalistic written-language word in a conversation, your listeners may mistake it for a more colloquial homonym. They may also assume that you have simply made a mistake, and question your grasp of Japanese. Therefore, it is important for you to acquaint yourself with conversational language as well as the language that you will need to decipher legal texts and articles in the financial press.

However, it is important to distinguish between colloquial speech and slang. These two categories of language are not identical—although they are commonly confused. "Colloquial", per Webster's dictionary, refers to language that is "used in or characteristic of familiar and informal conversation." On the other hand, "slang" means "language peculiar to a particular group." For any given slang expression, the "particular group" might be teenagers, the criminal element, or another sector of society with whom you may not wish to explicitly associate yourself.

If a person tells you, "The cops are coming," you will probably not assign any particular group affiliation to his choice of words. "Cops" has a neutral connotation, but it is clearly colloquial—intended for conversation rather than written texts. In a newspaper article, the term "law enforcement personnel" would probably be used. While not offensive, "cops" is not suitable for most formal written situations.

Just as a newspaper editor would never allow "cops" to appear in an article, most people would not use the more formal written language term in a conversational setting. When your coworker tells you about the wild party next door that kept her awake last night, she is not going to say, "law enforcement personnel came and broke it up." She will say, "the cops came and broke it up."

However, if she were to say "the pigs came and broke it up," she would be making an indirect identity statement. The term "pig," as a reference to law enforcement officers, is a usage that is limited to street hoodlums and other criminals. If you use this term, you lump yourself in with that group.

Similarly, "that's great" is a neutral colloquial expression to convey approval. It suggests no age, class, or group affiliations. Little old ladies, schoolchildren, Wall Street attorneys and teenagers can all say "that's great." The following expressions, though, have been closely associated with the under-twenty crowd at various points in recent decades. You may recognize some or all of them, depending on your age (and how many old movies you have seen).

"Groovy!"
"Tubular!"
"Totally rad!"
"Cool, man!"
"Totally awesome!"
"Bitchin'!"
"Far out!"

There is of course nothing wrong with being a teenager—but you don't want to go around saying "that's groovy," etc. if you happen to be forty-five.

Keep these issues in mind as you learn your new language. For nearly every language, there is an assortment of slang and "street talk" books that you can purchase. Before you use an expression from one of these books too freely, make sure that you are aware of the age and social group with which it is associated.

LEARN PROFANITY—BUT NEVER USE IT

Just as there is a definite distinction between colloquial speech and slang, there is also a difference between slang and profanity. Relatively early in the study of your new language, you will make a discovery: there are bad words in foreign languages, too. Just in case you have spent your entire life under the supposition that English speakers are uniquely profane, it may be comforting to know that Chinese, Germans, Japanese and others have their share of four-letter words.

Adding a smattering of profanity to a conversation may seem like a way to make your speech seem more authentic. There are dangers associated with this practice, though. First of all, you may not be sure about the potency of a particular word. As is the case with English profanity, the bad words used in other languages carry varying degrees of offensiveness. Dictionary entries often contain watered-down translations of swear words. As a result, you may make what you think is a mildly salty remark, only to be faced with a room full of aghast listeners a few seconds later.

Moreover, profanity from the lips of a nonnative speaker always comes across as particularly crude. If a native speaker swears in his own language, he can always claim that he slipped in the heat of the moment. When a foreign speaker swears, he cannot lay claim to the involuntary reaction excuse. No matter how well you learn Italian, you will never bang your shin on a piece of furniture in the middle of the night and spontaneously swear in Italian. If you curse in a foreign language, your listeners will know that it was premeditated. This has obvious implications concerning their impression of you.

Nonetheless, profanity is an area which interests many language students. We talked earlier about the slang and street talk books published for students of foreign languages, and the dangers of throwing those expressions around. There are also many books on foreign profanity—in every major language, from Spanish to Indonesian. It is not a bad idea to pick up one of these books and familiarize yourself with some of the entries contained within. But this area of study should be for defensive purposes only, so that you can understand what's going on in the unlikely event that a Chinese or a German speaker begins casting aspersions on your ancestors.

One final word on the profanity issue: When you speak a foreign language, you are a playing the role of a guest in another culture. You might look the other way if your Uncle Harry puts his feet up on your coffee table, asks if you've forgotten how much he likes beer, and lets loose a loud belch. But you don't expect the same behavior from social and business guests who are invited into your home. The same rule applies for profanity. It might be permissible for a native speaker, but it's not okay for you, as a guest speaker of their language.

READING IS (COMPARATIVELY) EASY, BUT WRITING IS HARD

I have been through the process of learning a language several times in my life, and I have had innumerable conversations with others who have learned foreign languages. Despite the varying backgrounds, native languages, and target languages of all these people, there are two statements that everyone seems to agree on:

1. Understanding the written word in a foreign language is easier than understanding the spoken word, and
2. Speaking in a foreign language is much easier than writing.

158

Rule #1 might not apply if you are learning Chinese or Arabic, but it certainly applies to any European language you might decide to study. You will achieve basic reading competency long before you have full confidence in your listening comprehension skills. There are several possible explanations for this. For one thing, printed words on a page do not move. If something is a little confusing, you can go over it several times before making a final judgment about what it means. On the other hand, the meanings conveyed in the spoken language are constantly moving targets. You only have a few seconds to grasp the gist of what someone says—and then the speaker moves on to the next idea.

In addition, written mediums tend to favor standardized language. Most people pay more attention to the rules of grammar and syntax when they write. Few individuals exercise the same discipline when they speak. As a result, the spoken word is full of slang, shortcuts, and regionalisms—all of which make the message more difficult to comprehend.

Speaking is easier than writing because your mistakes are more easily hidden in a conversation. Your words hang in the air for only a few seconds. When you write, however, your words remain on paper for future posterity to see and critique. A poorly written memo or email will definitely attract more notice than a poorly worded verbal explanation. The fact that writing is more demanding than speaking was probably apparent to you before you ever began to study another language. In your native language, speaking is often effortless, even involuntary. Meanwhile, composing a simple personal letter can require a monumental amount of mental exertion.

You can ease your way into writing in your foreign language. You don't have to start out with a twenty-page report or a highly nuanced piece of business correspondence. Until you are a competent writer, it is helpful to compose in the "bullet point" format rather than in fully developed paragraphs. For instance, if you write a business letter, compose an introductory paragraph and a closing paragraph, then list your main points as bulleted items in the main body of the letter.

The bullet point style is acceptable for most business situations. In fact, many businesspersons prefer this style, because it is often easier to read than the traditional paragraph format.

PAY ATTENTION TO THE DETAILS WHEN WRITING

Even if you write in bullet points, there are some errors that you should do your level best to avoid from the beginning. Mistakes in the areas of spelling, punctuation, and capitalization seldom prevent your written message from being understood, but they immediately peg you as someone who does not know the language well. With a little bit of effort, you can avoid mistakes that will make your writing stand out as "foreign."

It is especially easy to make spelling mistakes when writing cognates in foreign languages. When working with languages such as Spanish, words like *condición*, *minuto*, and *microfóno* are so close to their English equivalents that caution is needed to avoid the inadvertent use of the English spelling. (Incidentally, speakers of Romance languages have to watch out for the same mistakes when they write in English.) You should also remember to add accent marks to the vowels where needed.

The subtleties of spelling will increasingly become second nature as you continue to practice reading and writing in the other language. You will speed this process along if you resist the development of bad habits from the beginning.

Punctuation rules in foreign languages don't always seem to make sense. For me, the Spanish placement of an upside down question mark (¿) at the beginnings of interrogative sentences has always been particularly maddening. My patience has been similarly tried by the rules governing the usages of commas and quotation marks in Japanese.

Every language has a different set of rules for capitalization. In English, we capitalize the names of languages. In Spanish and French, the names of languages are not capitalized. When you write a memo in French, no one is likely to scream bloody murder if you capitalize the word for "English" (*anglais*), but this would not be correct French. Romance languages typically do not capitalize the words that refer to religions or nationalities, either. In Spanish, the name of the Catholic religion (*católicismo*) begins with a lower case letter.

A CRITICAL MILESTONE

Once you reach the intermediate stage in a language, you will be able to put together reasonably correct sentences and comprehend most of what others say. At this point, you will be having real "conversations." For a long while, however, communicating in the other language will require a deliberate act of effort. This is a struggle, because your concern for the mechanics of the language seems to detract from the content that you are discussing.

Persevere. Initially, everyone has to give as much attention to the nuts and bolts of the language as they do to the content being conveyed. Although you will often feel like you are trying to run a footrace in your wingtips or high heels, the awkwardness goes away with time and practice. Progress on this front is measured through a series of gradually increasing victories.

You will begin by having *simple* conversations in which you can focus solely on content. Then one day you will finish a lengthy, detailed conversation in your new language, and a few minutes later you will have an exhilarating realization: you were finally able to divert your attention from the language and focus on content. You will be recalling the particulars of the conversation, and you will be unable to remember at first if you had been speaking English or the foreign language—although of course, you will *know* that you had been speaking the foreign language the entire time.

This major milestone builds the conviction that you "speak" a language which you had formerly just been "studying." When you achieve this milestone you are well on your way to being able to use the language in a business context.

CHAPTER 14

TACKLING DIALECTS: WHICH VERSION OF SPANISH ARE YOU SPEAKING?

A TENNESSEE YANKEE IN THE ROYAL AIR FORCE

I remember seeing a TV news magazine segment about a fighter pilot from the Tennessee Air National Guard who, for some reason or another, had been dispatched to fly for a time with the British Royal Air Force. When the interviewer asked one of the RAF pilots to identify the most challenging aspect of the arrangement, the Englishman smiled wryly and replied, "the language barrier."

Although the British pilot was speaking in jest, the differences between various regional versions of English can be significant. Perhaps the most extreme illustration is found in the 1998 Scottish film, *My Name is Joe*. The actors in *My Name is Joe* all speak English, but the movie is fully subtitled due to the presence of heavy Scottish accents and regionalisms.

English is not the only language that varies by region. Languages such as Spanish, Arabic, French, and Chinese, which are spoken by far-flung populations, differ considerably according to the particular locale. In most cases, there is an agreed upon "standard" which is taught by educational institutions, and used to create instructional materials. For European languages, the acknowledged standard is almost universally the language as it is spoken in its European country of origin. (The one exception is English; American English is now generally preferred by foreign students over British English—though some European readers might disagree with me about this.)

162

SPEAKING SPANISH OUTSIDE OF SPAIN

A first experience with a dialect can be intimidating. Beginners are often nonplussed when a Spanish speaker from Guadalajara or Havana doesn't sound like the Spanish recordings in her university's language lab. Spanish has been spoken in the Americas for about five hundred years—ample time to allow significant divergences from the language of Spain. The variations between the Spanish currently spoken in Spain and the Spanish spoken in Latin America are significant. If you have only been exposed to the European standard, your ears will need some time to adjust. Moreover, the Spanish-speaking area within the Americas is vast—so Mexico City residents do not use the language exactly like the inhabitants of Buenos Aires.

WHEN "STANDARD" SPEAKERS ARE A SMALL MINORITY

Portugal—another former imperial power—carried its language to the Americas and Africa. If not for Portugal's colonial past, the language would today be one of the numerically less significant languages of Europe. There are only about 10 million residents in the tiny Iberian nation; but there are more than 186 Portuguese speakers living in Brazil. Add to that about 20 million Mozambicans, and millions of Portuguese speakers in other African nations. Today, only a fraction of the world's Portuguese speakers actually hold a passport from the country of the language's origin. Therefore, it is a tiny minority of Portuguese speakers who actually speak "standard" Portuguese. (The same could be said of Spanish; the population of Spanish-speaking America is many times larger than that of Spain.)

From a statistical perspective, Brazilian Portuguese is the most significant dialect of the language. If you first learn European, or Continental, Portuguese, you will have to acclimate yourself to some minor differences in Brazilian pronunciation and vocabulary. (On the bright side, a number of courses in "Brazilian Portuguese" are now available, so you may be able to acquaint yourself with it before you land in Brazil.)

I adjusted to Brazilian Portuguese during an extended stay near São Paulo after studying Continental Portuguese for several years in the United States. In my experience, the relatively uniform Brazilian Portuguese is much easier to adjust to than the multiple American dialects of Spanish. (Although there are courses in "Latin American Spanish", the variations in speech within Latin America usually force the authors of these courses to favor one of the various dialects within this region.)

MORE SUNDRY DIALECTS

France is universally regarded as the seat of French-speaking culture. French is also spoken in several other European countries, in Africa, and in the Canadian province of Quebec. The Canadian version of French seems to be particularly daunting for French students who are fresh from the classroom. I have seen dictionaries of Canadian French, but I haven't yet seen any full-length courses based upon the Quebec dialect.

Chinese dialects used to be a major obstacle to learning any universally serviceable form of spoken Chinese. Now the dialects are merely a manageable impediment. The Mandarin dialect has been embraced throughout China and Taiwan, but regional differences in usage and pronunciation persist. Having learned the Beijing dialect, it took me a number of years to get used to speakers from Taiwan, Shanghai, and other areas.

The dialect issue is not limited to global languages like French, Spanish and Portuguese. Even Japan—a country about the size of California—is home to numerous regional language variations. "Standard" Japanese is more or less the Tokyo dialect, but differences that emerged before the age of mass communications still exist. Residents of the Kansai region—the area around the cities of Osaka, Kobe and Kyoto—speak a distinctive version of Japanese which affects the way greetings, pronunciation, and verb endings are rendered in daily communications. (If you want to hear a bit of Kansai Japanese, rent *Black Rain*, a 1989 American film about two New York City policemen who get mixed up in a conflict in the Japanese underworld.) In my years as a Japanese language interpreter, I was also challenged by the unique dialects of Kyushu (Southern Japan), Okinawa, and Hokkaido.

DIALECTS BARK WORSE THAN THEY BITE

Now that I have sufficiently alarmed you over dialects, I have some good news: once you have the standard version of a language under your belt, you can usually adjust to a regional dialect with minimal difficulty. Unique English dialects—such as those of Wales, Ireland or Australia might cause confusion to the uninitiated ears of an Ohio resident. But no Ohioan has ever required an interpreter when navigating the streets of Melbourne or Dublin. Similarly, dialect confusion in a foreign language disappears with repeated exposure. While there are exceptions (recall the aforementioned Scottish movie that required subtitles) these exceptions are few and far between.

The caveat, of course, is that you must learn the standard version of the language well. Deciphering a dialect is normally a straightforward matter of untangling the standard language from the incremental modifications that have been applied within a particular region. Master the language of the Paris salons, and you will be ready for the rough-and-tumble watering holes of rural Quebec soon enough.

Should you go one step further, and actually try to speak in a regional dialect? Opinions will vary on this one, but my vote is—*no*. A dialect is, by definition, the nonstandard characteristic speech of a particular region. The standard language, by contrast, is universal across multiple regions. In this light, a foreigner who affects the regional speech of a dialect is kind of like a New Yorker who puts a gun rack in the back window of his BMW when driving through rural Kentucky. It is somehow just not convincing.

Once again, it is helpful to consider the matter from the opposite perspective: try to recall the last time you heard a nonnative speaker of English say, "howdy," "jolly good," or "right away, Bubba."

CHAPTER 15

WALKING, LEARNING, AND CHEWING GUM AT THE SAME TIME

MULTITASKING

I have a confession to make: I don't think that I could entirely give up television. Sure, I know that a lot of the programming is pure trash, but some of it is also pretty good. I have a particular weakness for CNN, the History Channel, and the Discovery Channel. In addition, I will grudgingly admit that I have consumed my share of more low-brow entertainment. (*Seinfeld* reruns are my particular weakness.) And as for movies—I have my own express lane at the local Blockbuster.

But my leisure activities don't stop there. I go to the gym everyday. I surf the Internet. I drive to parties and meetings with friends. I even go running, when the fickle weather in Ohio permits.

My time is also consumed by many activities that aren't necessarily fun. I spend an hour in the car each day commuting to and from my office. I have to clean the house, fold laundry, and prepare my meals. Once per week, I drive to the local supermarket and stock up on groceries.

Yesterday I got a haircut. I spent twenty minutes waiting in the barbershop. Two months ago I refinanced my house, and I spent about the same amount of time waiting in an office for the loan officer. Last month I went out of town on business, and I spent a total of two hours waiting in the airport.

I turn all of these situations—from watching a movie to waiting for a flight—into study sessions. This is the principle of *multitasking*—or doing more than one thing at a time.

If you are like most people, you confront an endless series of demands on your time. As a result, it may not be practical for you to set aside one or two hours everyday and say, "This will be my language study time." The solution, therefore, is to *blend* language study into your other activities.

Consider, for example, a leisurely two hours spent watching a DVD. Why not divert a bit of your attention from the movie to study German vocabulary? When you were a kid, your parents probably scolded you for doing your homework in front of the television. However, you are not a kid anymore—and you can quite effectively mix certain language study activities into your TV time.

I religiously study foreign language vocabulary while I watch TV. Sometimes I simply flip through my vocabulary cards. On other occasions I write out new vocabulary cards, referring to my unfamiliar words list and a dictionary. But I never just watch the DVD without injecting some productive study time.

If you adopt this technique, you will find that you actually enjoy movies, documentaries, and sitcoms even more, knowing that your ninety minutes in front of the television has moved you a bit farther down the road to language competency. Moreover, you will reach the point where you feel guilty when you try to watch TV *without* studying. Your vocabulary cards will become as indispensable to an evening of television as the TV Guide or a bowl of popcorn.

You can start each day with a productive dose of language study. Before you go to sleep, place a tape player beside your bed with a language-learning tape cued up and ready. When the alarm goes off, turn on the lights, put your feet on the floor, and turn on the tape player. Let the tape player continue to run as you brush your teeth, shower, and shave (or put on your makeup).

How long does it take you to clean, groom, and dress yourself in the morning? I spend about a half an hour on these activities. However, I use this time productively by listening to language tapes as I complete my morning preparations—and this only occasionally results in additional shaving cuts.

Place cassette players at strategic points in your house or apartment. In addition to the cassette player in your bedroom, you can also place a cassette player in the kitchen, living room, etc. This way, you don't have to lug your equipment from room to room. You can simply walk to another location in your home and hit another button.

If you ever eat alone in your home, then there is no reason why you can't turn on your language tapes while you eat your sandwich or Chinese carryout. Most meals take at least twenty minutes. That time could be used for mental as well as physical nourishment. Leave the tapes on while you eat dessert, clean the dishes, and feed the leftovers to your cat.

Tapes can also be employed in numerous situations outside the home. One of the most onerous tasks in my week is the trip to the grocery. I always seem to arrive at the store at the same time as everyone else, which means extra time maneuvering around the aisles and waiting in line. (In the checkout lane, I always seem to get behind the person who is buying enough food to see his entire family through a moderate ice age.) If the crowds are bad, the grocery store can consume up to an hour.

I address this problem by wearing my Sony Walkman into the store. Even with the headset, I am able to hear enough of my surroundings to avoid other carts and shoppers. I usually don't have to remove my headset until it is my turn in the checkout lane.

I often blend language studies into my daily trip to the gym. Before leaving the house, I simply throw my Walkman and a few cassettes into my gym bag, and I can then listen to language tapes as I lift weights or work out on the exercise bike. Since I usually spend about an hour at the gym, multitasking my workouts means that I get an extra hour's worth of language study.

There is nothing more frustrating than waiting for someone else. Nonetheless, such delays are a fact of life. You must wait for the dentist, the loan officer, and the accountant. When taking an out-of-town trip, you are dependent on the schedule of the airline. If you sign up for a class at evening college, you must wait during the fifteen or twenty minutes between your arrival on campus and the beginning of the class.

Why waste these ten- to thirty-minute chunks of time? With a little planning, you can turn the twenty minutes spent in the dentist's waiting room into a grammar review session, or the half hour at the auto repair shop into thirty minutes of vocabulary review.

The key is to make sure that you always have study materials on hand. Keep a grammar book in your briefcase. Leave a Walkman and several language tapes in the backseat of your car. (Several people have jokingly referred to my car as "the rolling language lab" because of the number of language study materials that I keep inside it. However, I am never left in a waiting room without something to study.)

Speaking of the car—most of us spend about an hour per day behind the wheel. If you spend all these hours listening to music or talk radio, then you are missing out on valuable language study time. You can advance your studies considerably in the time it takes to drive to and from work—especially if you use the *VocabuLearn* or the *Pimsleur* tapes (see the "Language Student's Buying Guide" near the end of this book).

I wouldn't suggest trying to study a language while you're on the job, but what about during your lunch hour? If you eat at your desk, you can listen to your Walkman without disturbing others. This is also a good time to tackle reading passages, grammar study, and of course—a great time to pull out your vocabulary flashcards.

The above techniques must of course be modified to fit your circumstances and lifestyle. If you carpool to work with three colleagues everyday, then it probably won't be feasible for you to listen to your tapes on the way to work. (However, you can certainly flip through your vocabulary cards when it is someone else's turn to drive.) Likewise, some of my suggestions about listening to tapes constantly around the house may not work if you are married and have three children. (But you should still be able to listen when you are shaving or putting on your makeup.)

The key is to look at the activities in your own life and ask yourself where there is room for multitasking. As a general rule, you can multitask any activity that doesn't require your full concentration.

ADVANCED MULTITASKING

I began studying Japanese around fifteen years ago, and I know the language very well. The same is true of Spanish. I have reached the point in both of these languages where I can no longer receive significant benefits from textbooks and other purely instructional materials. However, my abilities in these languages would deteriorate if I were to cease all contact with them.

My solution has been to use these languages as the medium for learning about other subjects. I recently read the popular business book, *Getting to Yes*, by Fischer, Ury and Patton. However, I read the Spanish-language version, *Obtenga El Sí*. When I finally got around to reading Steven Covey's book, *The Seven Habits of Highly Effective People*, I bought the Japanese-language version. When I get my daily dose of online news each morning, I make it a habit to select one of the foreign-language sites of CNN.com (You can take your pick of Spanish, Portuguese, German, Italian, Japanese, Korean, and Arabic.). I subscribe to *Newsweek en Español*, and to the Spanish-language version of *National Geographic*.

It is increasingly easy to purchase entertainment in other languages. I recently read the James Clavell novel, *Gaijin*, in Spanish. When the latest *Star Wars* epic, *Attack of the Clones*, was released as a DVD, I was pleased to find that a Spanish-language track had been included. I am a bit too old for the Harry Potter books—but I noticed that all of them are available in multiple languages. Whatever your tastes in movies and fiction, you will probably be able to buy what you like in the language of your choice.

There are many benefits to advanced multitasking. To begin with, a particular language, like any subject, grows old over time. You will not enjoy running through mechanistic vocabulary and grammar drills in languages that you have been studying for many years. Advanced multitasking allows you to study the language without enduring the normal rituals of study. The language becomes secondary, and the content of what you are reading or viewing becomes the primary focus of your attention. Additionally, using your second or third language as a medium for reading novels, catching up on the news, or learning economics is a very value-added form of multitasking. This approach will leave you with more time for other things—perhaps even the study of yet another language.

CHAPTER 16

MORE LANGUAGE LEARNING TIPS AND STRATEGIES

LEARN BY EXAMPLE

As your confidence grows in your new language, the ideas that you want to express will grow progressively more complex. You will soon grow bored of telling everyone what you ate for breakfast, where you live, and how long you have been studying Russian. You will recognize this phase when you enter it. This is the point at which you are no longer able to immediately find the words that you need in your beginner's textbook or in a phrase book.

Sometimes you will find that you are able to construct the more complex ideas by looking up the necessary words in a dictionary, and then applying what you know about the grammar of the language. However, this method will not be 100% successful. Every language has its own set of idiomatic constructions and irregular syntax. Consider the following English sentences:

"We'll be in trouble if we don't get down to business."

"If you rest on your laurels, you will fall behind the times."

"Only proactive measures can prevent the situation from getting out of hand."

"If we don't see eye-to-eye on this issue, then we should table the discussion for now and let the matter work itself out."

For a beginning student of English, you can imagine how difficult it might be to figure out constructions such as "rest on your laurels," "fall behind the times," and "see eye-to-eye." Some of these phrases might be

171

found in a good dictionary of idioms. But as a beginning student, you would probably bungle some aspect of any one of these expressions. Moreover, phrases such as "let the matter work itself out" might not be readily found in *any* dictionary or instructional text.

This does not mean that as a nonnative speaker, the higher levels of expression will be forever beyond your grasp. However, there is a threshold beyond which the textbook cannot carry you. When you reach this threshold, you should shift your attention from the canned example sentences in your textbooks to the sentences that you find in materials produced for native speakers.

Just as you keep a set of vocabulary cards, you should also start and maintain a set of example sentence cards. One day you will come across a sentence in a magazine article and say to yourself, *"I should remember that grammatical construction. It might come in handy someday."* All you have to do is write down the sentence on a 3"x5" index card and file it away. Now it is yours forever, to study and employ in your own conversations and writing.

The more varied your reading, the more varied will be your powers of expression. There are certain aspects of a language that you can only learn from reading financial newspapers. Other nuggets can only be gleaned from scientific and technical materials. And don't forget to read editorials and opinion pieces. These will teach you how to structure an argument and persuade in the language.

You can also feel free to copy sentences and turns of phrase that you hear people use in conversation. If someone says something that strikes you as useful, jot it down and add it to your sentence card collection. To succeed with a new language, you must become a connoisseur of the methods by which people employ it.

Professional journals and websites that pertain to your particular profession are especially valuable in this regard. If you are a computer programmer who is studying Spanish, then you will want to pay special attention to language that Spanish-speaking programmers use when talking about object-oriented design, program debugging, and multi-tier architecture. This will enable you be truly polished when you discuss these principles with fellow programmers in Madrid.

An Example from Japanese:

夏には卵は長持ちしない。

Pronunciation: *Natsu ni wa tamago wa nagamochi shinai.*
Translation: Eggs don't stay fresh for long in the summer.

My translation is somewhat colloquial. A word-for-word translation would not be as user-friendly. The core element of the above sentence, *naga-mochi suru* 長持ちする, is an odd beast - a combination of an adjective, *nagai* 長い(long) and the verb *motsu* 持つ(to have, to hold) attached to the verb *suru* する (to do).

From an English-speaker's perspective, this is an odd way of attacking the idea that "eggs don't stay fresh for long (or quickly spoil) in summer." But this makes perfect sense within the world of the Japanese language.

Japanese is full of little syntactical nuggets like this that you will need to commit to memory in order to become a truly competent speaker of the language. Insights like the one above cannot be laid out in a grammar book. The only way for you to learn them is through habitual listening and reading. You will then need to reinforce your knowledge by applying what you have learned in your own speech and writing.

HITTING PLATEAUS

For the first few months of your studies, it will seem that your knowledge and skill in the language doubles every two or three weeks. And this may not be far from the truth; when you are starting at the bottom, it is relatively easy for you to increase your knowledge by a factor of twenty-five, fifty, or even one hundred percent. At this stage, every textbook and cassette program is full of things that you didn't know before: new vocabulary, new grammar rules, new idioms, etc. You also have the momentum of novelty on your side.

After a while your rate of improvement will taper off. Progress will be measured in minor increments rather than leaps and bounds. Stimulation will be harder to find, as fewer language textbooks and tapes will be able to offer you something new. Nonetheless, you will know that you still have a long way to go before you reach fluency. You will have to keep moving, even though studying Japanese or Russian may at times feel like just another routine.

173

Plateaus eventually threaten all study, skill-building, and self-improvement efforts. When as a thirteen-year-old, I took my first guitar lesson, my instructor warned me, *"At first, you will be eager to practice everyday. But later on, you will go through periods when you don't feel like practicing. The students who keep practicing through these times are the ones who eventually become good guitarists."* Similar advice might be appropriate for language learners. Plateaus are inevitable, but they must be overcome.

There are several strategies that you can employ for overcoming plateaus. Depending on your circumstances, you might want to use all of these strategies, or just one or two of them.

BUY A NEW TEXTBOOK OR AUDIO PROGRAM

The first thing you might do is whip out your credit card, log on to Amazon or one of the specialty online language bookstores, and purchase some new materials. Plateaus often occur when your present collection of language materials is no longer teaching you anything new. You may be in need of some more advanced materials, or perhaps just a course which approaches the language from a different perspective.

You can often preempt plateaus by making regular additions to your language study library. The monthly purchase of a new book or a new audio course will help you to preserve your sense of novelty.

STEP OUT INTO THE REAL WORLD

Alternatively, you may want to provide yourself with some fresh "real world" doses of the language. Strike up a conversation with a native speaker of the language that you are studying. If possible, visit a setting where the language is regularly spoken. If you live in a major city, you likely won't need to purchase a plane ticket in order to accomplish this.

Periodic overseas travel does provide tremendous benefit for language learners. Nothing reinforces your desire to increase your skills like time spent on the ground in another country, where at every turn you can exercise your language skills in a different scenario. If time and resources allow, you might consider taking an annual "language vacation" to a country in which your target language is spoken.

TAKE A REST

A final possibility is that you may have been spending too much time focused on your language. As important as consistent study is, it is possible to hit a point of diminishing returns—where you need to step back from the subject to let all the information you've consumed soak in.

If you find yourself in a rut, perhaps you need to add variety to your mental life. Begin the study of another language, enroll in an evening accounting class, or read a book which interests you. You will probably find that the addition of such variety enables you to see your language through "fresh eyes."

DIVERSIFYING YOUR LINGUISTIC PORTFOLIO

The process of learning languages can be habit-forming. You will experience a genuine thrill the first time you are able to converse in a language that was incomprehensible two years earlier. Naturally, you will want to repeat the experience. Shortly after you reach a point of competency in your first foreign language, you will probably start shopping for your second one.

This realization raises a few questions. First of all, are two or three foreign languages better than one? My answer would be a conditional "yes." Every additional language that you learn increases the number of countries in which you can read the local press, conduct market research, and telephone any business or government agency without worrying whether or not you will be greeted by someone who speaks English. All things being equal, a person who speaks both Spanish and Chinese has more options than a person who speaks only one or the other. A person who speaks Japanese *and* Spanish *and* Chinese is more versatile still.

That having been said, there are several cautionary points to bear in mind. First of all, for business purposes, basic skills are of limited use. To truly say that you "speak" a language in the business world, you must have reached professional-level competency. Discussions of technical, accounting, and personnel matters require advanced language proficiency. It's fine to begin your second foreign language (or your third, for that matter) as long as you don't stop working to improve your first one.

175

> **For business purposes, high levels of skill are required.**
>
> I recently saw a television commercial on *CNN en Español* (CNN's Spanish-language station) that highlighted the embarrassments that can occur when a person overestimates his language skills in a business situation. The commercial was produced for the Spanish-speaking market by the car rental company Hertz.
>
> The camera opened on the office of a fictional car rental company called *"Autos Rebajados"*—which roughly translates as "Cut-rate Cars." The phone was manned by an American customer service agent who proclaimed his abilities in Spanish. However, it soon became clear that the customer service agent spoke very poor Spanish. Each time he answered the telephone, he consistently misunderstood the gist of what the person on the other end of the line was saying. The scene finally moved to the Hertz office, where an operator answered in fluent *español*.

THE RULE OF SEVEN

There is a limit to the number of languages in which you can practically expect to achieve business-level competency. I have read about linguists who have learned ten, twelve, or even twenty languages. While I don't doubt that there are individuals who can carry on basic conversations in twenty languages, I would be willing to bet that there are few who can discuss advanced theories in economics, finance, and engineering in so many tongues. *Remember: your goal should be to reach an advanced level of competency in any language that you study.* It would be better for you to truly master only *one* foreign language than to have a superficial knowledge of four or five.

Polyglots (individuals who speak multiple languages) sometimes refer to the "Rule of Seven". The Rule of Seven states that proficiency in seven foreign languages is the practical upper limit for most people. In other words, if you try to take on more than seven languages (in addition to your native one), you are unlikely to become highly competent in all of them.

My own research suggests that the upper limit may be even lower. The American Translators Association, or ATA (atanet.org) is a professional organization for translators and interpreters. I recently browsed through the translator profiles located in the ATA's online database. It was common to find translators and interpreters who worked with two or three foreign languages, but I was unable to find a translator who offered services in more than five foreign languages.

This might provide a good yardstick for planning your own language studies. Keep in mind that translators are language specialists, and *their* limit seems to be five foreign languages. For a person whose primary job function is not translation, I would estimate that the practical limit is about three foreign languages. However, this is not exactly dismal news. Three foreign languages should provide enough variety to keep most learners motivated and interested, without sacrificing a high level of attainment in each language studied.

Once you experience the fun of mastering one or two languages, you will probably find no less than a dozen that really interest you. In fact, I have yet to meet a language that I don't like. If I had unlimited time, I would study them all—from French to Bulgarian to Navajo. However, there are only so many hours that can be dedicated to studying new languages and maintaining old ones. Therefore, I would urge the part-time linguist to exercise discipline. Make a list of all the languages that potentially interest you, and narrow it down to three.

STRATEGIES FOR DIVERSIFICATION

How should you determine the languages on your list? There is a number of diversification strategies from which you can choose. You might decide to learn the languages of the countries that dominate your industry. For example, a person working in the automotive industry might first learn Japanese, then German, and then Korean. A similar strategy would be to look at the countries in which your company is most active. Are most of your employer's customers based in France, Germany, and Sweden? If so, then your future language studies are clearly mapped out for you.

Not everyone works in an industry or job where the choice is so obvious. There are other factors that you can use to decide. Many learners elect to study languages from the same family. If Spanish is your first foreign language, then you might opt for Italian and Portuguese as your second and third ones. (In fact, a person who speaks Spanish will understand a significant portion of Portuguese and Italian the first time she encounters them.) Other examples of closely related languages are Russian and Ukrainian, German and Dutch, Arabic and Hebrew, Thai and Lao, and Hindi and Urdu. If you first learn one of these languages, then you will have a significant head start when you begin the other one.

On the other hand, many serial language-learners crave diversity rather than familiar ground. After spending a year or two focused on Spanish, you might be anxious to step outside the provincial bounds of the Romance language family. For your next challenge, you may be ready for something entirely different, like Arabic or Chinese. A mastery over several languages that have no shared roots will give you wider geographic coverage, since languages with common roots are typically spoken in the same area.

THE FIRST ONE IS THE HARDEST

Language-learning is most difficult the first time around. Having gone through an entire lifetime communicating in only one language, some students have difficulty developing the second "channel" of thought and communication. The process becomes easier after the hurdle of the first foreign language is cleared. When you begin your second foreign language, you will have the advantage of the learning skills that you acquired while learning your first one. Although each foreign language is different, the learning process is very much the same each time around.

Moreover, beginning a second foreign language can actually help you to move past plateaus in the one you are currently studying. This notion seems counterintuitive—but it has proven true for me on a number of occasions, and others have reported similar results.

Here is how it works: suppose that you have been studying Spanish everyday for two years, and you now feel that you aren't making further progress. The solution—oddly enough—might be to pick up an introductory Russian course (assuming of course, that you want to learn Russian).

The first few chapters of your Russian course will give you a sense of the novelty that Spanish used to have. You will experience again the excitement of making initial strides in a language. The unfamiliarity of Russian will make you appreciate how much Spanish you have learned. Spanish will seem like an old friend. The result: you will be able to approach your Spanish studies with a renewed sense of enthusiasm.

A HARD ONE, THEN AN EASY ONE, THEN A HARD ONE

If you learn any of the hard languages (Chinese, Japanese, Korean, Arabic, Thai, etc.), make sure that you have really mastered the first language from this list before you attempt your second difficult language. If possible, stagger an easy language between the more difficult ones.

Suppose that your long-term goal is to learn Korean, Arabic, and Spanish, and you learn Korean first. After you have reached a basic level of competency in Korean, I would recommend that you make Spanish the second language that you study. Arabic and Korean are both among the world's most difficult languages. Therefore, you will likely appreciate taking a "breather" with a Romance language.

CHAPTER 17

LANGUAGE SKILLS AND YOUR CAREER

APPLYING LANGUAGE SKILLS IN SPECIFIC CAREERS

The average American will have an average of three to five distinct careers, and hold about ten to twelve jobs during his or her lifetime. You may already have an idea of how a foreign language could be useful in your current position. Nonetheless, if you are just getting started with languages, it may be helpful to examine how language skills are applicable in some other careers that you might be considering.

Sales

Many small- and medium-sized companies would like to expand into other markets, but they do not have the resources necessary to establish a branch office in another country. A sales professional with foreign language skills can be a valuable asset for such an organization. Often such individuals will be assigned a mixture of domestic and foreign accounts.

There is an especially high demand for bilingual salespeople among companies near the Mexican border. The economies of the Southwestern United States and Mexico are becoming increasingly intertwined. I was once recruited for a sales position with a machine tool distributor in Houston. The plan was for me to call on accounts in Texas, as well as customers in Mexico. (Interestingly, this distributor was also looking for a salesperson who spoke Vietnamese or Thai, given the high numbers of Southeast Asian immigrants in the Houston area.).

The only official language in Detroit, Michigan is English, but the presence of so many international automotive manufacturers in the area has created a demand for Japanese-, German-, and Korean-speaking sales representatives. Spanish is also becoming more important in the automotive fields.

180

If you would like to work in the international automotive industry but you don't want to move to Detroit, don't fret. There are internationally oriented opportunities elsewhere. Honda, a Japanese automaker, has plants in the United States, Canada, and Mexico. Toyota, the largest Japanese automobile manufacturer, is similarly spread out across North America, with plants in Kentucky, Alabama, Indiana, West Virginia, California, Ontario, and Tijuana.

Although the Japanese presence in the North American automobile industry receives the most attention, the Germans and the Koreans are also major international players. I recall several of my colleagues being recruited to work at the German-owned BMW plant in South Carolina in the early 1990s. Meanwhile, the Koreans are also building plants in the United States. Hyundai has recently constructed a plant in Alabama, where the company manufactures the popular Hyundai Sonata.

As foreign automakers continue to integrate into the American automobile industry, foreign suppliers are arriving as well. Japanese automotive components suppliers such as Nippon Denso, Yazaki, and Aisin all have well-established presences in North America. These companies are usually interested in both the Japanese transplant operations in North America (Honda, Toyota, and Nissan) as well as business opportunities with Ford, GM, and Daimler-Chrysler. If you speak Japanese and have a background in the automotive industry, you will surely be able to generate some interest among these companies.

Human Resources

In the age of the multinational corporation, human resources professionals need language skills to administer personnel policies and employee relations in overseas facilities. Standards regarding wages, work hours, and corporate hierarchy vary greatly between Europe, the United States, Latin America and Asia. Compared to his monolingual counterparts, the bilingual or multilingual human resources manager can more easily bring about a consensus in regard to these issues.

Human resources professionals who speak Spanish have especially strong prospects in California, Texas, and other states that have large Spanish-speaking populations. Moreover, the recent influx of guest workers from Mexico has heightened the demand for Spanish-speaking human

181

resources professionals throughout the country. Spanish-speaking human resources administrators are now sought in places where the demand did not exist ten years ago. I have recently come across ads seeking such individuals in Nashville, Cincinnati, and Milwaukee.

Law

There is a tremendous amount of disparity among the world's legal systems. While every country has laws against universal crimes such as theft and murder, we have yet to reach a global consensus in many areas of business law. What is perfectly legal in the United States may be forbidden in Japan, and what is accepted as a standard business practice in Japan may be forbidden under American law. In general, American business laws reflect a more laissez faire attitude than the rest of the world, but this is not always the case. For example, it is common in many countries for an employment ad to list age and gender requirements for a position. Such practices are forbidden under the laws of the United States.

Language skills give legal professionals the capability to research laws and case histories in non-English-speaking countries. Foreign language skills are also indispensable when dealing with government agencies throughout the world.

Purchasing

Selling your company's goods in other parts of the world is only one half of the international business equation. The global business environment favors national specialization. In certain industries, it will be highly probable that at least some of the equipment or production inputs that your company uses can be more economically purchased from vendors overseas.

Sometimes there is no choice. In certain technical fields, there are unique products that can only be purchased from South Korea, Japan, or Germany. In other situations, the labor-intensive nature of a production input requires that it be purchased from countries with lower manufacturing costs.

For manufacturing firms, sourcing and procurement involve extensive research and communications, which are difficult without proficiency in the local language. When a complex or mission-critical product is sourced, the supplier selection process often entails a lengthy period of evaluation. After a suitable supplier is selected, financial terms, shipping arrangements, and countless other details must be finalized.

If you are already a purchasing professional, then it would make sense to learn the language of a country in which a large percentage of your industry's inputs are manufactured. From a general perspective, the present growth of the manufacturing industries in Mexico and China make Spanish and Chinese solid language choices for purchasing agents and buyers.

Public Sector/U.S. Government

In recent years, government jobs have received renewed interest among professionals in the United States. The number of opportunities in the public sector has increased as well. Some of the fastest growing job categories in the public sector require language skills. In particular, there has been a marked increase in jobs related to law enforcement, intelligence gathering, and national defense. All of these job categories rely heavily on foreign languages.

According to a study conducted by the National Security Education Program (NSEP), "Analysis of Federal Language Needs," the need for language specialists in defense-related federal agencies has grown particularly acute in recent years:

> *"There is little debate that the era of globalization has brought increasingly diverse and complex challenges to U.S. national security. With these challenges comes a rapidly increasing need for a workforce with skills that address these needs, including professional expertise accompanied by the ability to communicate and understand the languages and cultures of key world regions: Russia and the former Soviet Union, China, the Arab world, Iran, Korea, Central Asia and key countries in Africa, Latin America and East Asia.*

Some 80 federal agencies and offices involved in areas related to U.S. national security rely increasingly on human resources with high levels of language competency and international knowledge and experience. Finding these resources and, in particular, finding candidates for employment as professionals in the U.S. Government, has proven increasingly difficult, and many agencies now report shortfalls in hiring, deficits in readiness, and adverse impacts on operations."
(Source: National Security Education Program (NSEP) Analysis of Federal Language Needs)

The U.S. federal government even founded a special NSEP scholarship program in the early 1990s in response to the problem. NSEP scholarships are awarded to university-level students to *"study those languages and cultures critical to U.S. national security"*.

The agencies with the strongest demand for language skills include the U.S. Customs Service, the Central Intelligence Agency, the FBI, the U.S. Secret Service, and the Drug Enforcement Agency. If you are interested in something even more adventurous, there is also a need for language specialists to work with the U.S. Coast Guard Intelligence Service. In conducting its annual survey of government-related language needs, the NSEP received some revealing feedback from Coast Guard Intelligence Service officials. The following comments describe the negative impact resulting from a shortage of qualified language specialists aboard Coast Guard vessels:

"lack of interpreters in Chinese, Russian, Polish, Japanese and Korean curtail any intelligence gathering which is critical to success of mission".... *"lack of interpreter reduced quality of right of approach questions"... "never determined nationality due to lack of interpreter"... "heavy workload for 2 Spanish speakers during two intense patrols; multiple daily interactions with immigrants"... "delay attributed to availability of interpreter being ashore and underway"..."Lack of Japanese interpreter resulted in no radio communications"*
(Source: NSEP)

Information Technology

The demand for IT professionals with foreign language skills has increased markedly in the past decade. The reason is the changing nature of the IT project market. Whereas the United States was once the singular destination for IT work, the demand for IT services has been expanding to the non-English speaking world. Europe, Japan, and Asia are just a few of the markets that increasingly require IT expertise.

Computer programmers and other technical workers will always be evaluated first on their technical knowledge. However, communication skills are also important. In order to properly design, program, and maintain solutions, IT professionals must be able to interact effectively with end users. In many cases, these end users don't speak English.

In IT project work, the program code itself requires relatively little translation, but language skills are frequently necessary in order to clarify business objectives and end user expectations. Someone must bridge the gap between the user who is expecting a particular level of functionality, and the Java programmer who must make the functionality happen. A large number of IT projects seem to fail because user expectations are not fully clarified. This risk is further increased when a language barrier is present.

I have experienced firsthand the role that language plays in a large IT project. During my employment at a large Japanese company, I worked on a major IT application development project with a team of American and Japanese programmers. On top of this, our end users spoke not only English and Japanese, but Spanish and French as well.

If you already have strong IT skills, then you can make yourself doubly valuable by adding language skills to your resume. As the IT industry becomes more and more competitive, "multiskilling" is a new buzzword for techies. Previously, it was standard practice for international IT consulting firms to hire separate individuals to fulfill linguistic and programming functions. Now, however, tighter deadlines and slimmer budgets have forced these companies to seek more programmers who can also speak foreign languages.

LANGUAGE SKILLS AND YOUR RESUME

In order to land a better job with your language skills, you must first make potential employers aware of your skills. This naturally leads to another question: How should you describe your language skills on your resume?

Most resumes are divided into standard sections, such as "Experience", "Education", etc. Near the bottom of your resume, you should have a section entitled "Language Skills." In this area, you will list the languages which you have studied, and your degree of accomplishment in each one. A sample "Language Skills" section might look like this:

Language Skills:

> Spanish: Extremely proficient in the written and spoken language. In my current position, I utilize Spanish daily to conduct business and technical discussions.

> German: Advanced proficiency in spoken and written German. I frequently utilize German to analyze product specifications from my company's European suppliers.

> French: Basic conversational skills and reading ability. I often travel to France to visit suppliers and attend key meetings.

As you can see, I prefer the term "extremely proficient" instead of the word "fluent" to describe your skills in a foreign language that you have truly mastered. To many readers, "fluent" applies only to a native speaker. The term "extremely proficient" informs the potential employer that you are *functionally* fluent in a language without making a claim to *native* fluency.

The above resume excerpt indicates that the applicant has extremely advanced skills in Spanish, moderately advanced skills in German, and basic skills in French. Always list your languages in the order of descending skill level. It is okay to list a language in which you presently have only basic skills. Just be sure that your resume does not overstate your abilities. At some point, you will be asked to demonstrate your proficiency in the language. (In most of my past positions, a native speaker of at least one of the languages I had listed was present in the interview.) Therefore, exaggerating your abilities is not to your advantage in the long run.

Notice also that I have listed at least one business function which the applicant is presently preforming with each language. She uses spoken and written Spanish as an integral part of her job. She uses her German reading skills to analyze product specifications. Even her basic French presumably comes in handy when she travels to France on business trips. It is important for you to explain how your language skills have made you a more effective professional.

You can also work your foreign language skills into the "objective" or "mission statement" that you place near the top of the resume:

> *"Seeking a challenging position in operations management, utilizing extensive global project management experience, and advanced Japanese and French language skills."*

> *"High volume industrial sales specialist, specializing in the Latin American market. Extremely proficient in Spanish and Portuguese."*

OPPORTUNITIES TO WORK OVERSEAS

Do you want to do more than just take an occasional business trip to a foreign country? Would you be interested in living in Asia, Europe, or elsewhere for an extended assignment of one, two, or three years?

There are four basic paths to acquiring an overseas position. Each option requires a slightly different level of skills, experience, and commitment:

Path #1: Find a job that involves immediate placement in an overseas position.

Multinational corporations sometimes open overseas positions to outside candidates. On Monster.com, I recently saw several positions that offered immediate assignments in Russia, Japan, and several European countries. If it is your desire to find an immediate overseas position in a professional field, it can be done.

These jobs are usually at the high end of the seniority and salary range. Therefore, the educational and experience requirements for these positions are typically quite stringent. If, however, you are a seasoned professional with a master's degree or two, you might be able to take this route.

Path #2: Take a job with a company based in your own country, with the plan of negotiating a later transfer to an overseas division.

There are numerous U.S. firms with overseas plants and branch offices. In addition to the better known companies like General Electric and Procter & Gamble, there are hundreds of lesser known American companies that have established foreign subsidiaries. I have a friend who is an engineer at an American medical technology firm. In the past three years, he has been offered opportunities to transfer to Germany, Japan, and China.

If you pursue this route, plan on two to three years of paying your dues in a key functional area within the company before getting a chance to transfer outside the United States. As a general rule, American companies only offer overseas opportunities to employees who have demonstrated their competency in a specific field (marketing, finance, engineering, etc.)

Path #3: Take a job with the American branch of a foreign company, with the expectation that you will have a chance at an extended assignment in the overseas headquarters.

Most of the Americans I know who have actually worked overseas have followed this route. If you are hired in the United States by Toyota, Honda, Bosch, etc., there is a reasonable chance that you will have an opportunity to work at their headquarters for an extended period.

As noted above, most of the Americans sent overseas by U.S. companies are senior managers. There are relatively fewer expatriate opportunities for employees just a few years out of college. Conversely, companies like Honda and Toyota send a large number of junior American employees to Japan for training. Although many of these trips involve one- to four-week stays, one- and two-year assignments are not uncommon.

If you go overseas as the employee of a foreign company, you will have a unique opportunity to immerse yourself in the culture. Almost all of your colleagues will be citizens of the foreign country, so you should have plenty of time to develop and hone your language skills.

When I made my first extended visit to Japan as the employee of a Japanese automotive components firm, I was the only American on the trip. While this type of experience offers true immersion in another culture, it also requires substantial flexibility.

Path #4: Take an overseas job teaching English, then start or continue your "professional" career later.

In most of the world's countries where English is not the primary language, it is possible for a native speaker of English with a four-year college degree to secure a one- or two-year position as an English teacher. This teaching position may be with a private firm that offers English lessons to corporate employees, or it may be a teaching job within the national school system.

I have met Americans who have taught English in Taiwan, Japan, South Korea, and Germany. All of them seemed to have enjoyed the experience, and many used their time on the ground to further their studies of the given country's language. This may be the perfect opportunity for you if you have not yet begun your primary professional career, or if you would like to take a year or two off. However, there are some caveats to consider.

First of all, these jobs are notoriously low-paying. In Japan, for example, the typical applicant is a fresh liberal arts graduate who just wants to spend a year in Japan. During my senior year in college, I seriously investigated several English teaching jobs in Japan, but abandoned the idea when I saw the bottom line. One private English school owner summed it up to me like this: "You're not going to get rich teaching English in Japan."

In addition, the time you spend teaching English overseas will be of little value on your resume if your ultimate goal is to be a marketing manager or an accountant. If you are right out of college, then this might not be a major consideration. More experienced professionals should think long and hard before they take this route.

TRANSLATING AND INTERPRETING

If you discover that you really love languages and you want to make them the focus of your career, rather than simply an added dimension of your resume, then the translator/interpreter field may be for you. I spent a number of years working in this area, both as a freelancer, as well as in a regular salaried capacity. The following observations may be helpful if you are considering this option:

Observation#1: The translation and interpreting field offers the best opportunities for those who are willing to work as freelancers and independent contractors.

In *Free Agent Nation* (Warner Books, 2001), Daniel H. Pink describes the phenomenon of the independent worker, "*someone who works for herself, generally alone, moving from project to project and selling her services.*" *Free Agent Nation* offers hope to those who would like to do serious work without becoming entrenched in the corporate lifestyle, complete with redundant meetings, office politics, and the company picnic.

In mainstream career paths, however, there are still some practical impediments to working as a pure freelancer at most companies. Traditional corporate roles such as sales, production control, purchasing, and accounting require extensive daily involvement within the organization. There is a constant need to attend meetings, huddle with the team, and go on business trips. Therefore, regular, onsite corporate membership is more or less a requirement.

Translation is different. Companies view translation as a temporary, provisional function. If a chemical firm plans to expand into non-English-speaking markets, no one in the boardroom says, "Let's create a translation department." Instead they say, "Let's outsource our translation needs to a dependable outside contractor."

It is often possible for a translator to complete an assignment for a company without making even a single visit to the firm's office. Email, fax machines, and courier services are more than adequate for transferring the source documents and the completed translations.

Although interpreting services are usually performed onsite, companies tend to have a similar attitude of "temporariness" about them—

even if the services continue for years. The typical scenario is this: an American manufacturer has entered into a joint venture with a Japanese firm. A team of Japanese engineers is going to be sent to the American company's headquarters for eighteen months to work on the project. The American company therefore wants to hire several translator/interpreters to work for the duration of the project—but no longer.

This gives the ambitious freelancer an attractive proposition: she can build a network of clients, and work for several companies at once. To a large extent, she will be able to determine the type of work she wants to accept, and set her own hours.

Technology has also changed the translation field. When I was working as a freelance Japanese translator/interpreter, I had to rely on a small network of individuals whom I had met through organizations like the Japan-America Society, etc. Today, translator/interpreters can ply their trade on the web, selling their services to clients worldwide.

Observation#2: Translation and Interpreting Do Not Pave the Way Up the Corporate Ladder.

There is, of course, a downside to the freelance nature of translation work—if you are addicted to the notion of an extended career with a single employer. Those who need to measure their progress on the corporate ladder, through a series of predictable promotions, and five- and ten-year gold watches, should think twice before becoming translator/interpreters.

When I was hired as an in-house translator/interpreter for a Japanese die casting company in central Ohio, I was told at the outset that my days were numbered. "We anticipate that we'll need you for around two, maybe three years," the human resources manager told me. "After that, our need may go away, and we'll have no choice but to let you go."

As it turned out, I ended up transitioning into a sales position, so the company never laid me off—but the story is nonetheless illustrative of the perils faced by those who want a traditional "career track" as a translator/interpreter. The only exceptions to this rule that I have seen exist at the very large multinational corporations such as Honda and Toyota, which constantly rotate new foreign employees to North America. I know of a woman who has worked at Honda as an in-house interpreter/translator for a number of years. Her position is presently quite secure, and it should

191

remain so in the foreseeable future. But she is an exception to the industry rule.

Even the in-house translators who remain employed with a single company face a very low glass ceiling. The corporate ladder is climbed by moving into the ranks of management, and you can't move into management as a translator. It just doesn't happen. This is not because there is a conspiracy in the corporate world against translators and interpreters. This is simply because a position such as "Vice President of Translation" isn't part of the game plan at most companies.

Obeservation#3: The Most Successful Interpreter/Translators Also Specialize in a Non-Language Area.

Remember how I admonished accountants and computer programmers to learn foreign languages in an earlier chapter? Well, here I am going to mention an important point that many translator/interpreters ignore: language by itself isn't enough. If you want to become a top-notch language professional in the translation field, then you have to become acquainted with something *other* than language.

Any person who knows two languages well can readily translate or interpret non-specialized content. However, very few customers hire a language specialist to handle general conversations or personal correspondence. In most cases, translators and interpreters are contracted for communications that involve business and technical matters.

This means that as an interpreter/translator, you will have to understand a lot of industry-specific terms and concepts. Suppose that you have been hired, for example, to interpret a discussion about a chemical process. You should be able to speak comfortably about valences, bonds, and atomic weights—in the foreign language as well as in your native tongue. This does not mean that a translator or interpreter working in the chemical industry would necessarily have to have a formal degree in Chemistry (although it would certainly be an advantage); but such an individual would need more than the smattering of basic concepts that most of us remember from high school.

Of course, there are only so many areas in which you can acquire true expertise. No one can master every subject. Therefore, the most successful linguists focus on a few closely related niches. If you are business-oriented, then you could specialize in translating and interpreting in the finance, banking, and insurance sectors. Alternatively, you might combine manufacturing, quality control, and industrial materials. The key is to select a small group of areas that form a logical combination.

Some novice translators and interpreters list every specialty under the sun in their online profiles and resumes. I recently came across the website of a translator who claimed to specialize in engineering, law, finance, the chemical industry, automotive manufacturing, and insurance. (And this translator had only a few years of experience.) He would have been far more credible if he had claimed expertise in only one or two of these areas.

CHAPTER 18

"BUT THEY INSIST ON SPEAKING ENGLISH WITH ME!"

"I get really annoyed when the assumption is made that I can't speak Mandarin... I find it extremely tedious to try and drudge through a conversation in stilted English when I can communicate quite well in Mandarin... I will also gladly speak English with those whose English is better than my Chinese. But otherwise ... I'm living in China, ya know?"

- Internet posting by a Westerner living in China (www.chinese-forums.com)

STRANGE FOREIGNERS AND FOREIGN DEVILS

There is a Chinese proverb which goes, *"Tian bu pa, di bu pa, jiu pa yangguizi shuo Zhongguohua."* ("Don't fear heaven, don't fear earth. Fear foreign devils who speak Chinese.") Similar sentiments have been expressed in Japan. During the postwar years, the term *"hen na gaijin"* was the label for a "strange foreigner" who spoke fluent Japanese, and understood the ins and outs of Japanese culture.

A group can be effectively isolated by a lack of language skills. Some governments have gone so far as to make the linguistic isolation of foreigners the law of the land. In nineteenth century China and Japan, Europeans were forbidden by law from learning the local languages. The feudal rulers in East Asia during this era saw European culture as a dangerous cultural and political influence. If Europeans could not communicate freely, then their power to corrupt would be minimal.

I am not aware of any twenty-first century laws that forbid English-speakers from learning a particular language. But not everyone is eager to see American businesspersons become accomplished linguists. In fact, some individuals would regard a widespread increase in American foreign-language fluency as a distinctly unwelcome development.

The vast majority of people you meet will appreciate your efforts to communicate in their language (especially after you become good at it); but there are exceptions. You will occasionally be puzzled by native speakers who seem to regard your interest in their language as irrelevant, annoying, or even threatening.

There are a handful of reasons why these attitudes exist. Some are based in cultural inferiority complexes, ethnic biases, and economic self-interest. Others are more innocent. In any case, you may one day be disturbed when a native speaker of your target language insists on speaking English with you despite your insistent efforts to converse in Japanese/French/etc. It is therefore beneficial for you to know where these people are coming from, and what motivates them.

WORK-RELATED/ECONOMIC SELF-INTEREST

Remember "the tiny superstar subset" described in the previous chapter about foreign languages and the business world? Let's suppose now that you are a German-speaking member of this elite group. You went through the trouble and expense of attending law school in the United States, and you are now working as an attorney for a prestigious law firm in Chicago. You were hired largely because the firm wants to take advantage of your German language skills to expand its business in Europe. Your abilities as a bilingual speaker of German and English have enabled you to cultivate a niche within the organization. You can do what no one else in the firm can do: communicate with German clients in their own language.

Now suddenly one of your American-born colleagues (who is also a competitor for promotions, high-profile assignments, etc.) begins brushing up on the German she studied in high school and college. At first you might not regard this as a threat. Your experience in the United States tells you that while many Americans dabble in foreign languages, few actually master any language but English. When she greets you one morning with a *Wie geht's?*—you chuckle appreciatively and tell her that you're fine, thanks—responding in English.

Then one day you overhear her speaking German on the telephone. Her German is still not quite as good as your English, but she is holding her own in the language which (until now) was your exclusive domain within the firm. Is this a new trend? Are any of your other American colleagues learning German?

195

You notice that one of the firm's partners who happened to be in the area is also listening. "Hey," he says aloud. "I didn't know this firm had *two* attorneys who speak German." He smiles at you and gestures at your American colleague who is speaking German. You smile and nod your head, but your heart isn't in the gesture. Your competitive advantage has just been seriously undermined.

As mentioned elsewhere in this book, the "tiny superstar subset" of foreign-born, bilingual professionals has had to cope with very little competition from native English-speakers until now. Many have made significant investments of time and money in staking out their niche as the intermediaries between the English-speaking and the non-English-speaking world. Simple human nature suggests that this group is going to be less than thrilled to see their American colleagues (who were formerly reliant on them) begin mastering foreign languages. Most people don't go out of their way to encourage potential competitors.

A disclaimer is in order here: many educated foreigners will go out of their way to help an English-speaker who is learning their language. There is no mass conspiracy among the foreign-born, educated elite. The above scenario is most common in organizational settings in which skills in a particular language are linked to career advancement. These are the same competitive pressures that create dog-eat-dog mindsets among professionals of all stripes.

CULTURAL BIASES

> *"I'm now in Vietnam and I can say I'm still learning Vietnamese too, many Vietnamese are willing to talk to me in their language, but many, especially those in the tourism industry aren't. I don't mind, and never get annoyed if they could pass their meaning to me effectively, I just insist to talk to them in Vietnamese, and some other friends (foreigners) found it funny to see me talking in Vietnamese, while the Vietnamese guy was talking in English."*

- Internet posting by a Westerner living in Vietnam (www.chinese-forums.com)

In my experience, native speakers of European languages (Spanish-, French-etc.) are almost always pleased when an American demonstrates an ability to speak their language. If you greet a Spanish-speaker with a few words of her

196

language, she will likely assume that you are fluent and begin rattling off in Spanish to you as if you were her next door neighbor in Mexico. (Spanish speakers are especially tolerant of the foreigner who puts forth a valiant if imperfect effort.)

Students of Asian languages seem to encounter the most frustration when trying to demonstrate their skills. Some even suspect a conspiracy. As one American writing online complained:

> *"I think from a Japanese perspective they don't want non-Japanese to really know and understand their language....its something important about having your knowledge/language a secret while knowing others..."*
> -Japan-Guide.com forum

There is a long tradition of mutual language learning among European societies; but the Westerner who speaks Chinese, Japanese, or Korean is still a relative novelty. Asian languages have not been internationalized to the extent that other languages have been. French, for example, is the language of Africans, Europeans, and Asians. English, Spanish, and Portuguese are also spoken by ethnically diverse peoples who live in many countries. Korean, Japanese, Chinese, and Vietnamese, by contrast, are largely limited to the original ethnic speakers of these languages. Therefore, the Westerner who speaks Korean is statistically "unusual," while the Westerner who speaks both English and French is not.

Despite the recent prominence of English, European languages have a long history of parity. The balance of linguistic power has shifted numerous times in Europe. France, Germany, and Spain still regard their languages as major forces in the world; and the European Union is formally committed to preserving linguistic equality. Both France and Germany have official agencies dedicated to the international dissemination of their languages.

Until very recently, however, linguistic interactions between Asians and Westerners occurred in the context of unequal relationships. Malaysia, Vietnam, Indonesia, Singapore, India, the Philippines, and parts of China were all colonies of European countries at some point during the nineteenth and/or twentieth centuries. In the context of colonial rule, language transfer occurred in a single direction: the Vietnamese learned French, the Indians learned English, etc. Although resentment lingers over colonialism, some

Asians still regard this one-way linguistic transfer as the natural state of affairs. But attitudes in Asia are changing.

JAPAN LOOKS WEST

Japan is a country that has long straddled the divide between East and West; and it provides an illustrative example of the cultural and linguistic ambivalence that exists in much of Asia. Japanese attitudes about Western culture have ranged from fanatical loathing to an equally fanatical embrace. These shifts have followed larger social and political trends, and they resonate in contemporary Japanese attitudes about English, and the global role of their own language.

The "Southern Barbarians"

During the 1500s, Christian missionaries from Europe arrived in Japan, where they built schools, churches, and monasteries to spread the Christian religion. Simultaneously, Portuguese, Dutch, and British traders landed on the Japanese islands and established commercial relationships with Japanese merchants.

Although the overall European presence was relatively small, the Western influence in Japan was growing. The Japanese referred to the visitors as 南蛮 (*nanban*), or "Southern barbarians," since the first European ships arrived from the south. Early Christian literature in Japan was called 南蛮文学(*nanban-bungaku*), or "barbarian literature." There was deep ambivalence about these hairy barbarians in Japanese society. Some people wanted to imitate them; others wanted to expel them.

The faction that wanted to expel the barbarians took control in the early seventeenth century. Japan was unified under the powerful Tokugawa Shogunate, or military government, in 1603. The new administration was especially concerned about the ill effects of Christianization. There were widespread persecutions of Christian converts; and by 1650 Christianity was all but eradicated from Japan. To vaccinate the country from further Western influences, a series of laws was passed that severely restricted the movements of Europeans. The European presence was limited to a small commercial establishment on an island near the port city of Nagasaki. This

198

arrangement was deemed acceptable because the barbarians were technically not living on Japanese soil.

Japan Reopens to the West

In 1853, Admiral Matthew C. Perry sailed into Tokyo Bay with a flotilla of U.S. warships and informed the Japanese government that the period of isolation was now over. The Japanese had been isolated for two hundred years, and they had no contingency plans for dealing with an invasion of technologically superior foreign forces. Under duress the Japanese government signed the Treaty of Kanagawa, which gave the Americans the right to trade and establish a consulate.

Paintings of the early Tokugawa rulers invariably depict the shoguns in traditional Japanese garb. The last Tokugawa shogun, Tokugawa Yoshinobu, posed for cameras in a nineteenth century-style European military uniform, complete with knee boots and epaulets. Japan was on the verge of another period of epochal change. During the last years of Tokugawa rule, contacts with Westerners increased, and the idea of permanent isolation was gradually abandoned.

Tokugawa rule ended in 1867. By 1868, Japan was under the rule of the Meiji Emperor, and an era of almost frantic Westernization began. The Japanese now realized that national survival depended on competing with the Western powers on their own terms, while still preserving the unique aspects of Japanese culture. The slogan of the day was 和魂洋才 (*wakon-yoosai*), or "Japanese learning, Western spirit."

Some erudite Japanese began a debate about the true essence of the "Japanese spirit." In previous centuries, the Japanese had borrowed heavily from their Asian neighbors. The kanji characters used in the Japanese written language, for example, were originally copied from the Chinese language and modified to fit the Japanese phonetic system. China had always been the foreign culture that the Japanese were most likely to imitate.

In the mid-nineteenth century, however, China was in decline. Great Britain had defeated the country in two wars fought over the opium trade. The British and other European powers were now carving China up into colonial possessions. China (and by extension, the rest of Asia) was no longer worthy of emulation. The Western countries were the new powers in the world. The Japanese expression 脱亜入欧 (*datsu-a-nyuu-oo*) means

199

"leave Asia and join Europe." This phrase became synonymous with the country's drive to modernize and catch up with the West.

Some Japanese intellectuals argued that Japan should adopt a Western language to make the transformation to modernity complete. Proposals were put forth to replace the Japanese language with French, German, Dutch, or English. None of these plans ever gained much momentum; but the psychological link between Western languages and modernization would be a recurrent theme in Japan's collective psyche.

Japan Becomes a Military Power

When feudal Japanese samurai warriors first encountered European firearms in the 1500s, they regarded the weapons as cowardly. The idea of killing an enemy from afar with a technologically advanced weapon violated the warrior's code of 武士道 (*bushidoo*), which emphasized ritualized, man-to-man combat.

By the late 1800s, however, Japan was focused on building a strong industrial economy that could supply the warships, cannons, and rifles needed to equip a modern military. The notion of 富国強兵 (*fukoku-kyoohei*)—"rich country, strong army"—emphasized the link between industrial and military might. In 1905, half a century after Admiral Perry forced Japan to open its doors, Japan put the West on notice by defeating Russia in the Russo-Japanese War. The subsequent Treaty of Portsmouth gave Japan domination over Korea, and possession of the southern half of the Northern Pacific island of Sakhalin. In World War I, Japan fought on the side of the Allies, and was the only Asian nation present at the Versailles Peace Conference.

The drive to create a new Japan modeled on the West did not stop with factories and warships. Japanese young people of the early twentieth century were also fascinated by the idea of Westernization; and America's budding youth culture reached Japanese shores in the era between the two World Wars. During the Jazz Age of the 1920s, young women in Japan wore bobbed hairstyles, and bands played trendy American music in Tokyo dance halls. English slang words from American movies began to pepper the speech of the more cosmopolitan Japanese. The term モー・ガー (moo-gaa), or "modern girl" described a Japanese woman who wore makeup and espoused non-traditional views, in imitation of the American "flappers."

The Japanese were once again actively importing foreign culture, as they had when the Southern Barbarians landed on the islands in the 1500s. And once again, there would be a backlash from Japan's more reactionary forces.

The Japanese Language During and After World War II

The Greater East Asia Co-Prosperity Sphere (大東亜共栄圏 *Dai-Too-A-Kyooei-ken*) was the name the Japanese gave to their empire in the Pacific. Beginning in 1894, with the Japan-Qing War (日清戦争 *Nisshin Sensoo*), Japan forged an empire that stretched throughout much of Asia.

The official language of the Greater East Asia Co-Prosperity Sphere was Japanese. Japanese became the language of administration, and it was mandatory in most schools. The legacy of this policy can be seen today in the many Korean, Taiwanese, and Filipino senior citizens who speak Japanese. Gone was the talk of replacing the Japanese language with a Western tongue. I once read an account of a Japanese soldier who used the pages of an English dictionary to make cigarette papers, based on his confidence in Japan's impending military and cultural triumph.

This sense of hubris was not to last. Within a few short years, Japanese attitudes about language would swing yet again in the opposite direction.

The Occupation Years and Beyond

Following her defeat in World War II, Japan was forced to accept a period of formal occupation by a Western army. Thousands of American troops were stationed in the country, and an American military government wielded more or less absolute power over all social, political, and economic institutions.

General Douglas MacArthur's SCAP bureaucracy (SCAP was an acronym for Supreme Command for the Allied Powers) remade Japanese society from the ground up. SCAP officials redistributed land, rewrote school textbooks, and censored newspapers. No significant aspect of Japanese life was left untouched by the post-World War II Allied Occupation that lasted from 1945 to 1952.

Japan's postwar period of forced Americanization was viewed ambivalently by the Japanese themselves. On one hand, most Japanese acknowledged that the country's military leaders had led them to ruin. Many Japanese eagerly embraced the new relationship with America; and General MacArthur himself became a demigod of sorts in Japan. When the general briefly considered a run for the White House in 1948, Japanese storekeepers adorned their windows with signs expressing support for his Presidential bid. Throughout the Occupation, MacArthur's office received a daily flood of cards, letters, and gifts from average Japanese citizens.

The Occupation had an impact on Japanese attitudes about language. In the 1930s and 1940s, Japan had forced the Asian peoples that it conquered to learn Japanese. English was disdained as the language of the Anglo-American enemy. Now, however, the Japanese were eager to learn English. An English language phrasebook published immediately after the war sold 3.5 million copies. The book, 日米会話手帳 (*Nichi-Bei Kaiwa Techoo*), or *Japanese-American Conversation Manual*, held the record as the bestselling book in Japanese history until 1981.

Nonetheless, mixed feelings about the Americans persisted. The Occupation was a source of humiliation, and the immediate postwar years were accompanied by extreme economic privations. Desperation led to widespread crime and corruption. The country seemed overrun by black marketeers, prostitutes, criminal gangs—and Americans. Most American Occupation forces behaved honorably; but those who did commit rapes, assaults, and murders were tried by the U.S. military government—not Japanese courts.

The Westernization of the Meiji Era had been championed by the Japanese themselves. The Occupation was a forced exercise in Westernization at the hands of the American war victors. The situation led to a national identity crisis—which persists to this day.

MacArthur himself ultimately disappointed the Japanese when he returned from Japan in 1951. Speaking before a joint session of the U.S. Congress, MacArthur said that the Germans were more guilty for their wartime aggressions because they were "quite as mature as we [the Americans] were." He then asserted that the Japanese "by the standards of modern civilization...would be like a boy of twelve."

MacArthur's disparaging comparison was of course reported in Japan, where it aroused disappointment and a reappraisal of the new relationship with America. Writing in *Embracing Defeat: Japan in the Wake of World War II* (W.W. Norton & Company, Inc. 1999), author John W. Dower describes how the Japanese received MacArthur's words as "*a slap in the face..[that] awakened people to how they had snuggled up to the conqueror. Suddenly, many felt unaccountably ashamed."*

The legacy of the Occupation years is a Japan that feels a lingering inferiority complex toward America. The established Japanese intelligentsia delights in using English loanwords, and lecturing the Japanese people about the inferiority of their own culture. In popular culture, there is a near obsession with "foreigners." In a country where nearly everyone is of Asian descent, Caucasian fashion models occupy a disproportionately high percentage of magazine ads and television commercials.

In a recent edition of the online version of *Japan Today*, a journalist went out into the streets and asked random young people, "What is the best way to make foreign friends?" American youths would likely be puzzled at the premise of the question itself, but the Japanese responses were very practical, indicating that many of the young people had actually given the issue considerable thought: "One of my friends has foreign friends, but I do not. I don't know the best way to go about it..."said one young man. One respondent was a particularly gregarious young woman who claimed to "have many foreign friends" She revealed that, "when I was on the train, I saw a foreign lady who was reading an English town magazine, which included event info from my college. So I invited her to the event."

At the same time, the anniversaries of the bombings of Hiroshima, Nagasaki, and the Tokyo firebombing (a lesser known conventional air attack that killed 100,000 civilians during World War II) bring newspaper editorials about the dark legacy of American militarism. And ads that display foreign models often run alongside articles that decry the violence, corruption, and superficial values of the United States. Books written for Japanese businesspersons routinely describe American employees as egotistical, unwilling to make sacrifices for the group, and "not as disciplined as Japanese workers."

In 1990, when Japanese economic growth was the strongest in the world, Japan Diet member Shintaro Ishihara's controversial book, *The Japan that Can Say No* made news on both sides of the Pacific. Shintaro's book was filled with a series of bold claims that called out for media attention. At a time when a decorated World War II veteran occupied the White House, Shintaro drudged up an old grievance from 1945: he alleged that racism had compelled the United States to drop atomic bombs on Japan rather than on Germany. The author further stated that Japan could swing the balance of power in the waning Cold War by supplying the Soviet Union with advanced microchip technology.

In 1991, two American authors reacted to the new Japanese spirit of self-assertion. *The Coming War with Japan* (Saint Martins Press) proposed a doomsday scenario that bore rough similarities to the events of the late 1930s: America and Japan would become rivals for raw materials and markets in Asia, leading to an inevitable collision course. Although the predictions contained in the book turned out to be dead wrong, authors George Friedman and Meredith Lebard presented a studiously crafted scenario that seemed [remotely] possible at the time.

Speculations of open conflict between the United States and Japan were quashed by a Japanese economic slowdown during the mid-1990s, and a series of global concerns that gave new relevance to the Japan-America alliance: North Korean nukes, an increasingly aggressive China, and Middle Eastern terrorism. Nonetheless, the attention showered for a brief period on the books written by Shintaro, Friedman, and Lebard casts light on the ambivalence and tensions that simmer just beneath the surface of one of the strongest alliances in the world. The generation that actually fought World War II is passing into history, but many Japanese alive today can still remember the Occupation years. Many more have heard second-hand accounts from their parents and grandparents. The uneasy sentiments of those years continue to affect Japanese attitudes.

Add to this mix the fact that the Japanese historically take pride in the "uniqueness" of their own culture. Japanese linguistics professors and sociologists frequently write about how "difficult" and "unique" the Japanese language is: No foreigner could possibly learn it. Some pseudo-scientific but popular books have even argued that there are biological links between Japanese ethnicity and Japanese language skills.

The result is the *hen na gaijin* ("strange foreigner") complex mentioned at the start of this chapter. When an American does demonstrate real ability in Japanese, some native speakers of the language interpret this as a challenge of sorts. First, the American has proved that the Japanese language is just another language that anyone with the right tools and motivations can master. Secondly, the American has reduced her reliance on the more cultured Japanese who have mastered English.

Needless to say, the "strange foreigner" complex relies on a blatant double standard. There is no equivalent of the appellation that can be turned around on the Japanese. Japanese who study in the United States and master

English are referred to as *kokusai-ka* ("internationalists") and not "strange Japanese".

SLASHING TONGUES IN SOUTH KOREA

South Korea was never conquered by American forces, but the small Asian nation has been forced to rely on American military might because of the nearby North Korean threat. Troop levels have been reduced in recent years, but America continues to maintain a controversial military presence in the country. Protesting this presence has been a right of passage for South Korean college students for several generations. Every year, South Korean riot police clash with angry students who demand the ouster of the American military.

At the same time, South Korea is home to almost slavish attempts to "Americanize." In 2003, Western news media reported that some South Korean parents were subjecting their children to a bizarre operation in the hopes of giving them the ability to speak English without a Korean accent. The surgery, called a frenotomy, involves the removal of a small portion of the frenulum (the tissue which links the tongue to the base of the mouth). This is supposed to resolve difficulties when pronouncing a foreign language.

Just as some Japanese believe that only an ethnic Japanese can (or should) learn the Japanese language, some South Koreans seem determined to link English language fluency to biological factors. The parents who pay for the frenotomies neglect to consider that Korean children who are adopted by parents in the United States speak English as naturally as native-born Americans of any other ethnicity.

Secondly (and perhaps more importantly) why should the presence of a Korean accent provoke such a severe inferiority complex? After all, the American who masters Korean will surely speak the language with at least a trace of a foreign accent. And Korean adoptees raised in America have as much trouble with the Korean language as Americans of other ethnicities.

*　　*　　*

The attitudes described above represent extreme viewpoints, and should not be taken as indictments of entire Asian societies. While some of these examples may strike you as eccentric or even racist, remember that cultural biases and prejudices also exist in Western societies. In Asia—as in the

205

West—the extremes represent only one end of the continuum. The average Japanese does not think that the foreigner who speaks his language is an oddball or a threat. And the vast majority of Korean parents do not subject their children to unnecessary frenotomies.

Asia is now establishing an identity of its own (versus an identity defined in opposition to or in imitation of the West). As this process continues, the more extreme Asian viewpoints regarding language will pass into history. In the meantime, smile patiently when a Japanese refers to you as a "strange foreigner" because you speak passable Japanese.

ARE YOUR ABILITIES IN THE LANGUAGE UP TO PAR?

This chapter opens with a quote from an American who was annoyed when Chinese speakers ignored his proficient Mandarin—and insisted on conversing with him in broken English. It is possible for us to come across as equally boorish when we are too insistent on using our broken Spanish or Thai. This is especially true when the other party really has mastered English.

Writing in *How to Learn Any Language* (Citadel Press, 1991), author and syndicated radio host Barry Farber noted that while a European would be extremely reticent to speak a language that he didn't know well, Americans can be very extroverted with even the most basic language skills. As Farber puts it, *"Give an American a word in another language and he's in action...Give him five phrases and he's dangerous."*

Our collective tendency to give our language skills the benefit of the doubt is a double-edged sword. When you use your language skills, you reinforce what you already know and expand your knowledge. Therefore, the "extroversion" of American language students is fundamentally an advantage. Nonetheless, this gregariousness should be tempered with an appropriate dose of humility during the early stages of learning. In other words, don't force a busy stranger to stumble through a difficult conversation with you in broken Italian if she speaks fluent English.

SOMETIMES THE PERSON SPEAKING ENGLISH TO YOU IS SIMPLY TRYING TO BE HELPFUL

Many (unfortunately, most) English-speakers who travel abroad have no interest in learning other languages. These monolingual travelers are delighted to encounter foreigners who can speak English. In the overseas tourism industry, the English-speaker who is unable to function unless someone assists him in English has become a cliché. Many English-speakers sigh with relief when the Mexican concierge or the Turkish shop attendant speaks to them in English. If these same foreigners take for granted that *you* don't know a word of the local language, they are making a reasonable assumption—based on their past experience with Americans, Britons, and Canadians.

If your hotel concierge or your tour guide speaks English with you, don't make a point of demonstrating that you could function just as well in the local language. This person is just trying to help you. Your interaction with him is likely to be short and superficial, so go ahead and continue the conversation in English as long as his skills are passable. You will have plenty of time to use your French or Chinese among the general population.

COPING WITH MIXED MESSAGES

English-speakers receive a variety of mixed messages from speakers of other languages. This chapter explored interactions with foreigners who—for a variety of reasons—would prefer to speak with us in English. Don't forget that this group is a minority; the vast majority of non-English-speakers resent the assumption that everyone, everywhere *should* speak English.

One of my former work colleagues recounted an incident that occurred in French-speaking Quebec: A man approached him out of the blue and started speaking in rapid French. My colleague, who does not speak French, communicated this deficiency in English. The stranger then replied, "Then what the [expletive] are you doing here?"

I have had no experiences that were quite this unpleasant. However, I do recall a woman in the Mexico City airport who mildly upbraided me because I mistakenly asked her the time in English, having assumed that she was an American. And for all their enthusiasm for studying conversational English, the Japanese are not above complaining about the monolingualism of Americans. In *Shogun Management* (HarperBusiness, 1993), author William C. Byham, Phd, recounts the frustrations of Japanese businesspersons when dealing with English-speakers and "[the resentment] that many Japanese managers feel....Why is it always our side that must do business in a foreign language?"

Sometimes it does make sense to communicate with others in English, even if you are capable of communicating with them in their own language. There is no shame in using English in superficial interactions abroad with foreigners who have been hired for the specific purpose of assisting English-speakers. Also avoid the temptation to overestimate your own abilities. Humility in regard to this point is especially important if you begin the study of a language while living in the United States—where most of the native speakers you meet will have already mastered at least the basics of English.

Those who learn languages for professional purposes will also continue to use English in certain situations. I have been using the Japanese language since 1988, and I have translated professionally for major corporations. This doesn't mean that I refuse to use English with native Japanese-speakers. On the contrary: my work in the United States often involves mixed groups consisting of Americans who don't speak Japanese, and highly educated Japanese who have been living in America for five years or more. In these situations, it usually makes sense to speak English. Simultaneously, my work confronts me with numerous situations in which Japanese skills are essential. In these cases, I can switch to my "Japanese mode."

Likewise, your work and travel abroad will be a mixture of superficial communications—in which English may serve as a lingua franca—and more in-depth communications that will rely on your abilities in Spanish, Russian, or Korean. The important thing to remember is that language skills give you the versatility to handle either situation.

CHAPTER 19

THE LANGUAGE STUDENT'S BUYING GUIDE

When you visit an online bookstore such as Amazon.com, plug in the words "French language" and click the search button, you might be presented with thousands of choices. A trip to your neighborhood Barnes & Noble is similarly bewildering; there are audio programs, self-teaching texts, and dictionaries, but which ones should you buy?

As someone who has been actively studying languages for about fifteen years, I have had a chance to try all the major language learning products at one time or another. I am happy to report that there are a lot of good materials out there. Language texts and audio programs are usually prepared by dedicated specialists who approach their task conscientiously. (No one figures to make a fast buck off a shoddily prepared language text— the market just isn't that big.) As a result, most items on the market are good investments. Only rarely have I been thoroughly disappointed by a purchase.

Nonetheless, it is a good idea to head to the bookstore (whether online or in the neighborhood) with a familiarity of the items that are available. Many language products are designed to fill a particular niche, such as vocabulary acquisition, or aural comprehension skills development. In addition, each product approaches the language from a slightly different angle.

Although I discuss the pros and cons of each book, audio course or other resource in the list below, I recommend all of these items. Each one represents a solid investment, in terms of effectiveness and value. After you have used some of these items, you will probably find additional products that interest you. Over time, you will no doubt become a connoisseur of language study materials yourself, with your own list of must-have products.

COLLEGE TEXTBOOKS

College textbooks are seldom entertaining, and they are not created with entertainment in mind. Moreover, college textbooks are expensive. These days, it is not uncommon for a new college textbook to have a price tag of more than $100.

Nonetheless, you should purchase a college textbook for the language you have decided to study—even if you have no intention of ever taking formal classes. College textbooks, their price and drabness notwithstanding, are treasure troves of grammar, vocabulary, and example sentences.

In the paragraphs below, we will explore some mass market courses that teach and entertain you at the same time. But you still need a no-nonsense, these-are-the-rules textbook to provide a thorough, scholarly outline of the language. (Later, you should also acquire a textbook designed for a second-year or advanced course.)

Despite the expense and inevitable dryness, a well-written college textbook will serve you as a reference for years to come. In fact, I still use an intermediate Spanish college text that I purchased for a class way back in the 1986 – 1987 academic year.

The easiest way to acquire a college textbook is to simply go to the source. Every college has a campus bookstore. Navigate your way to the textbook section, and look for the shelf that says "German," "Russian," or whatever language you have chosen to study. It is often possible to buy a used textbook, although these may be only slightly discounted from the price of a new book.

Many language textbooks written for the academic market today also include audio CDs. Purchase one of these textbooks if you can find one.

ENTRY-LEVEL MASS-MARKET COURSES

The products in this group each consist of a structured course book and audio cassettes or CDs. At the time of this writing, all of these packages can be purchased for less than $100, and most are priced at less than $50.

These courses can be ordered through Amazon.com, or selected from the shelves of the larger bricks-and-mortar bookstores, such as Barnes & Noble or Borders. However, be aware that publishers in general, and language material publishers in particular, are notoriously inconsistent in regard to inventory levels and availability. Publishers also have a tendency to discontinue items without warning. Therefore, if you see one of the items listed below on your next trip to the bookstore, it would be a good idea to go ahead and buy it—you might not find it again. The same goes for items you see listed in the online bookstores.

In the past, I have made the mistake of delaying a purchase on the assumption that I could always buy the item at a later date—only to discover shortly thereafter that the course had gone out of print. And a considerable number of the language courses that I have purchased—some as recently as recently as the late 1990s—are no longer available today.

Teach Yourself (NTC Publishing)

Each *Teach Yourself* language course consists of a book and two audio CDs. Most of the course books can also be purchased separately; but the CDs are worth the marginal extra expense. *Teach Yourself* courses are affordable, thorough, and engaging.

Compared to their competitors, *Teach Yourself* courses do a particularly good job of handling non-European scripts. The Thai, Arabic, and Chinese courses in this series are the best in their price range—if you want to learn to read and write.

There are top-notch *Teach Yourself* courses in exotic languages such as Hindi, Urdu, Punjabi, Korean, and Tagalog. If you are learning one of these less commonly taught languages, then your first step might be a *Teach Yourself* course.

As indicated above, one strong point of NTC's courses is their serious approach to non-Latin writing systems. In recent years, the company has also begun to develop an additional series of low-cost, concise textbooks for students struggling with scripts such as Arabic, Urdu, and Russian. (I recently purchased *Teach Yourself Beginner's Arabic Script*, by John Mace.) Be sure to investigate this series if your language studies take you outside the Western European sphere.

NTC also sells an advanced audio program series entitled *Improve Your Spanish/French/German*. The advanced courses are only available in the three most commonly studied Western European languages. These programs are good investments for intermediate students of Spanish, French, and German.

The Colloquial Series (Routledge Ltd.)

In terms of content, the *Colloquial* series is similar to the *Teach Yourself* series, although the *Colloquial* series places greater emphasis on spoken communication than on reading and writing. As a result, some of their courses rely on transliterations rather than authentic entries for non-Latin scripts. However, the *Colloquial* series contains a number of quality titles in the non-European realm, and some of these courses (such as *Colloquial Korean*) provide a thorough coverage of the necessary written elements.

The *Colloquial* courses provide extensive grammar explanations, which are especially important at the beginning stages. The courses in this series consist of a course book and an audio CD component. Although the dialogs in the audio portion are studio recorded, they are written and produced to closely approximate real-life situations.

Routledge has provided particularly good coverage in the South East Asian area. In 1995, *Colloquial Vietnamese* was one of the first quality mass-market Vietnamese courses to appear on the market. For beginning students of Bahasa Indonesia, *Colloquial Indonesian* is one of the best options currently available (although NTC recently produced a *Teach Yourself Indonesian* course that is also quite thorough). Routledge sells a *Colloquial Malay* course; and *Colloquial Cambodian* is perhaps the only up-to-date, readily available course for the seldom studied Khmer language. (A great number of the Southeast Asian materials on the market seem to date back to the Vietnam War era.)

Routledge also produces a number of reference grammars and dictionaries that are worth investigating. Unlike most of the industry, Routledge maintains an easily searchable website that can be found on all the major search engines. You can view their selection at www.routledge.com.

Hugo's Three Months Courses

The Hugo's *Three Months* courses each consist of a book and three audio CDs. Hugo's courses are well-produced, and contain invariably clean audio. There is a good mix of dialogs, reading passages, and example sentences.

Hugo's has traditionally stayed away from exotic languages and scripts. (The company produced courses in Japanese, Arabic, and Chinese—using transliterations rather than delving into the authentic writing systems.) Hugo's courses are produced in Great Britain, and the company has focused on developing a solid European language product line. During the mid-1990s, Hugo's also produced a business language series, and an advanced series, but I have not been able to find these in stores for a number of years.

Availability has been a major issue with the Hugo's language courses. If you see a Hugo's course that you want—buy it.

Just Listen 'n Learn

This series is published by Passport Books, a division of NTC Publishing. Each *Listen 'n Learn* course contains a course book and three cassettes. (The company is gradually making the transition to audio CDs.) This series is available in a number of languages, including Arabic, Chinese, Japanese, German, French, Russian, and Spanish. Advanced and business-oriented courses are also available. Unlike some of the other series, the *Listen 'n Learn* courses consistently stay in print.

The audio portions of many of the *Listen 'n Learn* programs contain extensive recordings of impromptu, on-location interviews. This is a contrast with most other programs, which rely solely on tightly scripted studio recordings. The advantage of the *Listen 'n Learn* approach is that you will hear the language as it is spoken for actual communication purposes in the real world.

Living Language "Ultimate" Series

Although these courses are a bit more expensive than most of the other packages in the mass market category, the *Ultimate* series provides the language learner with exceptional value. Whereas the above courses contain two or three CDs, each *Ultimate* course consists of a thick course manual and eight CDs. The first four CDs contain audio versions of dialogs from the book. The second four CDs contain annotated portions of the dialogs and additional example sentences, supplemented throughout by an English-speaking instructor who provides extensive grammar and usage explanations.

The *Ultimate* series is constantly expanding. Courses are currently available in a variety of languages, including Chinese, Japanese, Spanish, Portuguese, German, Italian, and French. Advanced level courses exist for most of these languages. The *Ultimate* advanced courses are useful even to students who have already attained a significant level of competency in a language.

Living Language is a division of Random House. You can view their course packages online at www.randomhouse.com/livinglanguage.

Spoken Language Services, Inc.

This company produces a number of cassette courses which emphasize speaking and listening skills. Spoken Language Services' main strength, in my view, is that they produce some quality full-length courses for languages that are often ignored by larger publishers, including Malay, Farsi (Persian), and Tagalog. They also produce some good supplemental materials for those studying Arabic. The Spoken Language Services website is located at www.spokenlanguage.com.

Visual Education

Visual Education is a "study aids" company located in Springfield, Ohio. They produce study cards and flashcards for a variety of topics, including mathematics, science, and Bible studies. They also have an extensive language-related product line. I have used their vocabulary and grammar card sets over the years while studying several languages. The material presented on each set of cards is quite extensive, and will serve the learner well through the intermediate/advanced stage.

In addition, Visual Education produces a "Think" series, each of which consists of study cards and an accompanying cassette. These are good, although they are not as flashy and entertaining as some of the other cassette courses described in this chapter. But once again, the content presented is quite solid.

Visual Education seems to be focusing on the study card niche, and their basic product line has not changed much since I first began using their materials about ten years ago. However, they are the only company I am aware of that sells vocabulary cards for Arabic, Korean, and Chinese! While their products form a supplemental part of your language-learning toolset, they are nonetheless worth purchasing. Additionally, Visual Education products are very reasonably priced, and almost always in stock. For more information, see their website, www.vis-ed.com.

Pimsleur

Pimsleur language courses are based on the *Graduated Interval Recall* and *The Principle of Anticipation* learning methods developed by Dr. Paul Pimsleur. Pimsleur was a celebrated linguist who received a Ph.D. in French from Colombia University. He subsequently taught French at UCLA, and was involved in the language programs of several other prominent universities. Through extensive research, Pimsleur determined that the components of a language are assimilated most quickly when they are absorbed through hearing. Therefore, the fastest way to learn a new language—according to Pimsleur—would be to focus on the listening component.

Whereas the courses from *Teach Yourself,* Hugo's, etc. divide the learner's attention more or less equally between reading and listening exercises, the Pimsleur courses focus exclusively on audio. Pimsleur courses do not contain thick course books. Instead, they consist entirely of cassettes or audio CDs, and often a small supplementary booklet.

Each Pimsleur course is broken down into discrete lessons. When a lesson opens, an English-speaking narrator gives a short introduction, and instructs you to listen to the conversation which is to follow. You then hear a dialog spoken between two native speakers in the target language. When the conversation concludes, the narrator explains each element of the exchange, and the native speakers repeat the words syllable by syllable.

Difficult words are pronounced several times, so that you can completely absorb the phonetic structures. The narrator also provides extensive instructions regarding usage, and native speakers break in with additional examples. Then the original dialogue is played again. Amazingly, you find yourself understanding a complete verbal exchange in a foreign language—although it had been total gibberish a short while ago.

In subsequent lessons, you are given impromptu quizzes on language that you learned earlier. Completely out of the blue, the narrator may ask, "What is the Portuguese word for engineer?" After a brief pause, a

215

native speaker pronounces the word, and you think to yourself, "Ah, yes, *that's* it." Pimsleur's technique of prompting you to recall the words you learned in previous lessons etches the course content deep into your memory. (This is the Principle of Graduated Interval Recall.) Repeated quizzing and reinforcement moves the components of the language from short-term memory to long-term memory.

The Principle of Anticipation works by forcing you to produce the right word or phrase to fit a situational context. For example, the English-speaking narrator may say to you, "A man has just offered you a cigarette. Tell him that you don't smoke." (By this point, you will have learned how to tell someone that you don't smoke in a previous lesson, so you should be able to retrieve the correct language—or a close approximation.) Then, for reinforcement, a native speaker recites the answer. This particular component of the target language is now engrained in your bone marrow.

Pimsleur courses can be purchased for a wide variety of languages. Some of the more exotic selections included are Thai, Vietnamese, Hindi, Armenian and Farsi. Pimsleur has also created intermediate and advanced courses for many of the more widely studied languages, like Spanish, French, German, Japanese, and Russian.

Despite the ingenuity of the Pimsleur system, the courses do have certain drawbacks. Although the language presented in each lesson is drilled (almost) effortlessly into your head, the amount of content in a single unit is small in comparison to the lesson content of more traditional courses. This means that the learner can complete an entire 30-lesson, 16-CD course with a fraction of the vocabulary that a much shorter (and cheaper) course can deliver.

Another issue is cost. At the time of this writing, full-length Pimsleur courses cost as much as several hundred dollars. In many cases, the language learner could buy four or five of the book and CD courses (*Teach Yourself*, *Hugo's*, etc.) for the cost of one Pimsleur course. If your language study activities are restricted by a tight budget, then the Pimsleur courses can quickly consume a large portion of the money you have allotted.

However, the cost may be justified if you are learning a language with difficult phonetics. By the time you have worked through a Pimsleur program, the pronunciation of Arabic, Vietnamese, or Russian will seem much less formidable. Moreover, the all-audio format of Pimsleur courses provides the commuter with an unparalleled "hands-free" study session.

I recommend the Pimsleur programs if a.) you can afford them, and b.) your schedule dictates a lot of hands-free study time. They are indeed a highly effective study tool.

FSI Courses

Foreign Service Institute, or FSI, courses have been developed by the U.S. State Department to assist members of the U.S. diplomatic corps in learning a foreign language. In principle, the FSI courses are similar to the mass market courses like *Teach Yourself*. However, most FSI courses contain around a dozen cassettes and a thick course book. FSI courses are also more expensive; a full-length FSI course usually costs several hundred dollars.

FSI courses rely primarily on grammatical drills, using example sentences. While FSI courses contain a lot of material, some students find them to be a bit on the dry side. Indeed, FSI recordings feature monotone speakers who drill you endlessly with example sentences like, "Where did you buy your new car, Mr. Jones?" Nevertheless, the knowledge that you can absorb from these courses is significant. If you can learn without being constantly entertained, then an FSI course will definitely be a worthwhile investment.

VocabuLearn (Penton Overseas)

Each *VocabuLearn* package consists of two cassettes or CDs, which are filled with "audio flashcards". There is also a compact booklet that contains a transcript of the audio material. *VocabuLearn* recordings are designed to assist the student with bulk vocabulary acquisition. A single unit of each program is dedicated to a particular category, such as nouns, verbs, etc. When you turn on a *VocabuLearn* CD, you will first hear a bell tone. Then you will hear an English speaker say, for example, "the grass", and a native speaker of the target language says, "*la hierba*" (if you happen to be listening to the Spanish language recordings). The process is then repeated— again and again, through a long list of words. In the middle of each side of a CD, another bell tone sounds, and the order switches: the foreign language word is spoken first, followed by an English translation.

I don't know exactly how long the *VocabuLearn* series has been around, but I have been using it since I began studying Japanese in the late 1980s. The *VocabuLearn* format is extremely simple, but also very useful.

These programs have a way of inserting large amounts of practical vocabulary into your head with repeated listening. On numerous occasions, I have been surprised to find new vocabulary items from these recordings falling into my consciousness at exactly the right moment.

The only down side of the *VocabuLearn* programs is tedium. Because there is no narrative or dialog to engage your interest, you may find your mind wandering after a while. I usually make it a rule to limit my use of *VocabuLearn* to thirty consecutive minutes.

It is also a good to idea to employ these recordings after you have soaked in a bit of the target language through other study materials. Since *VocabuLearn* essentially contains large amounts of vocabulary outside of any meaningful context, you may not retain much if you listen to the recordings before you are exposed to other materials. First work through a few chapters of a *Teach Yourself* course, or a few Pimsleur CDs. You will then find yourself recognizing some of the words on the *VocabuLearn* program, and absorbing many new ones.

VocabuLearn audio programs are available in a wide variety of languages, including Hebrew, Portuguese, and Armenian. Advanced *VocabuLearn* programs can be purchased for most of the major languages.

Immersion+ (Penton Overseas)

The daunting speed of real-life conversations is one of the most troublesome obstacles faced by the intermediate student of a language. Everyone seems to talk so fast. The student often feels that if people would just slow down, he would be able to understand everything. The problem is that real world conversations do not slow down, and the student must train himself to comprehend the language at this speed.

The *Immersion+* CDs are a tool that students can use to overcome the "everyone talks so fast" problem. Each *Immersion+* CD contains a series of conversations based around realistic situations. The dialog is first spoken at a natural speed, then at an artificially slow speed, and then again at the natural speed. As you listen to the slow reading, you will be able to catch the bits and pieces that you miss in the initial full-speed reading, then confirm your comprehension when you hear the full-speed reading again.

One of the strong points of this series is that the conversations are engaging and entertaining. The scenes are varied, and several different storylines are present throughout each CD. In one vignette, two elderly women discuss their dissatisfaction with local politics. Then two men are golfing and talking about the weather, and the chores they have to complete later. A woman and her friend are planning a shopping trip. A married couple endures a series of misadventures while going out to dinner.

At the time of this writing, *Immersion+* CDs are available in all the major Western European languages. They can be ordered direct through the Penton Overseas website (www.pentonoverseas.com), or through any bookstore.

MOVIES

There is a wealth of language study opportunities to be found at the neighborhood Blockbuster store. Movies are one of the most entertaining language study tools. The vast selection of movies available assures that you will never run out of new titles to view. Moreover, the DVD technology of recent years has given the language learner even more options.

When you are in the beginning stages of language study, a movie in the target language may seem like an impossible hurdle. The actors speak impossibly fast, and it seems that you can only catch a word here and there. Don't worry, though—movies are a good training device at any point in your studies, because they provide practice in recognizing sounds and anticipating dialogue through context.

Back in the days of VHS, the selection of films that could be used for language study was limited to the "foreign language titles" section of the video store. While many quality films are made outside of Hollywood, it was often difficult for me to predict whether or not a movie would suit my taste. Standards of entertainment vary from culture to culture. Moreover, the "foreign language titles" tended to be dominated by particular genres for each language. Japanese films were usually samurai epics, French language films were invariably artsy character studies, and every Chinese film seemed to feature a peasant struggling against an evil landlord.

Today, however, it is possible to study languages while viewing the familiar Hollywood offerings. DVD technology has added foreign language tracks to most films. For example, this past weekend, I watched the John Woo film, *Windtalkers*, in Spanish. I would have rented the film even if it had been available only in English, but the Spanish language track on the DVD enabled me to kill two birds with one stone.

To find out which language tracks are available on a DVD, look at the "Special Features" section on the back of the DVD package. You will see separate listings for the audio tracks and subtitles. When you insert the DVD into the player, you can access the language options by selecting the "Audio Setup" and "Subtitles" options on the main DVD menu.

A good study technique is to set both the subtitles and the audio track to the target language. This will help to improve your aural word discrimination capabilities, as you will be able to read the foreign words at the same time that you are hearing them. If you are still a beginner, then you may choose to turn on the English subtitles and the foreign language audio, to see if you can catch the gist of some of the dialog.

At present, many new DVD releases are limited to English, Spanish, and French language tracks. However, I have also seen new releases with Thai, Portuguese, and Chinese tracks. You will just have to check each DVD. (I recently purchased a Chinese movie on DVD that has a Mandarin and a Spanish audio track but no English audio track.)

You can purchase foreign language films (or Hollywood films with foreign language tracks) online. Amazon.com has a wide selection of movies in most languages. I have also found a number of foreign movies in the brick-and-mortar stores such as Borders and Barnes & Noble. (If you happen to be studying Japanese, you will benefit from the recent anime craze. My local Borders bookstore stocks no less than a dozen animated Japanese-language DVDs.)

When selecting a movie, try to select one that is heavy on dialog. There is no way to absolutely determine this factor from the package, but some general rules apply. Comedies and dramas usually contain more dialog than action films and monster movies.

Although movies are good study tools, documentaries and talk shows are even better. These formats consist entirely of spoken content. The language employed in these programs is typically more standardized than that contained in movies. Pronunciation is usually sharper, and the speakers do not compete with the sounds of car chases, gunshots, or other distractions that are present in movies. Documentaries and talk shows also tend to contain more sophisticated vocabulary.

The problem with documentaries and talk shows is that they are often difficult to find. Because of low market potential, they are not distributed through mass-market channels like Blockbuster and Amazon. The best way to acquire a foreign-language documentary or talk show is through a native speaker who is willing to tape a program when he or she makes a return visit to his or her home country.

Depending on where you live, you may have access to foreign-language television channels. I remember being able to choose from several Spanish channels during an extended business trip to El Paso. Cities such as Los Angeles, New York, and Miami also offer programming in languages other than English. In Cincinnati, it is now possible to gain access to Chinese, Japanese, and Spanish programming through cable and satellite TV. This is an investment that you may want to consider when you reach the intermediate stage in your target language.

Remember that movies and other television programs are supplements. Though helpful, these resources are only reinforcements for the language that you have learned through textbooks, vocabulary study, and audio courses. Don't be tempted to rely on them as your primary study device.

THE INTERNET

The Internet has opened up new worlds to the language student that were unthinkable even in 1994 or 1995. There is a lot of material freely available on the Internet that will be valuable for intermediate and advanced students. There is also a limited number of free tutorials which will serve the beginner.

On the Internet, you can locate news in any major language. One of the best sites for a wide variety of coverage is CNN.com. At present, CNN offers news in Spanish, Portuguese, German, Italian, Korean, Japanese and Arabic. Although much of the content throughout each of these sites is the same, there is a slightly different emphasis based on the region in which the language is spoken. For example, CNN's Spanish site provides more extensive coverage of Latin American issues.

As mentioned in a previous chapter of this book, MSN.com and Yahoo provide foreign language content in a number of languages. The foreign language links are easy to spot on either site. Once you have navigated to the area for a particular language, you will be able to access news, articles, as well as search engine capabilities in the language.

Most of the well-known foreign language newspapers, such as *Le Monde*, *El Pais*, and the *Yomiuri Shimbun* have their own websites. If you know the name of the periodical you want to find, you can execute a search engine query for it. If you just want to find out what is available, execute a search engine query for "Spanish language newspapers," for example.

If you have a high-speed connection to the Internet and a set of computer speakers, then you can take advantage of a world of audio and video foreign-language web content. In terms of the variety of languages offered, one of the best sites is the Voice of America (www.voa.gov). This site has broadcasts in practically every language on earth. Another good site is the NHK (*Nihon Hoosoo Kyookai*) site, located at www.nhk.co.jp. Although the site is primarily in Japanese, NHK broadcasts in all major languages.

For the beginner, there are some basic tutorials posted across the Internet that explain the basics of a number of languages. Most of these are personal web sites maintained by individual language enthusiasts or educators. The quality of these sites varies, but some of them are definitely worthwhile. Locating such sites is the most difficult aspect of using them, as they are scattered throughout the millions of web pages on the Internet. Among the search engine and general portal sites, Yahoo probably does the best job of organizing these tutorial sites into lists. When you navigate to Yahoo's home page, select "Languages" under the "Social Sciences" heading. Then select "Specific Languages," and you will be taken to a list of tutorial sites. *About.com* is another good place to look for online language tutorials. About.com maintains an extensive list of links for the more commonly studied languages.

EDUCATIONAL SOFTWARE

For a long time, I was skeptical about language-learning software. However, I recently tried it and I was pleasantly surprised. The onscreen environment adds a dimension to language study that cannot be precisely duplicated with a textbook, or even by a textbook with CDs. This is especially true when you are learning the pronunciation of a new language. Language software enables you to point and click on a word, phrase, or picture, and then instantaneously hear the correct pronunciation in the target language.

Two of the best known producers of language study software are Rosetta Stone (www.rosettastone.com) and Transparent Language (www.transparent.com). Both of these companies offer affordable, quality programs which should be especially helpful for the beginner.

SPECIALTY LANGUAGE STORES

Most of the language-learning materials described in this chapter can be purchased off the shelf or ordered through any major bookseller. However, language-learning materials represent a specialized market. Don't expect to drive to the neighborhood bookstore and find language materials as easily as the latest Stephen King novel or *Chicken Soup* book.

There are a number of retailers who specialize in serving the language student. Some focus only on the languages of particular area, while others stock materials for any language that you might possibly want to learn.

I have personally ordered from the retailers listed below. You can reach all of them over the Internet.

Audio-Forum: (www.audioforum.com) Audio Forum sells more than 280 courses in more than 100 languages. Audio-Forum is a particularly good source for the FSI (Foreign Service Institute) courses.

Cheng & Tsui: (www.cheng-tsui.com) Cheng & Tsui is a haven for students of any of the Asian languages. From Cheng & Tsui's website, you can order courses for learning Chinese, Japanese, Indonesian, Thai, Vietnamese, and Korean. Their inventory includes courses for intermediate and advanced students.

Sasuga Japanese Bookstore: (www.sasugabooks.com): This is the place to go for everything Japanese, from beginner's texts to authentic materials written for native Japanese speakers. They also sell an extensive selection of books about Japanese culture, business, and history. In addition, Sasuga has a walk-in location in Cambridge, Massachusetts.

China Books & Periodicals: (www.chinabooks.com) As the name suggests, this San Francisco-based store is focused on the China-related niche. Along with Cheng & Tsui, this store will become one of your primary resources if you decide to study Chinese.

GENERAL TIPS FOR BUYING LANGUAGE MATERIALS

- Always try to buy items that include a textbook as well as tapes or audio CDs. Reading comprehension and listening comprehension are two different animals. For most languages, your ability to understand written material will be several levels ahead of your ability to understand what is spoken. Therefore, you can never have too much recorded material that is supported by a textbook. Textbooks by themselves are helpful, and listening-only programs (such as the Pimsleur CDs described above) also have their place. But in my experience, nothing beats a thoroughly written instructional text paired with a solid audio component.

- No single book, audio program, or software is a "silver bullet" for learning a language. Therefore, you should buy as many items as you practically can. As indicated above, each product category fulfills a different need. In addition, each author or editorial team will include some elements of the language, and leave other elements out. Therefore, there is much to be gained by buying multiple products within the same category. A Hugo's course will compliment what you learn in a *Teach Yourself* course. *VocabuLearn* CDs will enhance your progress in the Pimsleur programs. It is never an "either/or" issue where language-learning materials are concerned. More is always better.

ADDITIONAL NOTES

- In recent years, there has been a trend for audio recordings to be produced on CD rather than on cassette. Many of the above courses can be purchased in CD format.

- If you don't have any luck finding a particular package on Amazon.com or BN.com, there are other means by which you might obtain the course. Brick-and-mortar bookstores often stock out-of-print titles that they still happen to have in inventory. It would also be worthwhile to search the shelves of a used bookstore, such as Half Price Books. Half Price Books sells used books, as well as publisher's overruns. They have an extensive selection in all book categories, including foreign languages. (I have found a number of out-of-print gems in their Cincinnati stores.) You can also purchase books through their online service at www.halfpricebooks.com.

- Your public library should have many of the above courses. Although you can't purchase a course from the library, this public resource may be the fastest method of gaining access to an out-of-print course.

- Out-of-print titles are sometimes revived. If you search for a title and are initially told that it is no longer available, continue to check again at two- or three-month intervals. You might even write or call the publisher, and ask them if there are any plans to give the item a second life.

EPILOGUE

FUN AND PERSONAL ENRICHMENT

This book has focused on the practical benefits of learning a foreign language. We have discussed language as a tool for getting a better job, closing a sale, and learning more about our strategic and commercial competitors. While all these hard-boiled reasons for learning a foreign language are perfectly valid, by themselves they present a one-sided picture.

When you learn a foreign language, you will have a chance to step into other cultures in a way that is simply not possible otherwise. Some of the fondest memories of my career are drawn from the time I spent in Aguascalientes, a medium-sized city in central Mexico. I interacted with many interesting people, a few of whom I am still in contact with today. I had a chance to deeply experience a fascinating country that is a mixture of the Spanish, Aztec, and Mayan cultures. As much as I love the United States, my adventures there could never have been exactly duplicated in the USA.

One of the benefits of exploring other cultures is that they will give you new insights into your own. You will discover some aspects of the foreign culture that you prefer. At the same time, you will also encounter aspects of the foreign culture that give you a greater appreciation for life in your own part of the world.

Most people undergo an initial "honeymoon phase" when they step into another culture, during which they believe that everything on the other side is inherently more sophisticated and enlightened. When I first began working with Japanese companies about 15 years ago, I was convinced that Japanese management practices were vastly superior to American management practices. My impressions were bolstered by the "Japanese-style management" craze that was currently sweeping through the American business and academic communities. I absorbed all the good press about Japanese companies: they emphasize teamwork, they take care of their own, and they focus on quality.

After a decade and a half working with Japanese companies, I can tell you that much of the good press turned out to be true. Japanese companies are, on average, more team-oriented and harmonious. In my opinion, they have fewer problems with management power plays and factional strife. And the quality of Japanese products is confirmed every year, when Honda and Toyota take a large percentage of the top spots in consumer satisfaction and industry surveys.

But I also discovered that not everything about Japanese companies is positive. They are typically more bureaucratic and less efficient than their American counterparts. Even the simplest decisions can require hours of meetings in the interest of building a redundant consensus.

In Japan, the company invades the employee's personal life to an extent that few Americans would find acceptable. In order to build group harmony, Japanese company employees often must spend their precious free hours drinking and socializing with their colleagues. This means that few Japanese workers have much time for family life or personal enrichment activities.

My exposure to Japanese culture has not lessened my appreciation for the aspects of American culture which I most value: individuality and personal freedom. Nor has my identity as an American prevented me from admiring the positive traits of the Japanese work and cultural environments.

When you can fully understand what is written and said on both sides of a national boundary, you have a basis for weighing the relative merits of "their ways" versus "our ways." This is perhaps the greatest reward in learning another language. You gain not only another mode of communication, but another way in which to see the world.

APPENDIXES

I. The World's Most Commonly Spoken Languages (as measured by the number of native speakers)

II. The World's Largest Economies

III. The Second Languages Most Demanded on Job Sites and Job Search Engines in the United States

IV. Languages Discussed in this Book Categorized By Degree of Difficulty

I. THE WORLD'S MOST COMMONLY SPOKEN LANGUAGES (AS MEASURED BY THE NUMBER OF NATIVE SPEAKERS)

1. Mandarin Chinese............................more than 1 billion
2. Hindi/Urdu (Hindustani).....................500 million
3. English......................................450 million
4. Spanish.....................................393 million
5. Russian.....................................275 million
6. Arabic......................................245 million
7. Bengali.....................................211 million
8. Portuguese..................................191 million
9. Malay-Indonesian...........................160 million
10. French.....................................129 million

II. THE WORLD'S LARGEST ECONOMIES*

1. U.S.A.
2. China
3. Japan
4. India
5. Germany
6. United Kingdom
7. France
8. Italy
9. Brazil
10. Russia
11. Spain
12. Mexico
13. Canada
14. South Korea
15. Indonesia

*There are various methods of assessing economic size, each of which tends to yield a slightly different list. The above list is based on Purchasing Power Parity, as calculated by the World Bank in 2004.

III. THE SECOND LANGUAGES MOST DEMANDED ON JOB SITES AND JOB SEARCH ENGINES IN THE UNITED STATES

1. Spanish
2. Japanese
3. French
4. Mandarin Chinese
5. German
6. Korean
7. Italian
8. Portuguese

IV. LANGUAGES DISCUSSED IN THIS BOOK CATEGORIZED BY DEGREE OF DIFFICULTY

Easy

Spanish, Indonesian, Italian

Medium Difficulty

French, German, Portuguese, Vietnamese, Romanian, Czech

Difficult

Korean, Arabic, Thai, Japanese, Russian, Hungarian, Bulgarian, Serbian, Polish

NOTES & BIBLIOGRAPHY

Introduction: English-Speakers Lost in Translation
- *Lost in Translation* (2003) Universal Studios

Chapter 1: Does an English-Speaker Really Need a Foreign Language?
- "How can Britain's language skills be improved?" BBC News, April 14, 2005
- "Language learning in the UK plummets as students stay at home" The Independent, online edition April 14, 2005
- Ambushed
- "Volunteers test OSU's foreign language skills" http://www.ocolly.com/new_ocollycom/show_story.php?a_id=25783

Chapter 2: The Truth and the Hype about "Global English"
- *In Europe, Going Global Means, Alas, English*, By John Tagliabue The New York Times May 18, 2002
- "French in the New Europe..." http://www.abc.net.au/rn/arts/ling/stories/s1121493.htm
- "English surpasses French as main EU language" Helsinki Sanomat 5/4/2001 http://www.helsinki-hs.net/news.asp?id=200104101E16
- The review quote from a review of the previous edition of this book, written by Amazon.com reviewer "Merion_operafan" on October 18, 2004.
- "What Global Language?" by Barbara Wallraff, 11/2000 The Atlantic Online
- 英語を話せないと、仕事の上で損？ http://www.ewoman.co.jp/report_db/pages/02_020624_5.html (translation by the author)

Chapter 3: The 21st Century Speaks Many Languages
- The interview with David Graddol is from the VOA Wordmaster program, broadcast on March 18, 2004

- "Scholar Sees New Trends in Sino-Japanese Relations" http://www.china.org.cn/english/2002/May/33302.htm
- "Toyota seen overtaking GM as No. 1 auto maker by 2010" May 19, 2005, Globeandmail.com
- "Toyota considers new U.S. plant" CNN.com September 9, 2002
- The comments concerning Azteca América are from Santiago Solutions Group president Carlos Santiago, speaking to the Miami Herald in May, 2005 (Azteca's lineup aims closer to 'home', May 17, 2005)
- "China and India: Rise of the New Global Powerhouses" by J. Ørstrøm Møller, inthenationalinterest.com 2003

Chapter 4: How Lingua Francas Become Lingua Francas
- *The Passion of the Christ* (2004) Fox Home Entertainment
- Katzner, Kenneth (1995) *The Languages of the World*: Routledge & Kegan Paul Ltd.
- Crystal, David (2005) *The Stories of English*, Overlook Hardcover
- Oppenheim, Leo (1977) *Ancient Mesopotamia : Portrait of a Dead Civilization*: University Of Chicago Press
- Mintz, Steven (2004) *Huck's Raft : A History of American Childhood*: Belknap Press
- Kater, Michael H. (2004) *Hitler Youth*: Harvard University Press

Chapter 5: Language and the Limits of Globalization
- "France Rejects European Constitution" By Craig Whitlock / Washington Post Foreign Service, 5/30/ 2005 http://www.washingtonpost.com/wp-dyn/content/article/2005/05/29/AR2005052900644.html
- "The Protectionist Problem" http://www.cbsnews.com/stories/2004/06/28/opinion/main626416.shtml
- Rifkin, Jeremy (2004) *The European Dream: How Europe's Vision of the Future Is Quietly Eclipsing the American Dream*: Jeremy P. Tarcher

Chapter 6: Languages and the Business World
- "Execs Looking to Europe Face Several Challenges" by Sharon Voros http://www.careerjournal.com/myc/workabroad/foreign/20010705-voros.html

- "Savvy Execs Can Speak Their Clients' Language" by Michael Chang http://www.careerjournal.com/columnists/perspective/20020107-fmp.html

Chapter 8: Foreign Languages and American Values
- "Foreign Language Pledges Irk Student" http://cbs2.com/water/watercooler_story_069091113.html
- *CNN en Español*, October 13th, 2003 (Translation by the author)
- "Illegal Aliens Cost California Billions," The Washington Times, December 6, 2004
- "Edward Trimnell on the Myth of Global English and the Costs of Americans' Monolingualism" TransitionsAbroad.com http://www.transitionsabroad.com/publications/magazine/0505/edward_trimnell_on_language_immersion.shtml
- "A Big Warning" by Pierre Thomas and Martha Raddatz http://abcnews.go.com/sections/us/DailyNews/911conversation020607.html
- "Osama and His Toy Soldiers" CBS News.com http://www.cbsnews.com/stories/2002/12/05/world/main531969.shtml

Chapter 10: Which Language Should You Learn?
- "China approves sweeping change" http://www.cnn.com/2003/WORLD/asiapcf/east/03/09/china.cabinet/index.html

Chapter 11: The First Steps in Learning a Foreign Language
- Seward, Jack (1968) *Japanese in Action*: Weatherhill

Chapter 18: "But They Insist on Speaking English with Me!"
- "What is the best way to make foreign friends?" *Japan Today.com* http://www.japantoday.com/e/?content=popvox&id=448
- Farber, Barry (1991) *How to Learn Any Language: Quickly, Easily, Inexpensively, Enjoyably and on Your Own*: Citadel Press

Printed in the United States
47917LVS00002BA/60